Hope Lies in the Proles

Hope Lies in the Proles

George Orwell and the Left

John Newsinger

PLUTO PRESS

First published 2018 by Pluto Press
345 Archway Road, London N6 5AA

www.plutobooks.com

British Library Cataloguing in Publication Data
A catalogue record for this book is available from the British Library

ISBN   978 0 7453 9929 4   Hardback
ISBN   978 0 7453 9928 7   Paperback
ISBN   978 1 7868 0189 0   PDF eBook
ISBN   978 1 7868 0220 0   Kindle eBook
ISBN   978 1 7868 0219 4   EPUB eBook

This book is printed on paper suitable for recycling and made from fully
managed and sustained forest sources. Logging, pulping and manufacturing
processes are expected to conform to the environmental standards of the
country of origin.

Typeset by Stanford DTP Services, Northampton, England

Simultaneously printed in the United Kingdom and United States of America

Contents

List of Abbreviations

BUF	British Union of Facists
CP	Communist Party
ILP	Independent Labour Party
IRD	Information Research Department
IRRC	International Rescue and Relief Committee
NKVD	Narodnyi Komissariat Vnutrennikh Del (The Russian Secret Police)
NUWM	National Unemployed Workers Movement
NCRNT	National Committee for Rescue from Nazi Terror
POUM	Partido Obrero de Unificación Marxista (The Worker's Party of Marxist Unification, Spain)
SIM	Russian Secret Police
SOE	British Special Operations Executive

For Lorna Chessum

Introduction: Discovering Orwell

My interest in George Orwell's writings goes back to the late 1960s when I was a left-wing student. My first encounter was not with *Animal Farm* or *Nineteen Eighty-Four* but with *Homage to Catalonia* which I read as an account of revolution by someone who had actually lived through and experienced it. It was certainly one of the most important books in my political formation, showing that working-class revolution was both possible and to be welcomed, and that the Communist Party was most certainly not on the side of workers' power but that its first loyalty was to the Soviet Union. This was a very useful reinforcement for my politics, shaped as they were by being the son of manual workers; my father struggling as a casual labourer for many years, brought up on the Harold Hill council estate and being, by the time I arrived at University, completely disillusioned by Harold Wilson's Labour government. The Wilson government's conduct in the 1966 seamen's strike and support for the Americans in Vietnam had permanently ended my youthful belief that the Labour Party was an agency for fundamental social change. I had naively expected a Labour government to support workers in struggle at home and to support national liberation struggles abroad. Workers control and workers power, the self-activity of the working class, were where my political loyalties lay. As for Communism, it seemed self-evident to me that the Soviet Union was a police state, a dictatorship over the working class; that this had been the case for many years, and that Communist Party members were, whatever their other virtues, really just so many dupes, serving Russian interests in the mistaken belief that they were advancing the interests of the working class.

Looking back at the books that most influenced me when I was a student, one of the things that struck me is that only one, Ralph Miliband's *Parliamentary Socialism*, was actually recommended as part of a University course! The most influential book was without a doubt Peter Sedgwick's edition of Victor Serge's *Memoirs of a Revolutionary*, which showed me what being a revolutionary socialist could involve. It was followed by Tony Cliff's *Russia: A Marxist Analysis*, that, as far as I was and still am concerned effectively settled the question of the class nature of the Soviet

Union. There were a number of other volumes that left their mark: Wal Hannington's *Unemployed Struggles*, Allen Hutt's *The Post-War History of the British Working Class*, C Desmond Greaves *The Life and Times of James Connolly*, George Lukacs' *History and Class Consciousness*, Emmet Larkin's *James Larkin*, C L R James's *Black Jacobins*, Kate Millett's *Sexual Politics*, Willie Gallacher's *Revolt on the Clyde* and Harry Pollitt's *Serving My Time*. My interest in the labyrinth that is Marxist philosophy was fortunately curtailed by reading Louis Althusser's *For Marx*, which convinced me that life was too short, something for which I remain very much in his debt. There were certainly other books that left a mark. But there in the midst of this somewhat eclectic reading list, which includes books by a good many CP members (how it was that people of the calibre of Wal Hannington, Harry Polliitt and others could apologise for, indeed celebrate the Stalin tyranny, remains a special interest), was *Homage to Catalonia*.

My initial view of Orwell at this time was that he subsequently moved to the right politically, eventually turning against revolution and the left generally and becoming a fully-fledged pro-American Cold Warrior. What changed this view was first of all, Peter Sedgwick's tremendous article (unfortunately only 'part 1' ever appeared), 'George Orwell: International Socialist?' that was published in the journal *International Socialism* in June 1969,[1] and secondly the publication in paperback of Sonia Orwell and Ian Angus's tremendous four volume *The Collected Essays, Journalism and Letters of George Orwell* in 1970. The four volumes, battered and well-read, still sit on my shelves. These changed my view of Orwell completely and since then I have regularly returned to the man and his work, indeed taken sustenance from his writings, both where I agree with him and where I don't. Orwell, it is important to remember was always 'a work in progress'. His ideas and attitudes were always developing, changing: through discussion and argument, influenced by his extensive reading and by the unfolding of events as he viewed and participated in them. Often what we read is a debate that he is conducting, sometimes with others, often with himself, while he works out where he stands. This makes him all the more interesting as a writer and thinker. And, of course, he often gave voice to the most outrageous prejudices, sometimes amusing but sometimes not. His hostility towards vegetarianism springs to mind as an instance of the first and his hostility towards feminism as an example of the second. But while we can go a considerable way towards interrogating his thinking at any particular point in his life, any attempt to predict how he would have responded to developments after his death is, no matter how well-informed, guesswork that inevitably tells us more about the politics and opinions of the person doing the guessing than it does about George Orwell's likely posthumous politics and opinions.

At the centre of my interest in the man is his politics: that he remained a democratic socialist up until his death, that for him socialism meant a 'classless society' where the rich and super rich had been expropriated, abolished altogether, that democracy, freedom of speech and civil liberties were essential to socialism, that the working class was the agency of socialist transformation, and that he recognised that in the last resort the ruling class would resist their own abolition and that resistance would have to be put down by force. Moreover, he had seen through Stalinism by 1937 and had soon after recognised that the Soviet Union was not socialist at all but something else. His eventual conclusion, that it was some kind of bureaucratic collectivism, was mistaken in my opinion, but whatever disagreements one might have with this theory, the theory that, for example, informs *Nineteen Eighty-Four*, it gave his writing on Stalinism an uncompromising strength and certainty that was to be very much welcomed. Certainly his commitment to the Labour Party and the Cold War were both pulling him to the right in the post-war years, but even in this period he recognised that Labour welfarism was not socialism and continued a dialogue with the revolutionary left, both the Anarchists and Trotskyists. He was still urging, as we shall see, that the only cause worth fighting for was a Socialist United States of Europe, an essential step towards a Socialist world, and that socialism could only be finally realised globally. While there was much in his writing with which I disagreed and actions that he had taken in his lifetime which I thought were mistaken (and in the case of his involvement with the Labour government's Information Research Department, positively deplorable), for me at any rate, his great flaw was and remains his sexism. That this was a failing he shared with most of the men of his time and many of ours does not make it any the less disappointing and it certainly should always be remembered and taken into account in any honest assessment of the man and his politics.

This book is not a biography of George Orwell. Bernard Crick's biography still remains the best single volume on the man for my money, followed by Peter Davison's short but altogether indispensable *George Orwell: A Literary Life* and Gordon Bowker's *George Orwell*. Instead it focuses in particular on his relationship with the Left in Britain. It is written in the confident expectation that Orwell and his writings remain crucially relevant in the times through which we are now living.

1

'Until They Become Conscious They Will Never Rebel': Orwell and the Working Class

In *Nineteen Eighty-Four*, Winston Smith, while pondering the overthrow of Big Brother, inevitably confronts the dilemma that all socialists who believe in the agency of the working-class have sooner or later to face up to. The moral case for democratic socialism is overwhelming. Certainly, the only worthwhile political objective, as far as Orwell was concerned at the time he wrote the book, was the establishment of a classless society where the ruling class, whatever its particular make-up, had been overthrown, deprived of its wealth and power forever, and the working-class was 'in the saddle'. This would make possible the introduction of a real democratic system rooted, as it had to be, in the achievement of genuine social equality. The working-class were oppressed and exploited, ground down both at work and at home, the victims of a system of privilege and of the most gross, indeed positively obscene, social inequality. And yet they had the strength to bring that system crashing down if only they recognised their situation, embraced the socialist cause, and acted in concert to remedy it. Nothing could stand in their way. Not even Big Brother. But they don't act. The problem, as Smith puts it, was that 'Until they become conscious they will never rebel, and until after they have rebelled they cannot become conscious'. Smith is clearly speaking for Orwell here, rehearsing problems that he confronted himself. *Nineteen Eighty-Four* does not, of course, resolve the dilemma. Indeed, before his arrest, Smith goes through moments of both hope and despair. As he puts it: ' . . . if there was hope, it lay in the proles. You had to cling on to that. When you put it in words it sounded reasonable: it was when you looked at the human beings passing you on the pavement that it became an act of faith'.[1] We shall return to *Nineteen Eighty-Four* and the working-class, but first: how did George Orwell, an

Old Etonian and a former colonial policeman, come to this commitment both to socialism and to the working-class as agency?

Looking back on his teenage years, Orwell remembered himself as a public school radical in the immediate post-war years. This was a period when, as he puts it, 'the English working class were in a fighting mood'. He describes himself as being 'a Socialist' at this time, but only 'loosely', without 'much grasp of what Socialism meant, and no notion that the working class were human beings'. He was both 'a snob and a revolutionary' whose knowledge of the working class came from books such as Jack London's *The People of the Abyss*. He could 'agonize' over the sufferings of the poor, but 'still hated them and despised them when I came anywhere near them'. As he puts it, 'I seem to have spent half the time in denouncing the capitalist system and the other half in raging over the insolence of bus conductors'.[2] How this schoolboy radicalism would have developed if he had gone on to University from Eton, we can only conjecture, but instead, he took a different path and joined the colonial police. This was, of course, a pretty decisive repudiation of even the loosest idea of socialism. He sailed for Burma in October 1922. He was to spend the next five years in the service of the Empire.

On his own testimony, when he gave up his career as a colonial policeman and returned home from Burma in the summer of 1927, he came back bearing 'an immense weight of guilt that I had got to expiate'. In Burma, he had been a 'part of the actual machinery of despotism' and still had 'a bad conscience' about it. He had faithfully served the interests of British Imperialism, one of those charged with imposing British rule, by force when necessary, on the native population. He later recalled 'the women and children howling when their menfolk were led away under arrest' and 'the scarred buttocks of the men who had been flogged with bamboos'. And this violence was all-pervasive, inherent in the colonial relationship. He guiltily remembered 'the servants and coolies I had hit with my fists in moments of rage' at their clumsiness and supposed laziness. He had come home ridden by guilt and determined 'to submerge myself, to get right down among the oppressed, to be one of them and on their side against their tyrants' as a personal recompense. It was at this point that 'my thoughts turned to the English working class'.[3] This particular trajectory is, of course, dependent on Orwell's own testimony. Nevertheless, it does identify a concern to both take the side of and to be accepted by the working class that remained with him for the rest of his life. With whatever reservations and doubts for George Orwell, 'if there was hope, it lay in the proles!'[4]

The Road to Socialism

Although Orwell was to later claim that he only really became a socialist sometime around 1930, there is evidence of an earlier commitment when he lived in Paris in 1928–29 and wrote a number of articles for the left-wing press. Moreover, according to Gordon Bowker, at this time, his aunt, Nellie Limouzin and her partner, Eugene Adam, became, informally at least, 'his political tutors'.[5] Adam was a former communist, now fiercely hostile to the Stalinist takeover of both the Russian Communist Party and of the Communist International. Orwell argued the issues of the day with him, with Orwell actually defending the Soviet Union at this time, and he provided Orwell with contacts on the French left, including Henri Barbusse. Certainly, Orwell's time in Paris gave him the opportunity to experience, if only briefly, life at the bottom of the employment market, experience that he duly recounted in *Down and Out in Paris and London*, but he also encountered a left-wing culture that is missing from that book although he acknowledged it elsewhere. In a review that he wrote for *The Adelphi* magazine and that appeared in May 1932 (before *Down and Out* was published), he described a massive demonstration he saw in Marseilles when on his way home to England from Burma. There was 'an immense procession of working people . . . bearing banners inscribed "*Sauvons Sacco et Vanzetti.*"'[6] This was 'the kind of thing that one might have seen in England in the eighteen forties, but surely never in the nineteen twenties'. Britain had experienced 'a century of strong government' that now kept public disorder in check. Whereas in Britain, public protest 'seems an indecency . . . in France everyone can remember a certain amount of civil disturbance, and even the workmen in the bistros talk of la revolution – meaning the next revolution, not the last one'.[7] He chose not to explore this particular aspect of French working-class life. Instead, he tells the reader of his reluctance to write for the Communist press in France for fear of the police. A detective had seen him coming out of the office of a Communist newspaper on one occasion and this had caused him 'a great deal of trouble with the police'. They were 'very hard on Communists, especially if they are foreigners'. Other than that his account covers only some ten weeks of his time in Paris, the period during which he was near starvation, working as a *plongeur*,[8] and, of course, this is the experience that he set out to explore in the *Down and Out*.

Back in Britain, Orwell had famously gone on the tramp. He had first begun these explorations in late 1927 and 1928, before moving to Paris, and continued them after his return to Britain in 1930–31. What they show is his determination, not just to sympathise with the poor and destitute but to actually get some first-hand experience of how they experienced life and to get to know them as individuals. He was going to show his middle-class readership, to the best of his ability, what their lives were like from the inside. His intention was to turn the tramping poor from a faceless mass who were to be both pitied and feared into human beings; to humanise them, acknowledge them as individual men and women. To be able to do this he had to become one of them. What even the well-meaning middle class had to realise is that the only real difference between them and the poor is income. As he puts it, the average millionaire is only 'the average dishwasher dressed in a new suit'.[9]

For Orwell himself, of course, there was more to it than just humanising the poor for a middle-class readership. It was all part of expiating the guilt that he felt at having been part of an oppressive Imperialist system in Burma. Identifying with the poor, being one of them, even if only temporarily, was something that was to concern him throughout his life and that his middle-class friends often commented on. One moment that captures this is when he ventures out dressed as a tramp in Lambeth. He sees another tramp walking towards him and then realises it is himself reflected in a shop window. Already he looks dirty, indeed it seems as if dirt leaves you alone 'when you are well dressed, but as soon as your collar is gone it flies towards you from all directions'. Now that he is dressed as a tramp, everyone he passes responds differently. And then there is a moment of epiphany: 'I helped a hawker pick up a barrow that he had upset. "Thanks, mate", he said with a grin. No one had called me mate before in my life – it was the clothes that had done it'. Of course, as soon as he spoke Orwell's accent was to identify him as someone well-to-do who was, for whatever reason, down on their luck, but such individuals were common enough for this to not occasion too much surprise or cause suspicion from the other tramps. The same was not true when he ventured into working-class communities in the North of England. There he was always an outsider.

By the time Orwell went north, under contract to Victor Gollancz to write a book on his experiences and investigations, he had been associated for some time with *The Adelphi*, a literary magazine that had moved to the left under the impact of the Great Depression and the collapse of the Labour government in 1931. It was edited by John Middleton Murray, assisted by Richard Rees, Max Plowman and the working-class novelist Jack Common, with all of whom Orwell became friendly. After the collapse of the Labour government and the break away of the left-wing Independent Labour Party (ILP) from the Labour Party, Murray had joined the ILP. *The Adelphi* was to become to all intents and purposes the ILP's theoretical journal. It reduced its price to 6d so that in the words of an editorial written by Richard Rees, 'we may reach the greatest possible number of socialist readers'. And according to one account it did succeed in building up 'a regular following of working-class people' in the Midlands and the North.[10] Orwell wrote for it regularly and was very much under its influence. From this point of view *The Road to Wigan Pier* can be seen as a product of his interaction with the more radical and revolutionary elements within the ILP. As we shall see further on, this was particularly true of the book's determined rejection of the politics of the Popular Front.

Orwell kept in touch with Jack Common by letter during his visit to the North. On one occasion, he mentioned how he had visited the Adelphi offices in Manchester where there were what he described as 'fearful feuds and intrigues'. A fortnight later, safely back down South, he again wrote to him, explaining that one of the reasons for the squabbling seemed to be people from different parts of the North 'declaring that theirs is the only genuinely distressed area and the others don't know what poverty means'. One suspects this was a Yorkshire – Lancashire dispute! There were also problems between the magazine's working-class and middle-class supporters, with working-class people complaining of the 'patronising airs' put on by some of the middle-class socialists.[11]

More seriously, towards the middle of April 1936, he wrote to Common about how 'this business of class-breaking is a bugger'. He blamed the problems on the middle-class socialists who gave him 'the creeps'. Not only don't they want to eat with a knife, but they were 'still slightly horrified at seeing a working man do so'. Many of these people were of 'the sort of eunuch type with a vegetarian smell who go about spreading sweetness and light and have at the back of their minds a vision of the working class all T. T., well washed behind the ears, readers of Edward Carpenter or some other pious sodomite and talking with BBC accents'. He thought working-class people were 'very patient' under all this provocation and in his own case he 'was never once socked on the jaw and only once told to go to hell, and then by a woman who was deaf and thought I was a rate-collector'.[12] Orwell was, of course, to discourse at some length on the problems caused by some middle-class socialists in the second part of *The Road to Wigan Pier*, something to which we shall return.

What of *The Road to Wigan Pier*? It was written very much as a political act, intended to show middle-class readers in the South, where economic recovery was underway, that there was still considerable unemployment in the North with all that entailed in terms of human misery and that this was being forgotten. It was also a political statement in support of the miners who were only now beginning to recover from their defeat in the Great Lockout of 1926. This was particularly important because the miners were still the decisive force within the labour movement. It was also a political act in another more personal sense because it saw Orwell nailing his colours to the socialist cause in a way that he had not so far done. This was particularly the case once Gollancz decided to publish *The Road* as a Left Book Club choice.

In the book, Orwell celebrates the work of the miner. They did an essential job: one that he thought would have killed him off in a couple of weeks, and yet they were underpaid and subjected to humiliating and dangerous conditions at work. One in six miners suffered a serious accident every year and one in 900 was killed. It was a casualty rate equivalent to a small war. They did the most dangerous job in the country. Watching them at work, he wrote, 'you realise momentarily what different universes different people inhabit'. Indeed, the whole world of the 'superior person' like himself rested on 'the poor drudges underground, blackened to the eyes, with their throats full of coal dust, driving their shovels forward with arms and belly muscles of steel'. He singles out one particular instance of petty injustice to exemplify the position these men found themselves in: a disabled miner 'kept waiting about for hours in the cold wind' for his pension, an afternoon wasted, completely helpless in the face of the arbitrary whim of the company, even though the pension was his by right. As Orwell points out, not even 'a down-at-heel' member of the bourgeoisie like himself would have to put up with such treatment.

Orwell would, of course, be completely unsurprised by the workings of the benefits system in Britain today. He would recognise it immediately for what it was. He would also have immediately recognised the zero-hours economy for what it is and the role of employment agencies, indeed in *The Road*, he actually discusses the vicious impact of casualisation on the working class. He singles out a Professor Saintsbury who recommended casualisation as 'the very secret and safety-valve of a safe and sound labour system generally'. He thought unemployment a positive good, helping to discipline the workers, but 'only so long as the unemployed are made to suffer as much as possible'. As far as the Professor was concerned the dole was both 'demoralising' and 'ruinous' for the unemployed worker who, as Orwell observes, he presumably thought should either 'sleep in the street' or go into the workhouse. Anyway, the government, according to Saintsbury, was under no obligation to ensure the 'continuance of life' of the unemployed. A lot of people thought as much, but once again, as Orwell observes, it took 'a lot of guts to be openly such a skunk' as Saintsbury. Why did working people tolerate these attitudes and put up with these conditions? It was the inevitable lot of a working class that had been defeated. Orwell goes on about how this whole business of 'petty inconvenience and indignity . . . is inherent in working-class life'. He wrote of how, 'a thousand influences constantly press a working man down into a passive role. He does not act, he is acted upon. He feels himself the slave of mysterious authority and has a firm conviction that "they" will never allow him to do this, that, and the other'. He recalled how when he was hop-picking, he had asked his fellow workers why they did not form a union to demand better wages and conditions and was told that 'they' would never allow it.

He looked at the plight of the unemployed, praising the efforts of the National Unemployed Workers Movement (NUWM). This was 'a revolutionary organisation intended to hold the working class together, stop them blacklegging during strikes, and give legal advice against the Means Test'. He had seen a lot of the NUWM, built from nothing by the efforts of the unemployed themselves and 'I greatly admire the men, ragged and underfed like the others, who keep the organisation going'.[13] In the diary he kept of his time in the North, he was less complimentary. On one occasion, he heard Wal Hannington, the NUWM leader speak at a meeting and dismissed him completely unfairly, it has to be said, as 'though a Communist entirely bourgeois'. Indeed, as far as he could see 'as soon as a working man gets an official post in the Trade Union or goes into Labour politics, he becomes middle class'. Orwell went round collecting membership dues door to door with the NUWM collectors who were very keen to help him with his book. It was on one of these occasions that he saw a young woman kneeling in the gutter in the bitter cold trying to unblock the drain with a stick. This image is one of the most powerful that he incorporates into *The Road*, although he changes the context in which it occurred for the book.

Despite all the efforts of the NUWM though, he does not see any evidence of revolt in the making. Once again in the diary he describes attending an NUWM social in support of the German communist leader, Ernst Thaelmann. Most of the people at the social are women, 'young girls and shapeless middle-aged women' (we shall return to Orwell's sexism in Chapter 8) but they are, he supposes, 'a fair cross-section of the more revolutionary element in Wigan. If so, God help us . . . There is no turbulence left in England'.[14] He comes back from the North deeply pessimistic and argues that unless there is another war there are almost certainly several million men who will 'never have another job this side of the grave'. While he criticises the working class for being strong on organisation but weak on leadership, his own proposal of providing the unemployed with allotments hardly seems an answer to the situation! As it is, the working class have neither turned revolutionary nor lost their self-respect. He certainly acknowledges the demoralising impact that unemployment has, but argues that working-class communities in the North have in the main come to turns with their situation, adapted to it and above all remained human.

Why did the unemployed and the underpaid not rebel in these circumstances? First of all, it is important to note that he was of the opinion at this time that 'attempted insurrections' would have been counter-productive in a 'strongly governed country' like Britain, resulting only in 'futile massacres and a regime of savage repression'. In reality, of course, a more likely response was reforms and concessions combined with repression. Nevertheless, the main reason for the avoidance of either complete despair or revolutionary outbreaks is, Orwell argues, the availability of 'cheap luxuries'. This post-war development has been 'very fortunate for our rulers'. The unemployed and the low-paid have survived at a 'fish-and-chip standard'. Indeed, 'fish-and-chips, art-silk stockings, tinned salmon, cut-price chocolate (five two ounce bars for sixpence), the movies, the radio, strong tea and the Football Pools have between them averted revolution'.

Before we move on to discuss the second part of *The Road to Wigan Pier*, it is worth noting that Orwell comments on the difficulty of what he called 'class-breaking' in his correspondence with Jack Common.

Class difference made intimacy impossible, he found. When even working-class men who were members of the Communist Party could not help but call the ex-public school socialist, who wanted to know about their working, living and housing conditions, 'sir', what hope was there? There was a plate glass of class difference separating him from them so that they could see each other but never actually touch. The intimacy that had been possible, indeed inevitable, on the tramp was not possible in working-class communities where outsiders from another class were treated with a mixture of suspicion, hostility and subservience. Which brings us to the allegation, for many years propagated by the Communist Party, that Orwell's politics were defined by his disgust at the smell of the working class. This was prompted by Orwell's assertion in *The Road* that middle-class people were actually bought up to believe that the working-class smell. As he makes absolutely clear in the book, he no longer had 'feelings of that kind'. It was Harry Pollitt himself who successfully attached this particular slander to the book in a review he wrote for the *Daily Worker*. As Bernard Crick has pointed out, the very fact that the CP leader himself felt compelled to go after the book was 'a sign of the importance he attached to it'. Orwell put this slanderous attempt to discredit him, almost certainly correctly, down to the fact that he was fighting in the ranks of the semi-Trotskyist POUM at the time the book came out and consequently as far as the CP leadership was concerned any method of attacking him was permissible. Indeed, they would have regarded his death in Spain at the hands of the Russian secret police as something that was perfectly legitimate, although they would, of course, at the same time have strenuously denied that any such thing had taken place. Orwell threatened legal action, among other things, if the slander continued.[15]

The Smell of Crankishness

It is the second part of *The Road to Wigan Pier* that was the most contro-versial, however. Here Orwell put on display his considerable prejudices against the middle-class left. The primary target was without any serious doubt some of the middle-class socialists around *The Adelphi*. He asks why it is that while existing social conditions cry out for socialism ('every empty belly is an argument for Socialism'), the socialist movement is so weak. Rather than identifying the appalling performance of the Labour government of 1929–31, leading up to the effective defection of Prime

Minister Ramsay MacDonald and Chancellor of the Exchequer Philip Snowden to the Conservatives as the main problem, he places the blame on the secret teetotallers 'with vegetarian leanings' who inhabit the left and alienate the working class. The left attracts all the cranks and just to be helpful in identifying the culprits he provides a quite extensive list: those to blame are the 'fruit-juice drinker, nudist, sandal-wearer, sex-maniac, Quaker, "Nature Cure" quack, pacifist and feminist'. The 'smell of crankishness' has to be dispelled. As for the middle-class Fabians, they don't really object to the misery capitalism inflicts but more to its untidiness. They don't see themselves as part of any movement of the masses, but rather as clever people imposing reforms from above on 'the Lower Orders' for their own good. Not that the manual working class escape their share of the blame. He states quite categorically that 'no working man grasps the deeper implications of Socialism'. For a lot of working-class people all that socialism amounted to was 'better wages and shorter hours and nobody bossing you about'. It was 'present society with the worst abuses left out'. As far as he was concerned socialism 'cannot be narrowed down to mere economic justice' but would involve change of such a 'magnitude' as to 'work immense changes in our civilisation'. He deals with those workers who actually do recognise the scale of the change socialism will involve, 'the more revolutionary type', by a convenient sleight of hand whereby they are no longer considered as being 'genuine' workers. And with somewhat throwaway phrases, he ensured the unforgiving hostility of the CP by both dismissing 'the stupid cult of Russia' and referring to Soviet Commissars as being 'half gangster, half gramophone'. Understandably, Orwell himself felt it was necessary to insist at one point that readers should 'please notice that I am arguing for Socialism, not against it'.[16]

Many of the problems to do with the struggle for socialism that Orwell was grappling with, not too successfully it must be said, in *The Road to Wigan Pier* were to be answered as far as he was concerned in Spain. He left to fight in Spain before the book was even published.

'The Working Class Was In The Saddle'

In *The Road to Wigan Pier*, Orwell was writing about a working class that had suffered massive defeats and was still on the defensive. The 1926 General Strike had ended in defeat and mass victimisation and the Great Miners' Lockout had ended with the strongest section of the working class starved back to work, their pay and conditions savaged and their union crushed. In many areas scab unions had been successfully established by the mine owners. All this had been compounded by the performance of the Labour government that took office in 1929, presiding helplessly over the onset of the Great Depression and the mass unemployment that came with it. This government had been preparing to impose cuts in benefit on the unemployed and in pay on public sector workers, breaking up only over how drastic the cuts should be. At which point the man who had led the Labour Party for many years, Ramsay MacDonald, effectively defected to the Conservatives, becoming Prime Minister in a viciously right-wing National Government that proceeded to push through a programme of massive cuts, inflicting immense suffering, hardship and misery on millions of working-class people. In these circumstances, Orwell's confusion in *The Road* can perhaps be forgiven. When he arrived in Spain to fight for the Republic against the military rebels and their fascist allies, he encountered a radically different situation.

What Orwell found when he arrived in revolutionary Barcelona was, as he later wrote in *Homage to Catalonia*, 'a town where the working class was in the saddle'. He had gone from a country where the working class was still experiencing the consequences of historic defeats and betrayals to one where the working class was in control and fighting for its life against armed reaction. As he recalled:

> Practically every building of any size had been seized by the workers and was draped with red flags or with the red and black flag of the Anarchists, every wall was scrawled with the hammer and sickle and with the initials of the revolutionary parties, almost every church had been gutted and its images burned . . . Every shop and café had an inscription that it had been collectivised; even the bootblacks had been collectivised and their boxes painted red and black . . . it was a town in which the wealthy classes had practically ceased to exist . . . All this was queer and moving. There was much in it that I did not understand, in some ways I did not even like it, but I recognised it immediately as a state of affairs worth fighting for.[17]

What he had encountered in Barcelona 'really was a workers' State'.

Instead of the 'class in itself' that Orwell had written about in *The Road*, in Spain he saw a 'class for itself'. Although he does not use this terminology, his description of the revolution in Barcelona makes absolutely clear that this was what he had seen. Whereas in Britain, the working class would have most likely resisted a military coup in 'the name of "democracy" and the status quo', the Spanish working class had staged 'a definite revolutionary outbreak'. The peasants had seized the land and 'many factories and most of the transport were seized by the trade unions'. The workers' uprising that had foiled the military coup was, 'the kind of effort that could probably only be made by people who were fighting with a revolutionary intention . . . Men and women armed only with sticks of dynamite rushed across open squares and stormed stone buildings held by trained soldiers with machine guns. Machine gun nests . . . were smashed by rushing taxis at them at sixty miles an hour'. Even leaving aside 'the setting up of local soviets etc', working men and women did not do this kind of thing 'for the preservation of capitalist democracy'.[18] In Britain, he had seen the working class living in a society the capitalists had made, adapting to it as best they could, whereas in Spain he saw the working class reshaping society in their image, overthrowing the class system altogether.

Nevertheless, when Orwell first arrived in Spain, he was more sympathetic to the position advocated by the CP: that the revolution should be put on hold in order to concentrate on the defeat of Franco. He had originally hoped to join the International Brigades, but any such move was blocked by Pollitt. In this respect, it is not too strong a point to argue that Pollitt saved his life, because it was most unlikely that Orwell would have survived Spain otherwise. If he was not killed fighting the fascists on the Madrid front then he would have almost certainly been disposed of by the Communist secret police. Indeed, Orwell later recognised as much himself. As he told Jack Common, if he had joined the International Brigades then he should 'no doubt . . . have had a bullet in the back for being "politically unreliable"', that or jail.[19] Instead, he joined the POUM militia.

The POUM militia was another revelation. Here he experienced 'a foretaste of Socialism, by which I mean that the prevailing mental atmosphere was that of Socialism'. Ordinary class divisions did not exist in the ranks of the militia, something 'that is almost unthinkable in the money-tainted air of England'. It was social equality that 'attracts ordinary men to Socialism and makes them willing to risk their skins for it'. For the majority of people, Orwell insisted, 'Socialism means a classless society or it means nothing at all' and in the POUM militia he found 'a sort of microcosm of a classless society'. The experience left his 'desire to see Socialism established more actual than it had been before'. For Orwell, one important aspect of this socialist microcosm was that class difference had broken down, been overcome, so that the plate glass between the classes that had proven unbreakable in the North of England, in Spain had been shattered by the revolution.[20]

Only after he had served at the front and returned on leave to Barcelona in May 1937, still hoping to transfer to the International Brigades, did he realise that the communist position was not one of putting the revolution on hold, but that they were in fact in the process of eliminating the revolutionary gains that had been made and suppressing the revolutionary left, with the POUM as their primary target. He took part in the unsuccessful May Uprising in Barcelona and subsequently when the CP moved to suppress the POUM had to flee for his life. These were decisive moments for Orwell. He had seen the working class in power in Barcelona so that revolution was no longer something to be merely read about but was now something that he had practical experience of. And now he found that far from helping carry forward the struggle for socialism, the communists were busy putting it down in the interests of Soviet foreign policy. The belief that socialism was possible and that the necessary agency for overthrowing capitalism and establishing it was the working class was, with whatever qualifications, to remain at the centre of his political thinking for the rest of his life. As was the grim recognition that the Soviet Union, far from being a beacon of socialism, was an obstacle to, an opponent of socialism, and, that CP members throughout the world, far from being fighters for socialism, were, in practice, whether they realised it or not, the servants of Soviet foreign policy. In the service of the Soviet Union, they would lie and slander and indeed, where possible and if necessary, some of them were prepared to kill their opponents on the left. Orwell later wrote to Cyril Connolly, complaining of all the lies, mostly communist inspired, that were being told about the POUM and the May Uprising in Barcelona in Britain, but still he insisted that 'I have seen wonderful things and at last really believe in Socialism, which I never did before'.[21]

'Revolutionise Britain'

Orwell's revolutionary commitment continued up to and into the early years of the Second World War. He thought/hoped that the defeats of 1940–42 would create a revolutionary situation that would see the overthrow of capitalism in Britain, the establishment of socialism and the launching of a revolutionary war against the Nazis. The influence of his experiences in Spain is clear, but at the same time he recognised that Britain was not Spain. A British revolution would inevitably be different from either the Spanish or Russian revolutions. Nevertheless, he remained insistent about the role of the working class as agency and a classless society as objective. Sometime during 1942, he wrote an article, 'Looking Back on the Spanish War' that rehearsed a number of important issues. Among them was his blunt declaration to the effect that 'the backbone of the resistance against Franco was the Spanish working class, especially the urban trade union members'. It was important (his word), he insisted, to remember that 'in the long run – the working class remains the most reliable enemy of Fascism, simply because the working class stands to gain most by a decent reconstruction of society'. This was, he made clear, true only in the long run, however. He certainly did not romanticise or idealise the working class. He made so much absolutely clear when he went on:

> In the long struggle that has followed the Russian Revolution it is the manual workers who have been defeated, and it is impossible not to feel that it was their own fault. Time after time, in country after country, the organised working-class movements have been crushed by open, illegal violence, and their comrades abroad, linked to them in theoretical solidarity, have simply looked on and done nothing . . . Who can believe in the class conscious international proletariat after the events of the past ten years. To the British working class the massacre of their comrades in Vienna, Berlin, Madrid, or wherever it might be, seemed less interesting and less important than yesterday's football match.[22]

Even worse were the 'betrayals' of struggles in the colonies: 'between white and coloured workers there is not even lip-service to solidarity'. Despite this harsh assessment, he still argued that this did 'not alter the fact that the working class will go on struggling against Fascism after the others have caved in'. While the working class was ignorant and so could be tricked by fascist promises in the short term, they would inevitably discover 'in their own bodies . . . that the promises of Fascism cannot be fulfilled'. To permanently win over the working class, the fascists would have to raise their standard of living in a way that was impossible and that they never intended to do anyway so that sooner or later the workers would again take up the struggle for a better world. As he somewhat crudely put it: 'The struggle of the working class is like the growth of a plant. The plant is blind and stupid, but it knows enough to keep pushing upwards towards the light, and it will do this in the face of endless discouragement'. He personalised this belief in the working class in his encounter, when he had first arrived in Spain, with a nameless Italian militia volunteer who had welcomed him to the struggle without question or equivocation and shaken his hand. This man had been born knowing what Orwell had had 'to learn out of books and slowly' at that. He was the embodiment of 'the crystal spirit' and the Spanish War, the Second World War and other wars still to come were at bottom all about whether people like that Italian soldier should 'be allowed to live the decent fully human life which is now technically achievable, or shan't they?'[23]

At the same time, Orwell was grappling with Britain's changing social structure and the implications of this for the socialist struggle. He explored this question in the short book, *The Lion and the Unicorn*, which he wrote for the Searchlight series that he and Tosco Fyvel edited in 1941–42.[24] Here he rejected the idea of what he described as an old-fashioned proletarian revolution still being possible in a country like Britain. Instead of the advance of industry eliminating the middle class as Marxist theory predicted, it had, in fact, grown. Indeed, a new middle class had come into existence and had expanded to such an extent that it was essential that the socialist movement embrace 'the people who are most at home in and most definitely of the modern world, the technicians and the higher-paid skilled workers, the radio experts, film producers, popular journalists and industrial chemists', along with 'doctors, lawyers, teachers and artists etc'. These were an 'indeterminate stratum' that could or rather had to be won over to socialism. In *The Lion and the Unicorn*, Orwell argued for the setting up of a new Socialist Party that would have 'its mass following in the Trade Unions' but that at the same time 'it will draw into it most of the middle class'. And, he thought that most of the 'directing brains' of this new Socialist Party would come 'from the new indeterminate class of skilled workers, technical experts, airmen, scientists, architects and journalists, the people who feel at home in the radio and ferro-concrete age'. It is worth making the point that Orwell remained convinced that the new Socialist Party he hoped for would inevitably meet with armed resistance when it set about overthrowing capitalism and that this resistance would have to be met with whatever force was necessary. The capitalist class would not surrender its wealth and power without a fight, although the ferocity of that battle would vary from country to country. As he made clear a socialist government in Britain 'will crush any open revolt promptly and cruelly' and 'will shoot traitors, but it will give them a solemn trial before hand, and occasionally it will acquit them'. This was the British or rather, as he would have put it, the English way of proceeding.[25] The belief that any real attempt to carry through a socialist transformation in Britain would inevitably meet with armed resistance was something that Orwell always adhered to.

'Blind and Stupid'

One criticism of Orwell has been that while paying lip-service to the working class as the agency of socialism, in reality he regarded working-class people, in his own words, as 'blind and stupid'. According to Scott Lucas, one of Orwell's most determined critics on the left, *The Road to Wigan Pier* revealed that Orwell certainly did not regard the working class as 'a potential force to be mobilised', indeed they were 'too passive, misguided or ignorant for this'. He had 'jettisoned' the working class in favour of 'the exploited Middle Class'. And even when he later seemed to put his faith in the working class, nevertheless there was still 'all the time the sensation of kicking against the impenetrable wall of stupidity'. Sometimes this very stupidity was an advantage that 'stood them in good stead' because if they had understood how desperate Britain's position was in 1940–41 they would have been 'squealing for peace'. Indeed, such was Orwell's caricature of the working class that it was 'like waiting for Dick Van Dyke's chirpy cockney in Mary Poppins to start a revolution'.[26] Coming at him from a CP perspective, Beatrix Campbell accused him of having a 'big brotherly view of the working class', as regarding them as 'dead common', as having an attitude towards them that 'edges on contempt'. At her most generous, she concedes that he might well think 'the working class is the revolutionary class, but he doesn't feel it'. But more generally, he 'cannot conceive of the working class itself as a thinking class'. He 'fails to give it any place in the revolutionary cast, other than in a supporting role, the proverbial extras'.[27]

The problem with these and other critiques from the left are not only do they not do justice to the politics of *The Road to Wigan Pier* or of *Animal Farm* but that they do not recognise the decisive impact that revolutionary Barcelona had on Orwell. In Spain, he had seen the working class 'in the saddle'. This was the decisive moment in his political formation. What his critics on the left take to be his dismissal, even contempt for the working class, is, in fact, his attempt to find a way of explaining to himself, of conceptualising the failure of the British working class to go from being a class in itself to a class for itself. Certainly, he does not do this successfully and his use of language is often ill-chosen, offensive even, but nevertheless when his overall political trajectory is examined, it is clear that with whatever qualifications, momentary doubts and temporary backsliding, Orwell remained committed to the socialist cause and to the working class as the people who would bring it to realisation right up until his death. What he saw as necessary was for winning the middle class over to the socialist cause, to the fight for a classless society, was for them to give up their snobbery and to recognise that they had nothing to lose but their 'aitches'.

The claim that Orwell had contempt for working-class men and women is also starkly contradicted by the fact that while he saw the economic failures of capitalism, whether in its liberal or fascist guise, as underpinning the role of the working class as the agency of socialist transformation, he also regarded the working class as the social group that had remained most human. During the 1930s, when many middle-class socialists had enthusiastically embraced Stalinism, believing or at least pretending to believe for reasons of political expediency the most outrageous lies, the working class's essential decency had kept them from such a betrayal. Not only that, after his return from Spain, he still longed for breaking down of the plate glass of class difference. George Woodcock remembered how at the end of the war, Orwell was living in a flat in Islington, 'a lower middle class outpost on the edge of a great workers' district'. Orwell was always 'highly conscious of the geography of classes, and the whole area around Canonbury Square, with its bombed out houses and flooded basements and ruins red in summer with fireweed, had the kind of seediness he liked . . . ' These 'marginal districts gave him the comforting illusion of nearness to the British workingman – that nearness he sought so often and so vainly'. When they went for a drink together in a local pub, 'George did not appear to know any of the workingmen who frequented the pub, and he certainly seemed out of place among them, a rather frayed sahib wearing shabby clothes . . . an old Etonian'.[28]

The problem that Orwell faced is explored quite nicely by the literary critic and New York intellectual, Alfred Kazin, who like Orwell was a contributor to the US journal *Partisan Review*. He arrived in Britain in February 1945 and in his memoir, *New York Jew*, he described the country he found himself in as 'a social battleground'. He was greeted at the docks by the slogan, HANDS OFF GREECE, scrawled on a wall. He was here to investigate the provision of education for British service men and women and for war workers on behalf of the Rockefeller Foundation. In this capacity, he met with and talked to soldiers, firemen, nurses and factory workers across the country. What he found was 'a burning sense of grievance among workers in the factories and soldiers fighting abroad or still in barracks. Their sense of injustice was irrevocable, a sacrament, a pledge of common feeling'. As he put it, 'Historic bitterness and grumbling fatalism gave the working class identity to itself, its sense of having been long marked out and put down'. This was the work of centuries so that 'the workers were their own people, belonged to nobody but themselves'. They had 'their separate speech, their pubs, their "low" feeding habits, their ancient bitter humor' and these were all 'sacred to themselves'. Indeed, the English working class, he thought, actually 'liked class differences. They thrived on the social drama'. He also managed to meet a number of British writers, journalists and left-wing intellectuals, but the man he most wanted to meet, George Orwell was, at the time of his visit, working as a war correspondent on the continent. Nevertheless, he discussed Orwell with other people and actually remarks on how one working-class Labour Party secretary in Limehouse simply dismissed him, despite his association with the *Tribune* newspaper, as 'not one of us'.[29]

No Feeling of Solidarity with the 'Coloured Working Class'

One other aspect of Orwell's attitude towards and ideas about the working class requires discussion here. He returned from Burma a convinced anti-imperialist and while the strategic urgency with which he regarded the fight against the Empire was subject to change according to the circumstances, his commitment to anti-Imperialism remained throughout his life. This anti-imperialism involved recognising the economic benefits that Britain gained through the exploitation of the colonies and the extent to which even the British working class were the beneficiaries of this exploitation. He regularly returns to this theme although the ferocity with which he grapples with it, once again varies. As early as *The Road to Wigan Pier*, he made the point that 'the high standard of life we enjoy in England depends upon our keeping a tight hold on the Empire, particularly the tropical portions of it such as India and Africa'.[30] This was something that he thought socialists often refused to face up to: that socialism and anti-imperialism were inseparable and that justice for working-class people in Britain had to involve justice for working-class people in the colonies. This would have to involve sacrifices at least in the short term. His anti-imperialism was most fierce after his return from Spain. What was often forgotten, he argued, was 'that the overwhelming bulk of the British proletariat does not live in Britain, but in Asia and Africa'. Further, that in India wages of 'a penny an hour' are perfectly normal, 'and we are at great pains to keep it so'. While the average annual income in Britain was 'something over £80', in India it was only 'about £7' which gave 'some idea of the real relationship of England and India'. This, he insisted was 'the system which we all live on'.[31] He had earlier (26 December 1938) written to Jack Common complaining about the weakness of anti-imperialism on the left which 'simply sickens me'. The problem was 'that the working class in England and France have absolutely no feeling of solidarity with the coloured working class'.[32] This had to change if there was to be any advance towards socialism.

He was still complaining of the weakness of anti-imperialism on the left in 1945, that there was no real concern about India at Labour Party meetings and no recognition that justice would have to be done to the colonies, not just independence, but economic justice as well.[33] And in the summer of 1947, he once again insisted that the British people, including the working class 'owed their high standard of life to direct or indirect exploitation of coloured peoples'. By world standards, the British worker 'is living above his income' so that socialism might well involve an overall fall in British living standards in order to do justice to workers in the colonies.[34] Socialism, Orwell insisted, would be better but not necessarily more comfortable than capitalism at least in the early days, but you could not have socialism in countries like Britain and France on the backs of the exploited workers in India and Africa.

'If there is Hope it lies in the Proles'

With the Second World War coming to an end, Orwell gave up his hopes for the emergence of a new Socialist Party and instead gave his support to the Labour Party as the best alternative on offer. There were occasions when he thought that the Labour government that took power in 1945 might actually be moving the country in a socialist direction, might actually confront the upper class, but these hopes did not last long. He soon realised that the Atlee government was not going to abolish the British ruling class and that its reforms were never going to fundamentally threaten their position. And, moreover, as far as he could see, the working class was happy with this. What the working class wanted was a better deal from their rulers, rather than their overthrow once and for all. This moderate reformism was why there was no ruling class attempt to overthrow the Labour government. From his point of view, while he supported the Labour government, despite considerable disappointment, he certainly did not believe that it was socialist and, indeed, thought the prospects for socialism were pretty grim (see Chapter 5). It is this pessimism that, at least in part, informs *Nineteen Eighty-Four*, although it is also important to remember that Orwell thought a totalitarian world was only one of the possible outcomes of post-war conflicts. And the fact remains that while his portrayal of a totalitarian state ruling by means of terror and lies is extremely compelling, the book through the voice of Winston Smith also powerfully endorses the belief that the working class is the agency whereby Big Brother can be overthrown and a better world created.

Winston Smith inhabits a recognisably Stalinist Britain where his own parents had disappeared in one of the first great purges in the 1950s. In his own lifetime, he can think of perhaps thirty people that he knew personally, other than his parents, who had disappeared. But this was a totalitarian regime that had moved beyond Stalinism. The degree of surveillance and the ability to manipulate, control and invent the 'truth' go way beyond anything actually achieved in the Soviet Union and its satellite states. As Eric Hobsbawm put it, *Nineteen Eighty-Four* certainly showed 'what Stalin would have wanted to achieve', but it was beyond the capabilities of the time. The book was science fiction, a projection into a horrific future.[35] Its portrayal of the working class was, however, very contemporary.

The 'proles' are not kept suppressed by the terrorist methods that are used against what we can usefully call the middle or managerial class but by the same methods that Orwell believed were used in the Britain of his boyhood through to the late 1940s. They were not worth the attention of the Thought Police, but could instead be left in ignorance and apathy, not even really human. This was most definitely not an attitude taken by either the Nazi or the Stalin regimes. Under Big Brother though, the proles were largely left to themselves:

> They were born, they grew up in the gutters, they went to work at twelve, they passed through a brief blossoming-period of beauty and sexual desire, they married at twenty they were middle-aged at thirty, they died for the most part at sixty. Heavy physical work, the care of home and children, petty quarrels with neighbours, films, football, beer and, above all, gambling, filled up the horizon of their minds.[36]

On one occasion, when he was walking through a working-class district, Smith sees two men having a fierce argument over something in the newspaper. They were arguing about the Lottery numbers! The Lottery, 'with its weekly pay-out of enormous prizes, was the one public event to which the proles paid serious attention . . . It was their delight, their folly, their anodyne, their intellectual stimulant'. When it came to the Lottery, men and women who could barely read and write were 'capable of intricate calculations and staggering feats of memory'.[37]

There were only a few Thought Police keeping an eye on the proles, 'spreading false rumours and marking down and eliminating the few individuals who were judged capable of becoming dangerous', but that was about it. Otherwise, they 'were beneath suspicion'. No real attempt was made to indoctrinate the proles because the Party did not want them to have any 'strong political feelings' of any description. Instead all that was required of the proles was a 'primitive patriotism which could be appealed to whenever it was necessary to make them accept longer working-hours or shorter rations'. Even when their hardships led to unrest, this led nowhere because 'being without general ideas, they could only focus on petty specific grievances' and 'the larger evils escaped their notice'.[38] And yet, as far as Smith is concerned if there is hope, 'it lies with the proles'. This is something that he debates with himself throughout much of the book.

Certainly the Party has contempt for the proles, but the idea that Orwell shares that contempt is false. Smith has his own moment of epiphany when he suddenly realises where the strength of the proles lay. They 'were not loyal to a party or a country or an idea, they were loyal to one another'.[39] He did not 'despise them or think of them merely as an inert force which would one day spring to life and regenerate the world. The proles had stayed human'.[40] There is a particularly pertinent passage in Emmanuel Goldstein's often skipped and little read *The Theory and Practice of Oligarchical Collectivism* that surely holds the key to Orwell's thinking:

> . . . if leisure and security were enjoyed by all alike, the great mass of human beings who are normally stupefied by poverty would become literate and would learn to think for themselves, and when once they had done this, they would sooner or later realise that the privileged minority had no function, and they would sweep it away. In the long run, a hierarchical society was only possible on a basis of poverty and ignorance.[41]

The problem is most certainly not stupidity, but rather poverty and ignorance.

As far as Smith is concerned, if only the proles could 'somehow become conscious of their own strength' then they could rise up tomorrow, 'shake themselves like a horse shaking off flies', and 'blow the Party to pieces'. Surely sooner or later, they must do it. The problem was that until they become conscious 'they will never rebel, and until after they have rebelled they cannot become conscious'.[42] Neither Smith nor Orwell ever resolves that particular conundrum so that the proposition that hope lies with the proles remains for Smith both 'a mystical truth and a palpable absurdity'. In the end, at the very moment of his arrest, Smith goes with the 'mystical truth'. When he is watching the working-class woman singing while hanging out the washing, he experiences a 'mystical reverence' for her', recognising that

> . . . everywhere, all over the world, hundreds of thousands of millions of people just like this, people ignorant of one another's existence, held apart by walls of hatred and lies, and yet almost exactly the same – people who had never learned to think but who were storing up in their hearts and bellies and muscles the power that would one day overturn the world . . . All round the world, in London and New York, in Africa and Brazil and in the mysterious, forbidden lands beyond the frontiers, in the streets of Paris and Berlin, in the villages of the endless Russian plain, in the bazaars of China and Japan – everywhere

stood the same solid unconquerable figure, made monstrous by work and childbearing, toiling from birth to death and still singing. Out of those loins a race of conscious beings must one day come.

For Winston Smith as for George Orwell, 'if there was hope, it lay in the proles!'[43]

2

'Why I Join the ILP':
Orwell and the Left in the Thirties

Orwell's return home from Burma and resignation from the colonial police set him on a new path, but it was his experiences during the 1930s that determined the direction that path took. Certainly, during his time in Paris, he had already identified himself with the left in a broad sense and this was to continue and deepen on his return to Britain. Here he found a defeated and betrayed Labour movement that was experiencing the rigours of 'austerity' at the hands of a Conservative-dominated National Government. First the defeat of the General Strike and the great Miners' Lockout in 1926 and then the debacle of the 1929–31 Labour government, which fell apart over the scale of the cuts to be imposed on the unemployed. The Labour Party was wrecked by this failure, leaving the working class – but most especially the unemployed to the tender mercies of the Conservatives. Orwell, as we have seen, was determined to experience life as it was lived by the casually employed and homeless, but the onset of the Great Depression and the arrival of mass unemployment changed the situation dramatically. Partly, it was because the Great Depression put systemic change on the agenda. The scale of the crisis of capitalism was such that reform, to many people, was no longer enough. What was needed was a radical transformation sweeping the old order away altogether. Clearly no such change was going to come from a Labour Party committed, in the words of Ralph Miliband, to 'MacDonaldism without MacDonald',[1] but if not the Labour Party, then where would it come? From the Communist Party? From the Independent Labour Party (ILP)? And, while the Conservatives were dominant in Britain, on the continent there was the rise of fascism, with the Nazis taking power in Germany in 1933 and strong fascist movements developing in other countries. In Britain, a former junior minister in the Labour government, Oswald Mosley had established the British Union of Fascists, hoping to replicate Hitler's rise.

At this time, while Orwell had reservations about the Communist Party, he still regarded it as being on the same side, as part of the struggle for socialism. This was, of course, to change after his experiences in Spain. Most congenial was the ILP, although he still had reservations. As we shall see, he was to actually join the ILP after his return from Spain, even if only briefly, the only political party he was to ever join. It was the *Adelphi* magazine that was to lead him towards the ILP.

'The ILP Was the Only British Party I Felt Like Joining'

The ILP had been founded as long ago as 1893, a reformist socialist organisation that, when electoral success failed to materialise, turned to the trade unions for support. It was one of the key constituents of the Labour Party when it was established in alliance with the trade unions in 1900. While in the years before the outbreak of the First World War, the Parliamentary Labour Party functioned as little more than the left of the Liberal Party, the ILP remained committed to reformist socialism and was very critical of the Labour Party leadership. This was the time of the Great Labour Revolt when massive strikes, often unofficial, swept over much of the country. In this period, the ILP lost some members to the more militant Marxist British Socialist Party and more to the struggle on the shop floor in industry. It declined from 887 branches in 1909 to 672 in 1914. The ILP was opposed to the First World War, but more from a pacifist than a revolutionary point of view. Of the 1,191 conscientious objectors put on trial during the War, 805 were ILP members. The ILP increased in strength as the war went on, particularly on Clydeside, where its members were involved in the great trade union struggles of the time, in militant rent strikes and in campaigning against the war.

After the war, the Labour Party's new constitution, committing the organisation to reformist socialism for the first time and establishing a system of individual membership, caused problems for the ILP. What was the point of its existence now that the Labour Party itself was, at least formally, a socialist organisation and that socialists could join it directly rather than through an affiliate like the ILP? An additional problem was, of course, that as far as the Party leadership was concerned, its socialist commitment was only nominal, something that got the membership out canvassing during elections, but that could be safely ignored the rest of the time. The ILP found itself increasingly at odds with the timid conservatism displayed by Labour in office, both in 1924 and in 1929–31.

Disillusion was such that in 1924 when the first MacDonald government was on the verge of collapse, the ILP leader, James Maxton expressed the opinion that 'the sooner they were out the better, as every day they were in led us further from Socialism'.[2]

Relations became considerably worse during the 1929–31 Labour government. Maxton's vocal opposition to the government provoked great hostility. A militant group of ILP MPs around Maxton increasingly opposed the government, over its use of repression in India, but most fiercely over its failure to deal with the problem of rising unemployment. Maxton made their position clear in the Commons: the Labour government had committed itself to carrying on capitalism, a system 'which has never removed poverty from the lives of the people, which has never got over that great margin of unemployment, which has always kept the tremendous gulf between the poor and the rich, a gulf that is widening'. Even given this, the ILP MPs would still support the government but 'on one condition, and on one condition only, that they will so arrange the affairs of this country that no unemployed man, his wife or child, shall have any dread of starvation or insult'.[3] The Labour government failed even this minimal test. It was not just a question of refusing to raise the level of benefits, but of also refusing to ameliorate the brutal way they were administered under the notorious 'not genuinely seeking work' clause so as to disqualify as many claimants as possible. MacDonald's Minister of Labour, Margaret Bondfield, became one of the most hated people within the Labour movement.

A good indication of how strained relations were was provided when ILP militant John McGovern was elected to the Commons at the end of June 1930. He encountered the bitter hostility of the great majority of Labour MPs, remembering how when he was first introduced in the House, the Labour benches 'remained cold and frigid', rather than cheering the newly elected member as was customary. This was, he wrote, 'an omen of things to come. Every effort was made to squeeze the ILP out of political life'. Labour MPs regarded the ILP, whose every criticism of the government was to be vindicated, with 'anger and bitter hatred'.[4] The Labour Party National Executive began refusing to endorse candidates who gave their first loyalty to the ILP. For its part, the ILP condemned the Labour government for its embrace of financial orthodoxy and warned that this would inevitably lead to further attacks on the unemployed. When this came to pass, the government broke up, not over the question of cuts to the dole, but over their scale. MacDonald demanded unanimous support for the cuts he proposed and when he failed to get it decided to bring down his own government. This was even though most members of the cabinet had voted in favour. As Fenner Brockway put it, those Labour ministers who refused to back MacDonald and Snowden over the cuts had only drawn back 'at the fifty-ninth second of the eleventh hour . . . from the edge of the precipice to which they had led their party for two and a half years'.[5] And they still refused to change policy even though they had refused the inevitable conclusion that policy had led to.

The general election that followed the fall of the Labour government with the former leader of the Labour Party campaigning against it saw the Labour Party lose 243 seats, reduced from 289 MPs to only 46. The Labour Party had fewer seats than the Liberals! The result was also a disaster for the ILP with many MPs swept away as part of the Labour rout. The Labour Party National Executive had refused to endorse 19 ILP candidates and stood rival candidates against them. It was, of course, absolutely predictable that the Labour Party took no action against the ministers who had supported MacDonald right up until the very last moment, but instead took measures to curb the left. The bitterness of Labour MPs against MacDonald's ILP critics was every bit as great as their bitterness against MacDonald. It was often reciprocated. McGovern, one of those 19 who was nevertheless re-elected, remembered in his constituency of Shettlestone, how his supporters 'chased the Labour candidate down public streets where he was rescued by the police and put on a bus . . . the Labour candidate lost his deposit'.[6] Despite such individual successes, however, the ILP contingent in the Commons was reduced to five. Refused the Labour whip, once Parliament reassembled, under Maxton's leadership, they acted as an independent party even before disaffiliation. Even so a split was still not inevitable, but the Labour leadership was not prepared to tolerate a leftwing opposition within its own ranks any longer, especially one that insisted that it was not just MacDonald and Snowden but the party leadership as a whole that bore responsibility for the policies that had led up to the debacle of 1931. At its March 1932 Conference, the ILP voted to disaffiliate from the Labour Party by 241 votes to 142. It is worth considering what was the essential difference between the Labour Party and the ILP at this time? The Labour Party was, as far as the ILP were concerned, only interested in patching up capitalism, at the expense of the working class if necessary, whereas the ILP proposed to begin the process of legislating capitalism out of existence as soon as they took office. The Labour Party were parliamentary reformists whereas the Maxton ILP saw themselves as parliamentary revolutionaries!

The decision to disaffiliate from Labour cost the ILP members. By November 1932 the number of branches had fallen from 653 to 450. Among the members who left were many of those holding elected office who regarded their chances of retaining their council seats and union positions as better if they remained within the Labour Party. In Glasgow, 40 of the ILP's 44 councillors resigned over disaffiliation. For many ILP members, it looked as if their commitment to reformism could best be realised within the Labour Party regardless of Labour's actual performance in office and they turned their backs on the ILP's attempt to develop a 'revolutionary' way forward. At the same time, the ILP also faced the determined efforts of the Communist Party to destroy it, first from the left during the Third Period turn and later from the right during the Popular Front turn. From a membership of 16,773 in 1932, the ILP declined to 11,092 the following year, a decline that continued relentlessly throughout the 1930s as it found itself crushed between Labourism on the one hand and Stalinism on the other. The relative success of the CP's Popular Front turn was to do the ILP considerable damage. By 1939, membership had fallen to only 2,441.

'Marxism has to be Hammered into a New Shape'

The Communist Party of Great Britain had been established in response to the October Revolution in Russia, to the Bolshevik's fight for survival that followed, to the spread of the revolutionary wave westwards and to the great upsurge in class struggle that took place in Britain at the same time. With the defeat of the revolutionary movements in Finland, Hungary, Germany and elsewhere, with the failure of the revolution to become international, the Stalin faction emerged triumphant inside the Soviet Union. It embraced the ideology of 'Socialism In One Country', launched a policy of forced industrialisation at the expense of the Russian peasantry and working class and imposed a murderous police regime on the country. In the course of the 1930s, millions of people were to die of starvation, were worked to death in the slave labour camps or were executed for supposed political crimes in the Soviet Union. An unprecedented 'cult of the personality' was imposed, celebrating Joseph Stalin in almost God-like terms. There was the introduction of slave labour on a massive scale. The great purpose of this terrible experiment was to transform the Soviet Union into a modern military force that was able to protect its interests as a great power. And, of course, the Stalin regime ensured its domestic security by recurring massacres together with the staging of fake public trials of the surviving leaders of the October Revolution, both eliminating and intimidating any potential opposition. What is astonishing in retrospect is that this murderous regime of torturers and exploiters was celebrated as a socialist utopia, as the hope of humanity, by many of the best socialist activists, militants, propagandists and theorists in every country in the world. This phenomenon has still not been adequately explained.

Communist Parties were established with varying degrees of success throughout the world. They brought together many of the most determined fighters against capitalism and imperialism, men and women who had often made tremendous sacrifices in the struggle for a better world; victimised, imprisoned, beaten and, in many countries, killed. They were committed to a revolutionary struggle for workers' power, hoping to spread the revolution and make socialism global. With the Soviet Union's embrace of 'Socialism In One Country', however, Communist Parties throughout the world were instead dedicated to a different purpose: to the service of the country where 'socialism' was supposedly being built, to the Soviet Union and its interests. Instead of Communist Parties pursuing the cause of revolution and of international socialism, their campaigns and struggles were subordinated to the interests of Soviet foreign policy. This subordination was not accompanied without difficulty, meeting with considerable opposition in some national parties, but a combination of loyalty to the country of the October Revolution, a massive and systematic campaign of lies to disguise the realities of life for the common people and to hide the extent of repression inside the Soviet Union and often considerable financial subsidies, in the end, carried the day. One of the Communist Parties where the transformation was accomplished with the least difficulty was the British.

The ease with which the British CP transformed itself from a revolutionary socialist organisation into a reliable instrument of the Stalin regime probably reflected its small size. How on earth could a party that had achieved so little success challenge the wisdom of the people who had carried out the October Revolution and were building socialism in Russia? Men and women who had devoted their lives to fighting for a better world for the working class, often making great sacrifices in that struggle, instead found themselves fighting in the service of what was in the 1930s, without any doubt, the most brutal and murderous tyranny in the world. Certainly the rank and file believed the lies they were told about life in the Soviet Union: that this was a country, the one country, where the workers' ruled, and they in their turn repeated these lies. The enemies of the Stalin regime became their enemies, the enemies of socialism, whether witting or unwitting, to be fought by any and all means. The CP leadership were not so innocent however. They might not have appreciated the actual scale of the repression or the appalling living and working conditions of Russian workers as compared with the privileges of the new Soviet ruling class that was forming, but they certainly knew that the Soviet Union was no utopia. Even accepting that they did not know how bad conditions really were, what is interesting was that they still realised that they had to cover up what they did know and engage in systematic lying.

The first great demonstration of the British CP's subordination to the interests of the Soviet Union was its acceptance of the so-called 'Third Period' turn imposed by the Communist International (Comintern) in 1928. As Orwell put it, every new turn required that 'Marxism has to be hammered into a new shape'.[7] The politics of the Third Period proclaimed that the world had entered a period of revolutionary struggle and upheaval where the seizure of power was imminently possible and that consequently every effort had to be made to rally the forces of revolution. It meant an unrelenting fight against the reformists, whether it was the German Socialist Party or the British Labour Party. They stood as an obstacle between the workers and the cause of revolution and had to be swept aside. What the Third Period involved was a phase of intense ultra-sectarianism and ultra-leftism that was to have disastrous consequences for Communist Parties throughout the world. In Germany, the Third Period turn made the rise to power of the Nazis possible, with the strongest labour movement in the world divided, and fatally weakened, by the German Communist Party's war against the Socialist Party. Instead of fighting for a united front against the Nazis, the Communists argued that the Socialists were the main enemy, condemned them as 'Social Fascists', an argument still being urged when both parties were banned and their members were being carted off together to the concentration camps.

The consequences of the Third Period in Britain were, in comparison, of minor significance, reflecting the weakness of the British CP. Here the policy nearly resulted in the collapse of the CP as it found itself losing members and increasingly isolated because of its ultra-sectarianism. Not only was the Labour Party condemned as 'Social Fascist' with CP members being urged to break up their meetings where possible, but the Labour left was subjected to the most determined attack for being best placed to mislead the workers. The more a Labour Party activist was actually involved in the day-to-day struggles of the class, the greater danger he or she posed in this sectarian universe. Not someone to fight alongside, someone to be won over, but rather someone to be denounced and exposed as an enemy of the working class. This Third Period turn was carried into the trade union movement as well, with the unions being condemned as 'Social Fascist' and the CP committed to the estab-lishment of breakaway revolutionary trade unions, once again a recipe for isolation. The only reason this turn did not result in the complete collapse and disappearance of British Communism at this time was the financial subsidies provided by the Comintern.

To some extent Communist hostility towards both the Labour Party and trade union leaderships was a perfectly understandable response to their performance in the post-war years. The Labour government of 1924 had broken strikes and attacked the CP, the trade union leadership had sold-out the General Strike in 1926 and left the miners to be defeated in isolation during the Great Lockout, and the Labour government that took office in 1929 had done nothing for the unemployed except preside over a catastrophic increase in their number. And more generally, the Labour leadership opposed any attempts at fighting back against the capitalist system and its iniquities except at the ballot box. Nevertheless, the labelling of the Labour Party and the trade unions as 'Social Fascist' was absolutely not something that arose out of the realities of the class struggle in Britain. It was imposed by the Comintern. What is also important is that the CP embraced not only the ultra-sectarianism of the Third Period turn, but also the strategic understanding that lay behind it. The British CP, which in this period was reduced to some 2,000 members, acted in the belief that revolution was imminent in Britain. A working class that all the evidence indicated was still reeling from defeat and very much on the defensive, was to be related to as if it was gripped by revolutionary fervour and ready to overthrow capitalism! There can be no serious doubt that if left to work out its own path, the CP would have responded to the reality of working-class defeat rather than the fantasy of imminent revolution. Its leadership included men and women with considerable experience of the class struggle in Britain, not least Harry Pollitt himself. Instead of the reality of a working class on the defensive informing their revolutionary politics, however, they subordinated themselves to the Comintern, allowing the Stalin regime to define their reality for them. Their priority became not how well they served the interests of the working class in Britain and abroad, but how well they served the interests of the Soviet Union.[8]

This impacted on the ILP. At the same time as the ILP was losing members to the Labour Party, it was also under attack from both inside and outside from the CP. During the Third Period it was viewed as a particularly dangerous enemy because it stood on the left, ready to mislead the workers when they took the revolutionary path. They had to be smashed. In 1932, however, while the CP had 2,500 members, the ILP still had 16,700. When the Comintern abandoned the Third Period turn, belatedly recognising the threat that Nazi Germany posed to the Soviet Union, and began arguing for united front action on the left to fight fascism, the attempt to undermine, weaken and destroy the ILP as a rival continued. And then when the CP duly embraced the Popular Front turn in 1935, it began attacking the ILP for being too revolutionary, as if the Third Period turn had never been.

'An Unholy Alliance Between the Robbers and the Robbed'

Orwell's attitude towards the CP before his experiences in Spain was certainly critical, but nevertheless he still regarded them as certainly being on the same side. Indeed he had a lot of time for the dedication and self-sacrifice of the rank and file membership, but already regarded the leadership as 'Russia worshippers' and as importing into Britain an alien politics that would deter the mass of the working class from embracing the socialist cause. He had at this time no idea of the enormity of the crimes being committed in the name of socialism in the Soviet Union or indeed of the twists and turns that the CP had already been required to make in the service of Soviet foreign policy. Looking at *The Road to Wigan Pier,* middle-class, fruit juice-drinking, nudist vegetarians were, at this time, much more of a problem as far as he was concerned than Stalinism. With the Labour Party discredited by the 1929–31 debacle, the organisation that he believed was most likely to lead the fight for socialism was the ILP. His road to this conclusion led via the *Adelphi,* which as we have seen had established itself as the ILP's semi-official theoretical journal. This was certainly the view of Richard Rees, one of the magazine's editorial team, who argued that his 'evolution into the full-bloodied socialist of *The Road to Wigan Pier* and then into the front-line soldier in Spain was partly, I believed, the result of our association over the past six years'.[9] In the course of the 1930s, Orwell was to write some of his finest articles for the *Adelphi* along with various book reviews and the occasional poem, indeed one of his poems; 'On a Ruined Farm Near the His Master's Voice Gramophone Factory' was actually reprinted in *The Best Poems of 1934*.[10] In July 1936, Orwell attended an ILP summer school and the following month he went to the *Adelphi* summer school where he gave a lecture. According to Rees, at the *Adelphi* school, which he describes as having 'the makings of an independent socialist university', Orwell surprised everyone with the extent of his knowledge of and understanding of Marxism.[11]

While Orwell was moving towards the ILP, the CP was adopting the Popular Front, or People's Front turn, as it was more generally known in Britain. Whereas the Third Period turn had been a product of the struggle for power in the Soviet Union itself and of Soviet fear of a war of intervention spearheaded by an alliance of 'bourgeois democratic' countries, with the installation of the Nazi regime in Germany and the rise of fascist movements across Europe, the situation had changed. Now it was fascism that was the great enemy and the Soviet Union looked for alliances with those countries it had only recently considered a threat. Communist Parties throughout the world were now to drop all talk of revolution, commit themselves to the defence of bourgeois democracy instead and work to build anti-fascist alliances right across the political spectrum. Marxism was to be hammered into a completely different shape. These anti-fascist alliances were to urge their governments to enter into alliance with the Soviet Union. This was the essence of the Popular Front. The domestic class struggle was to be subordinated to the need for maximum unity against fascism and in defence of the Soviet Union. Anything that risked alienating even Conservatives who were potential anti-fascists had to be dropped. Those organisations on the left that refused to accept this reordering of priorities were now attacked at best for assisting the fascists and at worst for being either under fascist control or actually fascist. The Trotskyists were, of course 'Trotsky Fascists', a label that was to be gradually extended to cover just about everyone to the left of the CP. All these enemies of the working class were attacked with all the venom that CP propagandists were by now the masters of. The ILP refused to give up the class struggle and remained committed to fighting for socialism here and now. It found itself once again under attack from the CP, but whereas this attack had come from the 'left' during the Third Period turn, now it came from the 'right'.

For many people, the Popular Front turn has come to be seen as the defining policy of the Communist Party as if everything else was some sort of aberration. Without doubt it was remarkably successful in rescuing the CP from the near oblivion of the Third Period and saw the party gaining influence in some areas of political and cultural life. Nevertheless, it is worth insisting at this point that the Popular Front turn was something imposed by the Comintern. While there is no doubt that many Communists across the world recognised what a disaster the Third Period turn had been in Germany and were fearful of the rise of fascism in their own countries, nevertheless the Stalin regime exercised total control over the Comintern. It was, in the end, Stalin's decision to change tack. If the Stalin regime had not felt itself threatened by the rise of fascism in the 1930s, then there is no reason whatsoever to believe that the concerns of national Communist Parties about the threat posed by fascism would have had any effect on Comintern strategy. The connection was coincidental rather than causal. That this was the case was to be conclusively demonstrated when Stalin allied with the Nazis in 1939 and across the world every Communist Party, no matter what the reservations some of their leaders might have had or the damage their organisations were inevitably going to suffer as a result, faithfully supported the policy. Overnight anti-fascism, the Communists' watch-word since 1935, was dropped.

The Popular Front turn had one other dimension. There was one criterion for inclusion in the broad anti-fascist alliance that was not negotiable and this was either silence about or enthusiastic support for the Stalinist tyranny in the Soviet Union. While Communists throughout the world were campaigning in support of bourgeois democracy at home, the Great Terror was sweeping away hundreds of thousands of men and women in the Soviet Union. A regime of torture, slave labour and mass execution was in place in Russia. And the great show case of all this was, of course, the Moscow Trials. The historic fact is that the Stalinist regime in the 1930s was more brutal and murderous than the Nazi regime at this time. Hitler's crimes were a product of war and conquest, inflicted, in the main from 1939 through to 1945, not on the German people unless they were political opponents or Jewish, but on the inhabitants of those countries the Nazis had occupied. Stalin's Great Terror was targeted at his own people. Communists and those sympathetic to their cause, the 'fellow travellers', had to either deny or ignore the Great Terror and to enthusiastically support the Moscow Trials. Not only that, they had to turn a blind eye to the export of the Great Terror abroad, not least to Spain. Those who refused to join in this disgraceful cover-up found themselves threatened, abused and slandered.

The CP faithfully implemented the Popular Front turn and covered up the Great Terror; indeed they covered up the Great Terror even when it consumed one of their own. Rose Cohen, a well-known CP member, and a personal friend of Harry Pollitt's, had married a Russian, Max Petrovsky, and emigrated to the Soviet Union. In March 1937, he was arrested and shot in September of that year. She was arrested in August 1937, and charged with being a British spy. She was tried and executed in secret on 28 November 1937. Pollitt tried to intervene on her behalf privately, but she had already been shot. Not only did the CP make no protest about the disappearance of one of its own, someone who Pollitt and others certainly knew was a loyal Communist, but when the British government attempted to intervene, the *Daily Worker* insisted that the affair was an internal Soviet matter. With considerable justice, Francis Beckett has described this article as 'one of the most weaselly and discreditable pieces ever written, with its fastidious refusal to even mention the name of a woman who every leading Communist in Britain counted as a friend'.[12]

Rose Cohen was not alone. Another party member, Freda Utley, had married a Russian, Arcadi Berdichevsky, who was arrested and worked to death in a labour camp. Having kept her British passport, she escaped arrest herself and almost certain death, and back home attempted to get the CP to intervene on her husband's behalf. She found herself to be suddenly a 'non-person', shunned by her former comrades. She later wrote: 'I had the greatest respect and liking for Harry Pollitt…To this day I find it difficult to understand how this British working-class leader . . . came to subordinate his conscience and sacrifice his personal integrity to become a tool of Russian tyranny'. She recounted her experiences in one of the most powerful contemporary critiques of the Soviet Union from the Left, *The Dream We Lost*, published in 1940.[13]

'A Powerful Instrument for the CP'

What of the Popular Front in Britain? It never succeeded in overcoming the opposition of the Labour Party, but had one great success: the Left Book Club that was launched at the end of February 1936. Its editorial board originally consisted of Victor Gollancz, John Strachey, a CP fellow traveller, and Harold Laski, a left-wing Labour Party intellectual. By the time it published its first books in May, it had a membership of 9,000, rising to 26,000 by the end of the year. It had reached over 39,000 by March 1937 and was to reach a peak in April 1939 when membership reached 57,000. Overwhelmingly, the membership was made up of white collar workers and middle-class professionals. Nevertheless, not only was this a remarkable success, but the Club also published the 'Left News', a 30 page magazine that combined campaigning for the Popular Front with eulogising the Soviet Union and defending the Moscow Trials. Considerable effort went into trying to organise the Club membership into local groups and at its height over 1,200 were active with four full-time organisers helping run them. These held regular meetings and became involved in various campaigns, particularly once the Spanish Civil War had begun. According to John Lewis in his history of the Club, by early 1938, 'it was by far the largest and most enthusiastic political movement in the country . . . its members found that here was an organisation actively inviting their co-operation, engaged in weekly lectures and discussions and a great variety of cultural activities, film shows, concerts and plays'.[14] There were groups organised for accountants, taxi-drivers, scientists, architects, teachers, actors and so on. Over 250 amateur theatre groups were affiliated. It ran Russian classes and even 'tourist trips to the Soviet Union'.[15] It was, as the ILP put it, 'a powerful instrument for the CP'.[16]

From the very beginning the Club was close to the Communist Party, something that certainly worried Gollancz on occasions. He tried to at least hide the appearance of CP domination over the choice of books by commissioning volumes by non-Communists such as Clement Attlee, G D H Cole and others. When Cole objected to how his book was treated and complained of a pro-Communist bias, Gollancz assured him, quite untruthfully, that this was not the case, pointing to a manuscript that they had accepted that was 'quite violently anti-Communist'. This was *The Road to Wigan Pier*.[17] Ironically, *The Road* was to be the Club's biggest selling volume at the time (44,000 copies) and, of course, it's most successful by far over time, remaining in print long after the Club's other volumes have been forgotten. An interesting light is thrown on Gollancz's own attitude at this time by his quarrel with another non-Communist author, H N Brailsford over his *Why Capitalism Means War* at the end of 1937. Gollancz objected to the last chapter which he considered anti-Soviet. First, he assured Brailsford that the Club had published books critical of the Soviet Union, but then went on: 'I feel that the Soviet Union . . . is not only justified but impelled to take every possible measure that can prevent the faintest chance of disloyalty or disruption within: and that therefore in this period the dictatorship of the proletariat through the Communist Party must be not only maintained but increased'.[18] Laski, however, insisted it be published. He did, however, draw the line at what he considered to be 'Trotskyite attacks' which he regarded as 'a declaration of war' on the Soviet Union.[19]

'Spilling the Spanish Beans'

While he was most sympathetic towards the ILP, Orwell still considered the CP as being on the same side whatever his disagreements. If he had been allowed, he would certainly have gone to Spain under the auspices of the International Brigades, and even when he was serving with the POUM, he made clear to both his ILP and Spanish comrades that he was sympathetic to the Popular Front strategy in the circumstances that obtained in Spain. The most urgent task was to maximise support against Franco and his fascist allies and this was best achieved by putting the revolution on hold so as to avoid alienating those elements of the middle class still loyal to the Republic. The POUM instead urged that the best way to defeat Franco was to carry the revolution through to the replacement of the Republic by a fully-fledged Workers' State that would raise the standard of revolt in Spain's colonies and make the revolution international.

What Orwell did not realise was first of all that under cover of the Popular Front, the Comintern was actually committed to rolling back the revolutionary gains made by Spanish workers and to destroying both the POUM and the anarchists. The Comintern was faithfully implementing the priorities of Soviet foreign policy which were, at this time, to form alliances with Britain, France and other powers against Nazi Germany. Workers' revolution in Spain would, it was feared, have driven those powers into alliance with Nazi Germany. Instead, the Communists were committed to defeating Franco and supporting the consolidation of a bourgeois democratic government, allied with the Soviet Union, in power. Suppressing the revolutionary left was a necessary part of this objective. Another concern of the Comintern's was with silencing those to the left of the CP who were exposing the Moscow Trials as a judicial massacre and conditions inside the Soviet Union as having nothing to do with socialism. They certainly did not want them leading a successful revolution in Spain with all the credibility this would have given to their anti-Stalinism. The Communist line was to condemn those who rejected the Popular Front as either objectively fascist or actively fascist and in Spain, where possible, to imprison, torture and to kill them.

When Orwell went on leave to Barcelona in May 1937 it was with the intention of transferring to the International Brigades. Instead he found the Communists engaged in rolling back workers' power in the city and supported the general strike and armed uprising called against them. If this protest had occurred after his transfer had taken place, then it is most likely that we would be pondering whether or not his death was an accident or an execution disguised as an accident! He would certainly not have remained silent while the men and women he had served with in the trenches were slandered as fascists. It was at this point that he realised that whatever the idealism of the Communist rank and file, the Communist Parties in Britain and elsewhere were not allies in the struggle for socialism, but were, in fact, primarily concerned with advancing the interests of Soviet foreign policy; and that they were prepared to do this by systematic lying and slander in a country like Britain, and by torture and murder in a country like Spain.

One last point worth making here is that the academic consensus at the present time is very much to endorse the Popular Front, even if the crimes of the Communists have increasingly had to be acknowledged. This was the only way to have defeated Franco. What this tends to overlook is that the Popular Front actually failed in Spain, that France and Britain did not come to the Republic's aid, and that the Republic went down to defeat. While there can obviously be no guarantee that victory would have followed, the POUM strategy of completing the revolution, raising the standard of revolt in Spain's colonies that were still in hands of the military, and appealing to the European working class on a revolutionary basis can certainly not be written off. The call to fight the bosses could have been a more effective rallying cry than the call to ally with them against fascism. The Bolsheviks had, after all, not defeated the White Armies and foreign intervention in the Russian Civil War on a massive scale by rolling back the revolution and embracing the Popular Front.

Having seen the Communists for what they were in Spain, Orwell was concerned to understand how they had come to abandon revolutionary politics and inevitably this led him to explore both the class nature of the Soviet Union and the history of the Comintern. His reading, once he had returned to Britain, convinced him that the Soviet Union was not socialist. A key text in this regard was Eugene Lyons, *Assignment in Utopia*, which showed as far as Orwell was concerned, that the Russian system was not 'very different from Fascism'. According to Lyons, a onetime Communist sympathiser, whose first-hand experience of life in the Soviet Union, had transformed his outlook, the Stalin regime had nothing whatever to do with any conception of socialism as human liberation. As Orwell observed: 'The GPU are everywhere, everyone lives in constant terror of denunciation, freedom of speech and of the press are obliterated to an extent we can hardly imagine'. There were 'periodical waves of terror'. At this time, he wondered whether the Soviet system was in fact 'a peculiarly vicious form of state capitalism'.[20] What is clear is that anyone on the left could have looked at the evidence regarding the realities of the Soviet Union at this time. The books and articles exposing the Stalinist regime for what it was were accessible to anyone interested, but most of the left refused to even look at them and instead preferred to read the books and articles that lied for and about the character of that regime, many of them published by the Left Book Club.

Orwell was also concerned to get an understanding of the development of the Comintern and of the British CP. He read, for example, the Trotskyist CLR James's *World Revolution*, 'that very able book',[21] and Franz Borkenau's *The Communist International,* which he actually reviewed. Orwell came away from this reading with an understanding of the development of Communist politics over the previous twenty-odd years, an understanding that was very deliberately hidden from new recruits to and sympathisers with the CP. Only recently, Orwell observed in his review, the Comintern had been through 'the "ultra-left" phase of 1928–34, the "social fascist" phase' when 'anyone who advocated a united front of Socialists and Communists was denounced as a traitor, Trotskyist, mad dog, hyena and all the other items in the Communist vocabulary'. As recently as five years earlier, 'Social Democracy was declared to be the real enemy of the working class' and 'Fascism was dismissed as something utterly without importance'. And now, with the Popular Front turn, anyone 'who cavilled at lining up with Liberals and Catholics was once again a traitor, Trotskyist, mad dog, hyena and so forth'. Most CP members were completely ignorant of this turnaround in policy. He ended his review calling for a socialist alternative, 'a movement which is genuinely revolutionary, i.e., willing to make drastic changes and use violence if necessary', but which did not lose touch with 'the essential values of democracy'.[22] The ILP was, he came to believe, this organisation.

As far as Orwell was concerned, he had seen workers' power in action in Barcelona, a classless society taking shape before his eyes, and it had been suppressed not by the fascists, but by the Communists acting in the interests of the Soviet Union. Now he found that the British Communists were slandering his POUM comrades and most of the left was either turning a conveniently blind eye to this or joining in. The Left Book Club faithfully followed the CP line, with Gollancz rejecting Orwell's proposed account of his experiences in Barcelona unseen. He had an article and a book review rejected by the New Statesman, indeed, the editor Kingsley Martin, even nearly thirty years later was to defend his actions with the statement that he would no more have published them than he would have published 'an article by Goebbels during the war against Germany'.[23] After some difficulty, he did succeed in publishing an account of what he had seen in Spain, 'Spilling the Spanish Beans' in the New English Weekly in two parts at the end of July and first week of September 1937. There was, he reported, 'a reign of terror' being carried out against the revolutionary left in Republican Spain. This was almost completely unknown in Britain where there was 'a quite deliberate conspiracy to prevent the Spanish situation from being understood'. One thing was clear though, and the left had to be told: 'Communism was now a counter-revolutionary force' and that the Communists are everywhere 'in alliance with bourgeois reformism'.[24] The ILP, however, stood by the POUM, fighting on their behalf, defending them against slander and persecution, and still championing the fight for socialism. Indeed, as early as July 1937, the minutes of the ILP National Administrative Committee had mentioned the possibility of a book by Orwell on his experiences in Spain to be entitled 'Barcelona Tragedy' that they were trying to interest Frederick Warburg in publishing.[25] It was, of course, to eventually be published as Homage to Catalonia. On 13 June 1938, Orwell joined the party and just over a week later the ILP newspaper, the New Leader, carried his article, 'Why I Join the ILP'.

'One Has Got To Be Actively Socialist'

Orwell starts off 'Why I Join the ILP' with a personal statement written from the point of view of a writer. Writers normally try to keep out of politics, he argues, but this option is being closed down because today 'the era of free speech' is coming to an end. As he points out, the freedom of the press had always been 'something of a fake, because in the last resort, money controls opinion', but now the spaces that remained for free expression are in danger of being closed down. Only a Socialist Party will defend free speech, which is in itself enough reason to become politically active. But, he goes on, there are more general reasons: 'It is not possible for any thinking person to live in such a society as our own without wanting to change it. Here, he makes the point that he has had 'some grasp of the real nature of Capitalist society' for 'perhaps ten years past'. He saw British imperialism at work in Burma and had seen the plight of the unemployed and, indeed, had tried to contribute to the struggle against 'the system' written about these issues. Now though, the 'tempo of events is quickening' and 'the dangers . . . are staring us in the face'. 'One has', he wrote, 'got to be actively a Socialist, not merely sympathetic to Socialism'. He was joining the ILP because it was the only party 'which aims at anything I should regard as Socialism'. He hoped for a Labour Party victory at the next general election, but 'we know what the history of the Labour Party has been'. What Orwell was embracing was the ILP's programme of legislating the overthrow of capitalism, but in the knowledge that this would be met with the armed resistance of the capitalist class and that this resistance would have to be put down by force: the lesson he had learned in Spain. He went on to write of how he had fought with the POUM militia in Spain and that although he had had reservations about their politics to begin with, they had been proven right. Now, he regarded their stance as the best way forward in Britain in order to avoid being led 'up the garden path in the name of Capitalist democracy' which was what he believed the Popular Front was all about.[26]

Orwell took a strong stand against the politics of the Popular Front over succeeding months. In mid-February 1938, he reviewed Fenner Brockway's new book, *Workers' Front*. Here Brockway championed socialist politics against the Popular Front, defended the POUM against Stalinist slander and repression, condemned the 'assassination' of Andres Nin and accused the Communists of carrying out a 'Counter-Revolution'. As far as he was concerned 'a Popular Front Government is inevitably timid' with the 'most moderate section . . . the Liberal Capitalists' effectively determining policy. As far as Orwell was concerned, Brockway was absolutely right when he argued that the Popular Front call for the working class and the capitalist class to ally against fascism was simply to call for 'an alliance of enemies, and, must always, in the long run, have the effect of fixing the capitalist-class more firmly in the saddle'. The Popular Front, he concluded, was 'an unholy alliance between the robbers and the robbed' and had already provided 'the nauseous spectacle of bishops, Communists, cocoa-magnates, publishers, duchesses and Labour MPs marching arm in arm to the tune of "Rule Britannia".[27] Instead, he advocated class politics, the fight for socialism, as the only way to defeat fascism.

For Orwell, the greatest danger posed by the Popular Front was that it was being used to prepare the country for war. This would ostensibly be an anti-fascist war, but, in fact it would be a war between rival great powers, the Soviet Union and the British and French Empires on the one side and the fascist powers on the other. It would have nothing to do with democracy or freedom. Not only was the Soviet Union not a bastion of freedom, but the British Empire was, as he pointed out on various occasions, nothing but a mechanism for exploiting cheap disenfranchised colonial labour held in subjection by force. Moreover, he was convinced that in the event of war, there would be a fascisation process in Britain whereby civil liberties would disappear, there would be repression of opponents of the conflict, increasingly authoritarian government, the suppression of working-class organisations and the whole process would be cheered on by the CP just as had happened in the Spanish Republic. Against this drive for war, he urged the formation, despite the difficulties of 'an effective anti-war movement'. He argued, on one occasion, for example, that

> The truth is that any real advance, let alone any genuinely revolutionary change, can only begin when the mass of the people definitely refuse capitalist-imperialist war and thus make it clear to their rulers that a war policy is not practicable. So long as they show themselves willing to fight 'in defence of democracy' or 'against Fascism' or for any other flyblown slogan, the same trick will be played upon them again and again: 'You can't have a rise in wages now, because we have got to prepare for war. Guns before butter' . . . every manual worker inwardly knows – that modern war is a racket . . .

He made clear here that he welcomed the support of pacifists in the fight against the coming war.[28]

In December 1938, the *Adelphi* carried a major article by Orwell, 'Political Reflections on the Crisis'. Here he once again condemned the Popular Front. It was a 'monstrous harlequinade in which everyone is constantly bounding across the stage in a false nose – Quakers shouting for a bigger army, Communists waving union jacks, Winston Churchill posing as a democrat'. While most people were still opposed to war, they were being prepared for it, coming to accept it as inevitable. He blamed much of this on the Labour Party, 'the so-called opposition'. Here Orwell was adamant that if you looked at the world and realistically weighed up the balance of injustice then the British Empire was a 'far vaster injustice' than fascism. As he pointed out, it 'is not in Hitler's power, for instance, to make a penny an hour a normal industrial wage; it is perfectly normal in India, and we are at great pains to keep it so'. The average Indian's leg is far thinner than the average Englishman's arm, and this was nothing to do with race, but everything to do with starvation. The coming war would be anti-fascist in name only. In reality, it would be fought to protect the British Empire, a system of injustice and exploitation 'far bigger' than Hitler's and 'in its different way just as bad'. Part of the Popular Front agenda was, he believed, to as far as possible minimise or even ignore the iniquities of British imperialism and the Labour Party acquiesced in this because in an imperialist country, left-wing politics are 'always partly humbug' and the Labour Party, in particular, 'when it comes to a pinch, are His Majesty's Opposition'. One point worth making here is that in 1938 there was considerable justice to Orwell's comparison between the relative iniquities and crimes of the British Raj and Nazi Germany. It was the war and Nazi mass murder in the lands that they occupied that changed this.[29] For Orwell, however, once again, the only hope was a new mass Socialist Party, but, on this occasion, he was not terribly hopeful, concluding that if 'any such party exists at present, it is only as a possibility, in a few tiny germs lying here and there in unwatered soil'.[30]

'Bitched, Buggered and Bewildered'

Among the people Orwell met inside the ILP at this time were two it is worth taking special notice of: Reg Reynolds and Ethel Mannin. Reynolds was a committed pacifist, who had worked alongside Gandhi against the British in India. When Gandhi drew up his 1930 ultimatum demanding an end to British rule in India, it was delivered to the British Viceroy by Reynolds. The campaign of civil disobedience that followed provoked the most violent response from MacDonald's Labour government. Over 60,000 people were arrested, thousands of protesters were beaten by the police, and hundreds were shot down. Prisoners who had supported a general strike in Sholapur in protest against Gandhi's arrest were sentenced to be flogged and the strike leaders were hanged. One man got seven years for carrying a Congress flag.[31] As far as Reynolds was concerned, Labour not only supported 'the crime of imperialism', but combined this with 'the nauseating vice of hypocrisy'. When he returned home to campaign against the Labour government's repression, his every step was dogged by Special Branch. As a good Quaker, he did everything he could to assist them.[32] Although he wrote for ILP publications and spoke at ILP meetings, he only joined once it had disaffiliated from the Labour Party. He resigned from the No More War Movement once the Spanish Civil War broke out, although only after trying to have civil wars exempted from any pacifist injunction on the grounds that fighting oppression was legitimate. Together with his partner, the novelist Ethel Mannin, he gave his support to the POUM and they both gravitated towards the Trotskyists within the ILP. In 1937, Reynolds published his *White Sahibs in India*, a powerful indictment of British rule. The book was published by Secker and Warburg and Reynolds was one of those who drew Frederick Warburg's attention to the fact that Orwell was writing a dissident account of the Spanish War, *Homage to Catalonia*, that Gollancz and the Left Book Club would not touch.

As for Ethel Mannin, she was one of the most remarkable people active on the far left in the 1930s. She was a life-long socialist, a champion of progressive education, of sexual liberation, as well as a successful popular novelist and travel writer. Towards the end of the 1920s her fiction was becoming increasingly informed by her revolutionary politics. In 1930, she had published the novel *Ragged Banners*, where one of her characters expresses amazement 'that the revolution's been delayed so long . . . Perhaps even yet we haven't suffered enough . . . Men's eyes have got to be opened . . . Starvation, that's what makes revolutions'. Her 1934 novel, *Cactus*, had the ghost of a German soldier proclaiming 'Russia in 1917, Germany in 1919, England in 1926, Austria in this year of revolt 1934 . . . Soon out of the rich warm soil of Spain will come revolt, from the Basque country and Catalonia'. Once again workers and soldiers councils would be set up, 'for that is the history of mankind, which is the history of revolt'. She visited Russia for the first time that year and came home 'very close...to becoming a Communist'. Her second visit in 1935 saw her beginning to become disillusioned with the Soviet Union, a process that was completed by the 'Hitleresque purges'. From sympathy with the Soviet Union, she moved towards first Trotskyism and then Anarcho-Syndicalism. She became a friend of the American Anarchist, Emma Goldman, working alongside her in the struggle against fascism in Spain and becoming involved in the effort to 'help make it known...there was also a social revolution behind the anti-fascist struggle, a great section of the working masses not merely fighting to preserve the capitalist status quo, but for a new social order'.[33] In 1938, Frederic Warburg published her shamefully neglected volume, *Women and the Revolution*, the first book of its kind published in Britain, which she dedicated to Goldman. As she made clear in the Dedicatory Introduction, even though the book was dedicated to an anarchist, she still considered herself a Marxist and a supporter of the POUM at this time. She wrote:

My own revolutionary faith insists that despite the Communist International and its betrayal of the Revolution in Russia, its wrecking of the Revolution in China in 1927, and its sabotage of the Revolution in Spain in the struggle against Franco in the interests of its foreign policy – the deterioration of the Marxian ideal into a dictatorship of the few over the many is not inevitable, and that by educating the masses through a truly free workers' democracy the ideal of the Libertarian Society of Anarchism may ultimately be achieved.

In the book, she ranges from the French Revolution through women's experience of the Industrial Revolution, the suffrage movement, women's opposition to the First World War, the Russian Revolution (celebrated very much from an anarchist perspective), Rosa Luxemburg and the German Revolution, the Chinese Revolution, the Irish Revolution and up to the Spanish Revolution. The Spanish Revolution had suffered a massive setback in May 1937, she conceded, when 'the counter-revolution had got to work' and now the Communists were committing 'frightful atrocities...against the Anarchists...imprisonments, executions and persecutions'. She still hoped that 'all is not lost'.[34]

The revolutionary couple had become interested in Orwell's work when *The Road to Wigan Pier* was first published, impressed by 'its shrewd observation' and irritated by 'its many superficial judgements'.[35] Mannin had reviewed the book for the ILP's *New Leader*, expressing the wish that the author had confined 'himself to facts and figures'.[36] Reynolds, it has to be said, confessed to both drinking fruit juice and wearing sandals in his memoirs! It was Orwell's involvement in Spain, however, that determined Mannin to meet him. When they met him, he was recovering from the wound in his throat and Reynolds remembered him as someone who 'saw the world through tired eyes' and gave an impression of 'disillusionment and gloom'.[37] They were all three of them involved with the international campaign for solidarity with the Spanish revolutionary left, Solidarida Internacional Antifascista, that Emma Goldman had been instrumental in setting up, and in the ILP campaign against the coming European war. Mannin herself responded to defeat in Spain by embracing a full-blooded pacifism in 1939, while Orwell and Reynolds both took a stance that can be best described as 'anti-militarist'. She was prepared to see the fascists in power if it avoided war, whereas both Orwell and Reynolds still argued that while imperialist wars were to be opposed, wars of liberation and the fight against oppression, injustice and fascism still had to be supported. Mannin's pacifism, as we shall see, even saw her, on occasions, flirt with anti-Semitism! Orwell himself wrote an anti-war pamphlet in the course of 1938 that was never published and has unfortunately been lost.

As war approached, he seems to have been both gripped by despair at the weakness of the ILP and by the infighting that wracked the party, but at the same time determined to continue the fight. He wrote to the anarchist Herbert Read in January 1939 about the need to 'start organising for illegal anti-war activities' and again in March to discuss the possibility of at least keeping 'a left-wing but non-Stalinist review' in existence and the need to establish 'printing presses etc. in some discreet place' so as to be ready as war approached. In both letters he assumed that Britain was going to undergo a 'fascising' process that would inevitably mean 'wage reductions, suppression of free speech, brutalities in the colonies etc.'.[38] When war came, however, both Read and Orwell were to support it.[39] Orwell quietly resigned from the ILP, although a good case can be made that his view of the way forward always remained close to the political strategy it advocated at this time, except that as far as he was now concerned, it had disqualified itself by its opposition to war. Mannin reacted to Orwell's turnaround with absolute fury: 'Is it because you like fighting for its own sake? Or what? . . . I don't understand it. It leaves me bitched, buggered and bewildered . . . I thought you thought it all crazy this smashing in of Nazi faces. For the luv of Mike write a few lines to enlighten our darkness'.[40]

3

'Giants are Vermin':
Orwell, Fascism and the Holocaust

In his invaluable 'Personal Memoir' of George Orwell, Tosco Fyvel writes approvingly of his concern to explore 'the limitless immorality of totalitarianism' and yet, at the same time of how he made no attempt to arrive at 'any close knowledge of' or even had any 'special interest in Hitler and Hitlerism'. Orwell's focus was overwhelmingly on Stalinism and its crimes, and on those who acted as its apologists. This meant that he neglected in his thinking 'the supreme revolutionary force for evil active in his lifetime', that is Nazi Germany. This, as Fyvel acknowledges, 'is a fairly large statement to make', although he argues that 'it is borne out by the facts'.[1] How valid is the assessment? After all, we are discussing a man who fought against fascism in Spain and was seriously wounded, indeed nearly killed in that conflict, who tried unsuccessfully to enlist to fight the Nazis when war broke out in 1939, who was to argue, often ferociously, against pacifism and the anti-war left, was to urge revolutionary war as the only way to defeat the Nazis and then went on to work at the BBC, essentially as a propagandist, assisting in the fight against the Axis powers. All of Orwell's work at the BBC can be legitimately considered as a contribution to the fight against fascism, however ineffectual that contribution might have been. And yet, even so, it does seem that Orwell was more concerned with investigating the realities of Communist rule in Russia than he was with investigating fascism and, more particularly, Nazi Germany. Why was this?

Partly this can be put down to the fact that he felt that the left did not have to be persuaded about the danger posed by fascism and Nazism whereas once he had returned from Spain, he was overwhelmed by the need to fight against the left's illusions in the Soviet Union. It was not just a matter of exposing the nature of the Communist regime presiding as it did over mass starvation, carrying out the Great Terror with all that involved in terms of the routine use of torture, mass executions and the reintroduction of mass enslavement. What appalled him was the way that this regime was celebrated by much of the left, not just by the Communist Party but by many in the Labour Party as well, celebrated as socialism no less. Another factor worth remembering as well, of course, is that in the 1930s, the harsh reality was that the Stalin regime actually was considerably more murderous than the Hitler regime was at that time. Stalin's crimes in the 1930s can be seen as a product of the drive towards breakneck industrialisation and preparation for war, whereas Hitler's crimes in the 1940s were to be a product of war and conquest. And, as far as Orwell was concerned, much of the left was actually putting itself at the service of Soviet foreign policy. Another factor, as we shall see, was Orwell's embrace of the theory of totalitarianism whereby Communist Russia and Nazi Germany were seen as converging, both becoming examples of a new kind of tyranny, oligarchic or bureaucratic collectivism.

What this chapter will attempt is to lay bare Orwell's commitment to the fight against fascism, the development of his understanding of fascism and Nazism, the theoretical basis that underpinned his 'mature' consideration of these movements and lastly his understanding of the Holocaust and its significance.

'In Retreat Before the Onslaught of Fascism'

While *The Road to Wigan Pier* is best remembered for its investigation into the social plight of the working class in the depressed North and for its idiosyncratic critique of the left, it also deserves some consideration for its account of the fascist menace at that time. In the second part of the book, Orwell tries to engage with both the crying need for socialism and the fact that instead of going forward, 'the cause of Socialism is visibly going back'. As he put it: 'At the moment Socialists almost everywhere are in retreat before the onslaught of Fascism, and events are moving at terrible speed'. Indeed, even while he was writing these words, 'the Spanish Fascist forces are bombarding Madrid, and it is quite likely that before the book is printed we shall have another Fascist country to add to the list'.[2] This fear certainly informed the urgency of his critique of the left, if not its accuracy! While he castigated the middle-class socialist 'cranks' for alienating the working class from the socialist cause, he was also concerned with the danger of the middle-class being handed over to the fascist cause. Before looking at his discussion of the attractions of fascism for people like himself and the danger this posed for the socialist cause, it is worth considering his actual encounter with Mosley and his Blackshirts in the North.

On 15 March 1936, Orwell went to a British Union of Fascists (BUF) meeting at the Public Hall in Barnsley. There were some 700 people there, including about 100 Blackshirts. Mosley spoke for about 90 minutes and to Orwell's horror was loudly cheered when he finished. He wrote in his diary that Mosley was a very good speaker, but that the speech itself 'was the usual claptrap – Empire free trade, down with the Jew and the foreigner, higher wages and shorter working hours all round etc. etc'. Mosley spoke from 'a Socialist angle' and 'easily bamboozled' his mainly working-class audience. He put the blame for everything on 'mysterious international gangs of Jews'. A few days later, in a letter to Richard Rees, he described Mosley as having talked 'the most unutterable bollox' at the meeting and wondered sceptically whether he believed what he was saying himself.[3] He also complained in his diary about the treatment meted out to questioners and hecklers who were forcibly removed from the meeting and, on one occasion, as far as he could see, treated with 'quite unnecessary violence'. He saw one man attacked with 'several Blackshirts throwing themselves upon him and raining blows on him while he was still sitting down and had not attempted any violence'. Once they had been thrown out of the meeting, those evicted were arrested by the police, even if they had been the victims of an unprovoked assault. As he put it, they got 'both a hammering and a fine for asking a question'. Much later, he was to remember the meeting in *Tribune* (7 December 1945) as showing how the police had 'collaborated with the Blackshirts in "keeping order"'. He resolved to write a letter of complaint to *The Times*, although without much hope that it would be printed. When they ignored his letter, he sent it to the *Manchester Guardian*, but they ignored it as well. More seriously, Orwell hunted down some of the people who had been thrown out of the meeting and discovered that one of them, a woman heckler, had been hospitalised. A few days later, he was in the audience at a Communist Party public meeting to protest about the police and the Mosleyites where 6 shillings was collected 'for the defence of the young men arrested in the Mosley affair'.[4]

What is interesting when one compares his diary account of Mosley's meeting with the discussion of fascism in *The Road* is how different in tone and purpose they are. In the diary, he writes more from the point of view of the working-class activists trying to combat the Mosleyites, being beaten up and arrested for their trouble and is concerned to make some sort of public complaint about Blackshirt violence. In both *The Road* and elsewhere, his concerns were radically different. He did not take the BUF that seriously as a threat. In a review of Wal Hannington's *The Problem of the Distressed Areas* that he wrote in November 1937, for example, he praises both Hannington and the NUWM for their fight against mass unemployment, low wages and poverty, but disagrees with Hannington's assessment of the fascist threat. For Orwell, Mosley is 'merely a red herring in a black shirt'. If 'English Fascism ...ever comes', it will not look like Mosley or Hitler, but will be 'a lot subtler'.[5] He expanded on this in *The Road*. Here he doubted that Mosley would ever be more than a joke as far as most people were concerned, 'a Gilbert and Sullivan heavy dragoon'. While he certainly needed watching, because you never know, here he argues that a successful English fascism would, for a start, not call itself fascist. It will most likely not seize power but will instead install itself in power under false colours. What would take power in Britain was 'a slimy Anglicised form of Fascism'. Its banner would be 'the lion and the unicorn instead of the swastika'. For Orwell, even at this time, fascism was conceived more as a system of government than as a mass movement, a line of thinking that, as we shall see, was to become more strongly held after his experiences in Spain.

In *The Road*, however, his immediate concern was to discuss the attraction that fascism had for the middle-class, to emphasise how urgent a problem this was and how important it was for the left to counter it. It was obvious why the capitalist-class embraced fascism, but what was its appeal for the middle class and for the intelligentsia. To fight fascism, it was necessary to understand it. While, in practice fascist regimes were 'merely an infamous tyranny', serving the interests of the capitalist-class, they did not win support on that basis. He went on:

> Everyone who has given the movement so much as a glance knows that the rank-and-file Fascist is often quite a well-meaning person – quite genuinely anxious, for instance, to better the lot of the unemployed. But more important than this is the fact that Fascism draws its strength from the good as well as the bad varieties of conservatism... Probably it is very easy, when you have had a bellyful of the more tactless kind of Socialist propaganda, to see Fascism as the last line of defence of all that is good in European civilisation. Even the Fascist bully at his symbolic worse, with rubber truncheon in one hand and castor oil bottle in the other, does not necessarily feel himself a bully; more probably he feels

himself like Roland in the pass at Roncevaux, defending Christendom against the barbarian.[6]

Fascism, from this point of view, was, at least in part, a rejection of the heartless nature of the socialism that was on offer from the left, a revolt against 'hedonism and a cheap conception of "progress"'. What the left had to do was 'to examine the Fascist case, grasp that there is something to be said for it, and then make clear to the world that whatever good Fascism contains is also implicit in Socialism'. While Orwell's discussion of fascism is problematic to say the least, the danger he identified certainly was not. The danger was that if something was not done then the middle class would be handed over to the fascists. He could envisage a middle class absolutely 'crushed down to the worst depths of poverty' and yet still regarding the working class as its enemy. This middle class would constitute a 'ready-made Fascist Party'. Consequently, it was vital that the socialist movement 'capture the exploited middle class before it is too late'. It was crucial to 'capture the office-workers, who are so numerous and, if they knew how to combine, so powerful'.[7]

The situation was 'desperate'. There was a real danger of 'Fascist domination in Europe' and the only force that could meet the challenge was the socialist movement. He was absolutely insistent that the 'capitalist-imperialist governments' will not fight the fascists, indeed he thought that the British ruling class 'would probably prefer to hand over every square inch of the British Empire to Italy, Germany and Japan than to see Socialism triumphant'. And if socialism did not triumph, then the alternative was a totalitarian world, 'economically collectivist . . . with all political, military and educational power in the hands of a small caste of rulers and their bravos'. What was coming was 'the slave-state or rather the slave-world'. It would be 'a world of rabbits ruled by stoats'.

How to fight this? He ruled out any embrace of the politics of the Popular Front which would only produce 'some kind of pale-pink humbug even more ineffectual than the parliamentary Labour Party' and anyway would involve allying with socialism's 'very worst enemies'. Instead, the 'sinking' middle class, the 'bank clerk dreaming of the sack, every shopkeeper teetering on the brink of bankruptcy', had to be won over to the Socialist cause. There was a very real danger, he thought, 'that in the next few years large sections of the middle class will make a sudden and violent swing to the Right'. The millions of office workers 'have the same interests and the same enemies as the working class', but, at the moment, 'nearly all of them would side with their oppressors and against those who ought to be their allies'. A middle class 'crushed down to the worst depths of poverty' might still remain 'bitterly anti-working class' and consequently constitute 'a ready-made Fascist Party'. This had to be avoided. The middle class had to be won over to the socialist cause. The only way to achieve this, he argued, was to 'bring an effective Socialist party into existence . . . a party with genuinely revolutionary intentions . . . numerically strong enough to act'. Such a party had to win over the middle class. There was going to be a real struggle because 'our plutocracy will not sit quiet under a genuinely revolutionary government', this was certainly the lesson of Spain as far as he was concerned, but when the time came he hoped that 'we of the sinking middle class . . . may sink into the working class *where we belong* [my emphasis] . . . after all, we have nothing to lose but our aitches'.[8]

One last point worth making about this discussion is that it pre-dated Orwell's time in Spain. In many ways his experiences in Spain reinforced the way his thinking was already tending. This very much reflected the influence of revolutionaries within the ILP. It was an aspect of Orwell's critical engagement with the left, an engagement that was to continue for the rest of his life. And, of course, it is very difficult to argue that he did not take the threat from fascism seriously in the months before he went to Spain.

'Have a Whack at Franco'

In his autobiography, *Towards Tomorrow*, Fenner Brockway remembered Orwell coming into the ILP Head Office 'to talk about going to Spain'. He was 'attracted by the libertarian Socialism' espoused by the ILP, but disillusioned by the in-fighting between Communists and Trotskyists in the London branches. He told Brockway that 'all he wanted to do was have a "whack" at Franco'.[9] He had no preference as to whether he joined the ILP contingent in the POUM militia or the International Brigades, but the decision was taken for him. The CP general secretary, Harry Pollitt, considered him politically unreliable and vetoed his joining the International Brigades. When he arrived in revolutionary Barcelona, he duly joined the POUM. Now volunteering to go and fight against Franco and his fascist allies in Spain would, at first sight, seem to indicate someone taking a pretty determined stand against the fascist danger. Even here though, we have the seriousness of Orwell's anti-fascism called into question.

Bill Alexander, a former International Brigade commander, savagely attacked Orwell for his lack of anti-fascist fervour, in a volume of essays, *Inside the Myth*, edited by Christopher Norris, and intended to systematically denigrate both the man and his politics. As far as Alexander was concerned, fascism did not make Orwell either 'angry' or 'concerned to do something'. Indeed, he had no deep feelings about fascism at all and Alexander describes his position as 'almost one of neutrality'. More generally, Orwell had 'no sense of identification' with working-class people, 'no sense of "there but for my family background go I"'. He had no understanding of 'the realities of Spanish life'. What he did have was 'his British upper-class arrogance' and moreover he was only in Spain to write a book, to provide 'the establishment with a best-seller to obscure and denigrate the real issues of the struggle against fascism'. This attempted character assassination was part of the Communist Party's longstanding vendetta against Orwell and in particular against his account of his experiences in Spain, *Homage to Catalonia*. To be fair though, Alexander does regret that Orwell was not allowed to join the International Brigades because in their ranks he might have found 'steadfast courage', 'comradeship and trust in humanity' and a 'purpose and cause'.[10] Orwell's own belief that he would probably have died seems a much more likely outcome. He did actually try to transfer to the International Brigades once he was in Spain, but the Barcelona Rising intervened. If he had transferred, one significant difference that Orwell would have encountered and one feels would have been unable to keep quiet about was that whereas officers in the POUM were elected and shared the same meagre rations as the rank and file, in the International Brigades staff officers enjoyed a considerably better cuisine than the other ranks![11]

The opening of the Moscow archives has allowed an insight into the British battalion that Alexander and co have been determined to hide in all the years since the end of the Spanish War. According to James Hopkins, out of the 2,063 British volunteers, no less than 400 were considered 'unreliable', whether from drink, cowardice or 'Trotskyism', a catch-all that covered any dissent from the official CP line or criticism of the Soviet Union and the Moscow Trials. Indeed, many of those accused of cowardice and other misdemeanours were, in fact, men who had become disillusioned with the CP's line and conduct, had tried to return home, and were smeared accordingly. Hopkins writes of a 'relentless' purge of those considered 'political unreliables' within the battalion. They were the victims of 'character assassination, surveillance, imprisonment, and, in isolated cases, worse', and all this has been categorically denied for the past eighty odd years. Indeed, any attempt at even raising these issues has been portrayed as slandering the memory of those who died fighting fascism. Similarly, the activities of the Russian secret police, the NKVD, busy attempting to carry out a Spanish replica of the Great Terror, have been strongly denied. As Hopkins points out, there is an 'unspeakable irony' in the fact that one of those prominent in denying NKVD activity in Spain, Nan Green, for years the secretary of the British International Brigade Association, was herself 'one of those who fell into its hands'. She was denounced by Bill Rust, the *Daily Worker* correspondent in Spain, a member of the CP leadership and, a particularly contemptible Stalinist,[12] who accused her of having an affair with a wounded Brigader who he believed to be 'either a Trotskyist or fascist' and a letter had supposedly been found among her possessions 'full of criticisms of the Soviet Union'. She was eventually cleared of the allegations, but never subsequently spoke of the experience. And, as Hopkins insists, Harry Pollitt himself certainly knew the truth of what went on within the International Brigades.[13] As for Orwell, he always refused to criticise the rank and file Brigaders, regarding them as courageous men and women fighting for democracy and freedom, but whose idealism was hijacked by the Communist Party. They had been duped into serving the interests of Soviet foreign policy. The ILP MP, John McGovern put it best perhaps when he remarked that there were in fact two International Brigades in Spain, 'one a fighting force drawn from the Socialist Movement of the world' that was to be admired and the other 'an International Cheka' that was committing fearful crimes against the Socialist cause and needed to be exposed.[14]

For Orwell though the great lesson to be learned in Spain did not concern fascism. When he went to Spain, he had been more sympathetic to what he believed to be the CP position of putting the revolution on hold in order to win the war and, indeed, he had continued arguing this position while serving with the POUM militia. Needless to say such a discussion would never have been tolerated in the International Brigades. He remained unconvinced of the POUM position, however, and, as we have seen, was preparing to transfer to the British battalion when he went on leave to Barcelona in May 1937. Here he realised that not only were the Communists rolling back the gains the revolution had made, effectively restoring capitalism, but they were also engaged in a systematic campaign against the revolutionary left, the POUM and the anarchists. His decision to stand on the barricades with the POUM in Barcelona was without any doubt one of the most important decisions he ever made. From this episode and its aftermath, the lesson he drew from Spain was that International Communism stood revealed as a counter-revolutionary force, that the left was blind to this and that it had to be told.

What he also experienced at first hand was the scale of the lies, smears and slanders that the Communists and their supporters were prepared to concoct and propagate against their opponents on the left, preparing the way for their arrest, imprisonment, torture and even murder. His realisation of the extent to which the Communists were prepared to lie and deceive was to inform his attitude towards them for the rest of his life. As he complained after he returned home, the reporting of the Barcelona Rising in the left and liberal press 'beat everything I have ever seen for lying' and he was personally being attacked by the *Daily Worker* 'with the most filthy libels, calling me pro-Fascist etc'.[15] Bill Alexander's essay is only a pretty mild example of all this, of the denigration that Orwell and others serving with the POUM were subjected to, but nevertheless it is still best seen as part of the campaign of lies and slander that had already been underway for nearly fifty years when it appeared in *Inside the Myth*. Far from Orwell being 'neutral' in the fight against fascism, he had fought in the trenches and been shot in the throat, only to find himself being condemned, at the time, not for being 'neutral', but for being in league with the fascists and consequently having to flee for his life from the Communist secret police, something we shall return to in Chapter 6. As far as Orwell was concerned the great lesson of Spain did not concern the nature of fascism, which the left was, of course, already very much aware of, but rather the brutal realities of Stalinism which the left either denied or chose to ignore.

Orwell did briefly discuss the nature of the Franco regime in the pages of *Homage to Catalonia*. Here he describes it as not so much an attempt 'to impose Fascism as to restore feudalism'. The Franco regime was an old-fashioned reactionary military dictatorship allied with the fascist powers. What concerned him, however, was the crackdown on the POUM and the anarchists showed that the Popular Front government in Spain, under Communist influence, was actually beginning to move 'in the direction of some kind of Fascism'. The prisons were filling up with revolutionaries, including men he had served with at the front, the factories were being handed back to the bosses and Spanish Anarchism, a great mass movement, was being destroyed. A Republican victory, he argued, would see the triumph of capitalism and consequently would not be of any real benefit to the workers, but it was still worth fighting for because it would prevent the restoration of feudalism. No matter how repressive the Republic was towards the workers, it would still 'be anti-clerical and anti-feudal', and 'Franco's regime would certainly be worse'. Moreover, Orwell thought it vital that a defeat should be inflicted on the two fascist powers, Italy and Germany, indeed, as he put it, 'it was time they got a beating, it hardly mattered from whom'.[16] What we see here is arguably the first instance of Orwell advancing the 'lesser evil' argument that was to become a characteristic of his political practice over the coming years.

Once back in Britain, Orwell, as we have seen, joined the Independent Labour Party, became a strong opponent of CP-sponsored attempts to establish a Popular Front and opposed the coming war. As he wrote to Geoffrey Gorer in September 1937, when war came it would inevitably be accompanied by the imposition of fascism, 'not of course called Fascism', and with the full support of the Communists. 'This', he went on, 'is what has happened in Spain'. Moreover, British rule in India was already 'just as bad as German Fascism'. The only way to fight against fascism was to fight for the overthrow of capitalism. All that supporting a capitalist-imperialist government in a war against fascism achieved was 'simply letting Fascism in by the back door'.[17] In retrospect, this completely misread the dynamics of British politics at this time and Orwell was to admit this once war actually broke out. Nevertheless, this was the position that he advocated with considerable conviction on his return from Spain.

'We Cannot Struggle Against Fascism Unless We Are Willing to Understand it'

While Orwell had attempted to explore the dynamics of fascism as a mass movement in *The Road*, on his return from Spain he turned more and more to discussing it as a system of government, as an example of totalitarianism. One of the conclusions that he drew from his thinking around this issue was that there were fundamental similarities between the Soviet and the Nazi regimes. According to Bernard Crick by 1940–41, his 'main intellectual concern . . . was with the totalitarian hypothesis: that the Nazi and Bolshevik regimes would move towards a common form of "oligarchical collectivism"'.[18] In fact, he was considering this notion even earlier. In June 1938 in a review of Eugene Lyons' *Assignment in Utopia*, he had tried to decipher 'the truth about Stalin's regime . . . Is it Socialism or is it a peculiarly vicious form of state-capitalism?' After reading Lyons' account of how 'the town proletariat, theoretically the heirs of the revolution, having been robbed of even the elementary right to strike. . . have been reduced to a status resembling serfdom', with 'freedom of speech and of the press . . . obliterated to an extent we can hardly imagine', with 'periodical waves of terror . . . incredible confessions' and everyone living 'in constant terror of denunciation', Soviet Communism 'does not seem to be very different from Fascism'. The convergence thesis seemed more than vindicated by the ease with which the anti-fascist Soviet Union and the anti-Communist Nazi Germany allied with each other in August 1939.

The most important intellectual sources that Orwell drew on for a theoretical underpinning to the convergence thesis were the writings of Franz Borkenau and later of Dwight Macdonald. Borkenau, an Austrian, was a former Communist and Comintern official, still a Marxist of sorts at this time, who had already published an account of his own experiences in Spain, *The Spanish Cockpit*, that Orwell had reviewed comparatively favourably in July 1937. Although Borkenau was not by now a revolutionary, he was concerned with the truth, in particular with acknowledging the fact that the Communists were pulling the Republic 'violently toward the Right'. Indeed, Borkenau had himself been arrested, suspected of 'Trotskyism'.[19] Orwell was to later praise *The Spanish Cockpit* rather more fulsomely than in his earlier review as 'the best book' on the early months of the Spanish Revolution. He also reviewed Borkenau's *The Communist International* in September 1938, praising it as 'a profoundly interesting book' although he disagreed with Borkenau's argument that the only political choices available were fascism or a reformed, recon-structed liberal democracy. As far as Orwell was concerned, there was a third alternative: 'a movement which is genuinely revolutionary, i.e., willing to make drastic changes and to use violence if necessary, but which does not lose touch . . . with the essential values of democracy'. There were the germs of such movements 'in numerous countries', Orwell insisted.[20] Clearly, he was already engaged with Borkenau's work when in May 1940, he reviewed his book *The Totalitarian Enemy*. In his review, Orwell remarked on what an 'eye-opener . . . the Hitler-Stalin pact' had been for many people. Having started from opposite ends, the two regimes were now 'rapidly evolving towards the same system – a form of oligarchical collectivism'. He hoped that Borkenau would go on to explore the proposition further. As Orwell insisted, 'We cannot struggle against Fascism unless we are willing to understand it' and the theory of totalitarianism was the key. A new oligarchical system of government had emerged that had overthrown both the working class in Russia and the capitalist-class in Germany. Instead of a collectivised economy signalling the liberation of humanity, in the hands of this new bureaucratic oligarchy it had become a terrible new kind of tyranny.[21] This was, of course, the world of *Nineteen Eighty-Four*. It is worth making the point here that as originally conceived *Nineteen Eighty-Four* did reflect this convergence, but with the defeat of the Nazis that dimension was supplanted by the more pressing need to expose Stalinism. As early as September 1943, Orwell considered fascism as effectively defeated, or as he put it, 'that particular dragon is almost certainly slain'.[22]

Borkenau, it is important to remember, was not the only source for this theory. Orwell also encountered it in the pages of *Partisan Review*, where Dwight Macdonald advocated a more explicitly Marxist version of the theory of bureaucratic collectivism. In the United States the theory had been developed as a Trotskyist heresy and was advanced by MacDonald and others as the key to understanding the modern world. Whereas Trotsky himself still believed the Soviet Union to be a 'workers' state' where power had been usurped by the bureaucracy, some of his followers, among them MacDonald, had broken with him, insisting that it was instead a new kind of exploitative and oppressive class society altogether.[23]

'I Have Never Been Able to Dislike Hitler'

What did Orwell have to say about Nazism during the early days of the Second World War? In March 1940, he reviewed *Mein Kampf*. Here, he actually wrote that he had 'never been able to dislike Hitler', that 'there is something deeply appealing about him' with his 'pathetic, doglike face'. Now to be fair, Orwell had also remarked on one occasion on how Stalin had a 'likeable face' and he did make clear that if he was in a position to kill Hitler then he would do it without hesitation. Even so, this discussion seems, as Tosco Fyvel put it, at the very least, 'pretty silly'. It is important to remember, of course, that this was written during the so-called 'Phoney War' and before the attempt to exterminate Europe's Jewish population had begun. And Orwell does go on to discuss Hitler's programme as revealed in the pages of *Mein Kampf*: the creation of 'a horrible brainless empire in which nothing happens except the training of young men for war and the endless breeding of fresh cannon-fodder'. Hitler appealed, he argues, to the need that people, or more properly, men, had at least intermittently, for 'struggle and self-sacrifice, not to mention drums, flags and loyalty-parades'. This was something socialists had to face up to. What is interesting is that there is no discussion of Nazi anti-Semitism.[24]

Orwell engaged with the nature of fascism and Nazism on a number of other occasions in the course of 1940. In August, he reviewed a play by Clifford Odets, *Till the Day I Die*, in which the Gestapo attempt to recruit a young Jewish member of the anti-Nazi underground as an informer in the early years of the regime. He remarks on the scene where the young man has his fingers crushed by a rifle butt as 'a little too horrible perhaps', but 'Heaven knows how many such things have happened in real life in the last seven years'. Certainly, Orwell's squeamishness, even at this time, shows a failure to appreciate the brutality of Nazi rule as it was already being practiced in occupied Poland, let alone what was to come. Nevertheless, he was far from alone in this underestimation of what the Nazis were capable of and of what horrors the war was to bring.[25] More interesting is his review of Charlie Chaplin's film, *The Great Dictator*, that appeared in the magazine *Time and Tide* in December 1940. In many ways he is very critical of the film ('it has very great faults'), but at the same time admits that when he saw it, the audience 'laughed almost continuously and were visibly moved by the great speech at the end'. The speech 'is really tremendous . . . one of the strongest pieces of propaganda I have heard for a long time'. But what, he asks, is Chaplin's appeal? Partly it is his reassertion of the tried and tested fact that 'giants are vermin'. In a world where the 'supermen' are everywhere taking control, Chaplin demonstrates the wisdom of the 'common man'. Indeed, he is 'a sort of concentrated essence of the common man', demonstrating 'the ineradicable belief in decency that exists in the hearts of ordinary people'. Atrocities that intellectuals can explain away ('Jew-baiting defended by pacifists' is one example he gives), the ordinary person just knows that 'it isn't right'. The Government should be heavily subsidising the film, even trying to smuggle it into Germany.[26]

One other point worth making here concerns Orwell's embrace of the theory of totalitarianism. While the Soviet Union remained allied with Nazi Germany, the proposition that the two regimes were converging seemed unproblematic. Once the Nazis invaded the Soviet Union, the situation became more complex. In May 1944, he wrote an interesting reply to a correspondent, Noel Willmett, in which he remarked that while the Nazis would 'soon disappear', this would only strengthen Stalin, 'the Anglo-American millionaires', and 'petty fuhrers of the type of de Gaulle'. While he thought that the world was definitely going in a totalitarian direction and that there might well emerge 'two or three great superstates' with regimes powerful enough to insist that two and two made five, Britain had not gone totalitarian yet, no matter what the 'pacifists etc. may say'. Still the future looked pretty grim, so why did he support the war? He went on: 'It is a choice of evils – I fancy nearly every war is that'. Even given everything he knew about the Soviet Union, he would still support it against the Nazis, because it 'cannot altogether escape its past and retains enough of the original ideas of the Revolution to make it a more hopeful phenomenon than Nazi Germany'.[27] There was another side to this particular advocacy of the 'lesser evil' argument which was that the Nazis also embodied the principle of counter-revolution so that their victory would have strengthened reaction everywhere and also demoralised the left, both non-Communist and Communist. Moreover, Hitler had never 'persecuted the rich, except when they were Jews, or when they tried to oppose him…the monied class have always been on his side'.[28]

Whereas during the period of the 'Phoney War', Orwell could write of his inability to personally dislike Hitler (although he would have killed him given the chance), as the war progressed and evidence of Nazi horrors mounted, he become more determined in his condemnation of Nazism. In *Tribune* in August 1944, he insisted against pacifist sceptics that 'the case against the Nazis must be substantially true'. As far as he was concerned 'Nazism is a quite exceptionally evil thing, and it has been responsible for outrages quite unparalleled in recent times. It is definitely worse than British Imperialism, which has plenty of crimes of its own to answer for'.[29]

'To Kill Off Every Jew in Europe'

In his discussion of Orwell's lack of attention to Nazism, Fyvel observed that he seemed to know little about 'Saukel's empire of millions of expendable slave labourers, at least in precise detail' and that the index of his four volume collected writings did not even mention 'Auschwitz, that hell on earth'. Why was this? While he does not go so far as to suggest that Orwell's failure to engage with the enormity of the Holocaust was due to anti-Semitism, he does note that there were others, most notably Malcolm Muggeridge, who accused him of anti-Semitism. For his part, he argues that Orwell never really got to grips with the phenomenon of anti-Semitism and that this also explained why he was 'a convinced anti-Zionist'.[30] How valid is Fyvel's argument?

Certainly Orwell came from a background where a low level anti-Semitism was both pervasive and acceptable. He was certainly guilty of making use of crude and vicious anti-Semitic stereotypes himself on occasions. The worst examples of this are on display in *Down and Out in Paris and London*. Here he celebrates his friendship with an exiled White Russian officer, Boris, and positively relishes the man's anti-Semitism. Boris tells him of an old Jew who tried to sell his own daughter which was 'the Jewish national character for you'. Before the Revolution, Boris tells him, 'we thought the Russian officer's spittle was too precious to be wasted on a Jew'. And for good measure Orwell recounts an episode where he had an argument with a Jewish shopkeeper and what a pleasure it would have been 'to flatten the Jew's nose'. One could 'Trust a snake before a Jew'.[31] He abandons this casual but still vicious anti-Semitism with the coming to power of the Nazis in Germany and Oswald Mosley's embrace of anti-Semitism. Orwell himself more or less acknowledged this much later when discussing the poet T S Eliot's 'antisemitic remarks' of the 1920s in a letter to Julian Symons at the end of October 1948. If they had been made after the Nazis had come to power 'they would have meant something different'. Casual anti-Semitism before 1933 was just an expression of prejudice which did not preclude having Jewish friends or necessarily endorse discrimination and persecution. After 1933 it did. There is, it has to be said, a strong element of special pleading here. Just about any Jewish reader of *Down and Out* would have been fully aware of the Tsarist regime's brutal persecution of Russian Jews, a persecution that culminated in wholesale massacre of tens of thousands of men, women and children carried out by the White Armies during the

Russian Civil War. Perhaps as many as 150,000 people died as a result of these pogroms, one in ten of Russia's Jewish population.[32] These pogroms were often accompanied by mass rape. This was the largest slaughter of Jewish people before the Holocaust. His Jewish readers would certainly not have seen Boris as some kind of amusing eccentric, but as their oppressor, as someone who very likely had Jewish blood on his hands. It is hard to believe that Orwell was unaware of this dreadful history, but its significance was certainly not appreciated. He went on to argue that anti-English jokes would take on a completely different complexion 'if 6 million Englishmen had recently been killed in gas vans'. Prejudice was not of that much significance if it was not accompanied by persecution.[33]

These remarks seem to capture the limitations of Orwell's attempts to understand the particular history and significance of anti-Semitism, and he certainly made the attempt, both during and after the war. He focussed his attention on anti-Semitism as a casual prejudice and altogether neglected the strategic place that anti-Semitism had occupied in much conservative and fascist thinking over many years, especially since the Russian revolution. He never successfully engaged with the political anti-Semitism that advocated discrimination, persecution, pogroms, expulsion and even mass murder. In the whole of the *Complete Works*, the *Protocols of the Elders of Zion*, for example, get only one passing mention.[34]

How much did Orwell know about the Nazi attempt to exterminate Europe's Jewish population? When he was working at the BBC, the news broadcasts that he both wrote and read out on a number of occasions referred to the massacre that was taking place. On 12 December 1942, he broadcast that the Polish government-in-exile had just revealed 'the full facts about the systematic massacre of the Jews in German-occupied Poland'. He told his audience that well over one million Jewish people 'have been killed in cold blood or died of starvation and general misery'. This 'brings home to us the nature of Fascism, the thing we are fighting against'. The following week, he returned to the subject which 'has caused the most profound horror all over the world'. He reported on the Foreign Secretary, Anthony Eden's statement, on 'these cold-blooded massacres' in the House of Commons and the promise that those responsible would be punished. He also reported attempts to get 1,000 Jewish children in 'occupied Europe' to safety, commenting that this scheme and the popular support it had received 'shows that the people of this country have not forgotten what cause they are fighting for'. And some weeks later, on 27 February 1943, he told his listeners of how in a recent speech, Hitler had 'said . . . quite plainly' that 'he intended to kill off every Jew in Europe'.[35]

Two things stand out here. First, that he was not aware of the true scale of the crime that the Nazis were engaged in at this time, although he was far from alone in this, and second that he was unaware of the government's secret determination, a determination in which Labour ministers were wholly complicit, not to rescue Jewish refugees, even children, from Europe.[36] There is no evidence that Orwell ever read Victor Gollancz's powerful 32 page pamphlet, '*Let My People Go': some practical proposals for dealing with Hitler's Massacre of the Jews and an appeal to the British Public,* that came out at the end of 1942 and sold an incredible 250,000 copies in three months. Gollancz castigated the government for its inaction, promising future retribution but doing nothing in the here and now in the way of rescue. The pamphlet is not included in his extensive pamphlet collection and he never referred to it, although it still seems incredible that such a voracious devourer of pamphlet literature as Orwell never came across one of the most powerful and best-selling pamphlets published in Britain during the war. And he does not seem to have been in any way involved in the activities of the National Committee for Rescue from Nazi Terror (NCRNT) that had been established by Eleanor Rathbone MP, William Beveridge, Gollancz and others in March 1943. When the NCRNT sponsored a gallop poll on the question of rescue, 78 per cent of those questioned supported letting refugees into the country at least as a wartime emergency measure. The NCRNT's campaigning caused the government considerable difficulties, but they rode the situation out, always promising that action was under consideration but without any intention of doing anything.[37]

Orwell regularly discussed the ebb and flow of anti-Semitism on the Home Front in his 'London Letters' to *Partisan Review.* He thought it was increasing in the course of 1943, to the point of becoming a 'problem'. He recorded his shock at hearing working-class men and women coming out with sentiments such as 'Well I reckon 'itler done a good job when 'e turned 'em all out'; and this after everything that had and was happening! People 'did not want to remember their suffering'. There were not going to be any pogroms in Britain, but the rising tide of popular anti-Semitism, he felt, 'causes people to avert their eyes from the whole refugee problem and remain uninterested in the fate of the surviving Jews of Europe . . . you switch off the wireless when the announcer begins talking about the ghettoes of Warsaw; that is how people's minds work nowadays.'[38] And even at this time, there were people in Britain denying that the mass murder of the Jews was taking place. In November 1943, Orwell reviewed Douglas Reed's book *Lest We Regret*. Although he had opposed appeasement and supported the war, Reed, was a vicious anti-Semite. He regarded Britain as 'Jew-haunted plutocracy' and absolutely denied that the Jews had ever 'been persecuted in Germany, or not to speak of . . . all the stories about pogroms and so forth are just "propaganda"'. The problem was, as Orwell saw it, that Reed 'is a persuasive writer . . . capable of doing a lot of harm'.[39] An additional problem was that the government did very little to counter domestic anti-Semitism, regarding it as something that was best ignored rather than something to be fought against.

'Revenge is Sour'

Certainly, as we have seen, Orwell acknowledged the mass murder of Europe's Jewish population, but it never became a central concern. He seems to have regarded it as a large-scale pogrom rather than as a new kind of phenomenon altogether. Even though he could criticise people who knew 'almost nothing about the extermination of German and Polish Jews' and put ignorance of this 'vast crime' down to their anti-Semitism which caused it to 'bounce off their consciousness', he never developed the conceptual tools for an understanding of the enormity of the Holocaust himself.[40] This was, it has to be said, the situation for most people at the end of the war. It is best seen as an intellectual failure from which he was not exempt, rather than something specific to him. What was more specific, indeed peculiar to him, though was his distaste at the punishment of collaborators and the like. He certainly made some telling points: on one occasion, for example, he argued that while all manner of 'petty rats' were being hunted down, 'almost without exception the big rats escape'. Nevertheless, his description of 'the present hunt after traitors and Quislings' as one of the most 'morally disgusting' episodes of the war was clearly excessive to say the very least. Even worse was his 9 November 1945 column in *Tribune*. 'Revenge is Sour', where he described how he had been shown around a prisoner-of-war camp by someone he described as 'a little Viennese Jew', in fact, a US officer. In front of Orwell the man kicked awake a sleeping SS General, a man certainly guilty of the most appalling crimes, and then went on to humiliate another SS man who had been trying to pass himself off as an ordinary soldier. Incredibly, Orwell criticises 'the Jew' for his behaviour, which although on one level, was, he concedes, completely understandable, because 'even a wanton kick to a prisoner is a very tiny thing compared with the outrages committed by the Hitler regime'. Indeed, he even admits that it was 'very likely his whole family had been murdered'. But nevertheless this Jewish kick aimed at an SS General becomes the occasion for a discussion of how 'the whole idea of revenge and punishment is a childish dream'.[41] One can only sympathise with Tosco Fyvel's outraged response to Orwell's crass insensitivity when he read this piece:

> I said to Orwell that here in Hitler's so-called 'Final Solution of the Jewish Question', one had the greatest deliberate crime committed in man's history, yet all Orwell did was mention it in one brief and dismissive sentence in a lengthy article telling how one Jewish officer kicked one SS man, an action Orwell referred to as 'getting his own back'. This surely was standing history on its head.[42]

What makes this all the more surprising though is that he was to write for the US journal, *Commentary* that was to make part of its mission in the immediate post-war years the memorialisation of the Holocaust! This publication had started out as the *Contemporary Jewish Record* which was published under the auspices of the American Jewish Committee. Orwell had published his article, 'Anti-Semitism in Britain' in its pages in April 1945. It became *Commentary* in November of that year, edited by Elliott Cohen, reinventing itself as a more self-consciously Jewish *Partisan Review*. The first issue carried an article by Orwell on the British general election along with a tremendously powerful editorial on the Holocaust written by Cohen. He wrote: 'As Jews we live with this fact: 4,750,000 of 6,000,000 Jews of Europe have been murdered. Not killed in battle, not massacred in hot blood, but slaughtered like cattle, subjected to every physical indignity – processed'. As the magazine's historian, Benjamin Balint, points out, at a time when the Holocaust was still being pretty much ignored, 'the magazine's early issues were filled with descriptions of the devastation of Jewish life in Romania, Hungary, Greece and Yugoslavia'. In an article published in the magazine in 1949, the historian Solomon Bloom argued that 'it is imperative to know everything about the Holocaust'. And among the magazine's claims to distinction was the publication of the first firsthand account of the Warsaw Ghetto Uprising. At this time, *Commentary* was also distinctly unsympathetic to Zionism.[43] None of this seems to have deepened Orwell's understanding of the Holocaust.

Fyvel also put Orwell's lack of sympathy for Zionism down to his anti-Semitism, but in fact Orwell regarded Zionism as a kind of European colonialism that was being put in place at the expense of the Arab population in Palestine.[44] In November 1946, he suggested in *Tribune* that the Labour government should consider 'inviting, say, 100,000 Jewish refugees to settle in this country'.[45] What he did not know, of course, was that the Attlee government was determined to keep Holocaust survivors out of Britain even while recruiting some 200,000 East European workers to come to live and work in Britain. Included among those to be welcomed into Britain was a surrendered Ukrainian SS Division, 8,000 strong. Orwell, it seems, knew nothing of this and it remains something barely known even to this day.[46]

4

'A Long Series of Thermidors': Orwell, Pacifism and the Myth of the People's War

On 23 August 1939, the German Foreign Minister, Joachim von Ribbentrop, arrived in Moscow, landing at an airfield bedecked in Soviet and Nazi flags and banners, 'the swastika juxtaposed with the hammer and sickle'. There had been a problem getting enough swastika flags for the event so they had been taken from local film studios where they had been used in the making of anti-Nazi films! There were handshakes and smiles all round, not least when the Gestapo officers accompanying Ribbentrop met their NKVD counterparts. Meeting with Stalin and Molotov, Ribbentrop concluded his Non-Aggression Pact, complete with its secret clauses partitioning Poland, conceding Romanian Bessarabia and effectively handing Finland, Estonia and Latvia over to the Russians. Once the proceedings were concluded, they celebrated with champagne and Stalin proposed a toast to Hitler: 'I know how much the German nation loves its Fuhrer. I should therefore like to drink to his health'.[1] It was, dare one say, impossible to tell the men from the pigs.

This momentous event sent a shock-wave throughout the international left, exposing Communist Parties everywhere as the creatures of the Kremlin with their policies determined by the exigencies of Soviet foreign policy that had everything to do with the most cynical, unscrupulous and brutal exercise of great power politics and nothing whatsoever to do with the struggle for socialism. One particular accompaniment to the Pact that is worth noticing here is that the NKVD handed over to the Nazis in the course of 1939–40 some 350 German and Austrian refugees, mainly Communists, including Jews, who had been swept into the prisons and labour camps as part of the Great Terror. Presumably, this was a gesture of good will.[2] Within days, Nazi Germany attacked Poland (1 September 1939) with the Red Army invading on the 17th.

How did British Communists deal with this surprise development? For the past four years, as part of the Comintern's Popular Front turn, the CP, as we have seen, had made the fight against fascism central to its politics. The threat posed by fascism and by the Nazis, in particular, was such that everything had to be subordinated to that fight. The CP became the great defender of 'democracy', with, as we have seen, revolutionary politics abandoned for fear of alienating prospective allies in the fight. And those on the left who refused to endorse this stance found themselves slandered as fascist sympathisers, fascist agents or, more straightforwardly, as plain fascists. The CP had, of course, applauded when the Great Purge in the Soviet Union had swept up most of the men and women who had led the October 1917 Revolution, condemning them as 'Trotsky-Fascists' and celebrating their execution as traitors and spies, indeed often as having always been traitors and spies. Nearer to home, this murderous dimension to Popular Front politics had been acted out in Spain, where the Communists had set about destroying the revolutionary left. And now, the Soviet Union had actually allied itself with the great fascist enemy!

What is interesting is that while the new turn certainly cost the CP some members, it did not do more damage. Instead, after some hesitation and misunderstanding, party members managed to convince themselves that the Soviet Union had no alternative other than to ally with Nazi Germany, indeed the Pact was something of a diplomatic triumph, once again demonstrating Stalin's genius and that it was a blow for peace. The ability of committed Communists to believe these sophistries is hardly surprising when one recognises that before the outbreak of the Second World War, the harsh reality was that the Stalin regime had already been engaged in mass-murder and the massive use of slave labour for some years, whereas the Hitler regime had not yet started down that path. Even as late as the publication in 1985 of Noreen Branson's volume of the official history of the British Communist Party covering the Pact and its impact, it was still referred to as only being concluded because there was 'little alternative'. She did acknowledge, however, that there were 'some clauses not made public at the time'.[3] Hardly an adequate response! But while most party members proved able to swallow almost anything, the Pact did the CP tremendous damage on the left generally. Non-party members, many of them regarding the CP as leaders in the fight against fascism, were not so prepared to regard the Pact as some sort of triumph. Among them was Victor Gollancz.

According to Ruth Dudley Edwards, Gollancz 'saw the Pact as a complete betrayal of his huge moral investment in selling the Soviet

Union to the members of the Left Book Club'. Whatever the excuses and justifications, 'he could not countenance . . . Stalin's accommodation with those whose intrinsic evil was beyond question'.[4] Gollancz was concerned to prevent the Left Book Club being altogether taken over by the CP and subordinated to the new turn, hoping, as far as possible, to minimise the damage it was inevitably going to suffer both as a result of the Pact and of the break with the CP. When the Nazis actually invaded Poland, at first it looked as if there might be some common ground with the CP. The *Daily Worker* condemned the German attack, endorsing the British declaration of war and proclaiming that this was 'a war that CAN and Must be won'.[5] The party published a pamphlet written by Harry Pollitt, *How to Win the War*, with 50,000 copies printed at one penny each. Here he warned that it would be a mistake to stand aside from the fight, contributing 'only revolutionary-sounding phrases while the fascist beasts ride roughshod over Europe', indeed it 'would be a betrayal of everything our forbears have fought to achieve in the course of long years of struggle against capitalism'.[6] This stance suggested common ground, but by the end of September the Comintern position, condemning Poland, Britain and France as the aggressors had been made clear: revolutionary defeatism. This certainly caused some problems within the CP with Pollitt replaced as general secretary and Johnnie Campbell replaced as editor of the *Daily Worker*, but it made a complete break between Gollancz and the CP certain.

Pollitt and Campbell were replaced by the arch-Stalinists, Rajani Palme Dutt and Bill Rust respectively, who faithfully followed the new line. Indeed, Pollitt was to actually privately complain that once Rust was installed as editor, the *Daily Worker* quickly began to have the smell of the 'pure Goebbels type of fascist propaganda about it'.[7] The Russian attack on Finland in November 1939, an open act of imperialist aggression that CP members once again felt obliged to faithfully defend, exacerbated relations even more.[8] The struggle for control of the Left Book Club continued into early 1940, with the break with the CP only really becoming final in May of that year. Gollancz now found himself the victim of Communist lies and slanders.

'Inside the Whale'

One consequence of Gollancz's break with the CP was a reconciliation, albeit temporary, with George Orwell. According to his own almost certainly apocryphal account, Orwell turned his back on opposition to war with the Nazis after a dream he had the night before the Hitler–Stalin Pact convinced him that he was 'patriotic at heart'.[9] Now a shared support for the war and hostility towards the CP brought them together. In January 1940, he wrote to Geoffrey Gorer that he had recently seen Gollancz who was 'furious with his Communist late-friends, owing to their lies etc'. This, he hoped, might mean that 'the Left Book Club may become a force for good again, if it manages to survive'. He wrote to Gorer once again in April, expanding on his meeting with Gollancz, the first time, he told him that they had met in three years. Gollancz had fallen out with 'his Communist pals, partly over Finland etc, partly over their general dishonesty which he's just become alive to'. Orwell confessed to being somewhat astonished when Gollancz, who had, of course, rejected *Homage to Catalonia* unseen, actually 'asked me whether it was really true that the GPU had been active in Spain during the civil war' and even more so when he admitted that he had not known that the CP 'had ever had any other policy than the Popular Front one'. He thought such ignorance inexcusable.[10] Gollancz was to publish Orwell's essay collection, *Inside the Whale*, in March 1940, even agreeing, to Orwell's surprise, to include *Homage to Catalonia* on the list of his previous books printed on the flyleaf!

Inside the Whale consisted of three essays, 'Charles Dickens', 'Boys' Weeklies' and 'Inside the Whale', the last of which was to occasion a sustained and quite disgraceful attack on Orwell by a former Communist, the historian E P Thompson in 1960, an attack to which we will return (see Chapter 7). What of 'Inside the Whale'? The essay is a celebration of the American writer, Henry Miller, the author of *Tropic of Cancer* (Orwell's copy of the book had been seized in a police raid on his home searching for obscene books in the summer 1939). He acknowledges Miller's limitations as a novelist, but is fascinated by what he describes as his 'mystical acceptance of the thing-as-it-is'. What this involves today is, among other things, acceptance of 'concentration camps, rubber truncheons, Hitler, Stalin, bombs, aeroplanes, tinned food, machine-guns, putsches, purges, slogans, Bedaux belts, gas masks, submarines, spies, provocateurs, press censorship, secret prisons, aspirin, Hollywood films and political murders'. What Miller's stance involves today, Orwell concluded, is the passive acceptance of a civilisation that is in a state of decay. Whatever one might feel about this, it means that

Miller 'is able to get nearer to the ordinary man than is possible for more purposive writers. For the ordinary man is also passive'.

What this discussion leads up to is a critique of the politicised literature that began to become fashionable 'in the years 1930–35'. Indeed, from 1935 up until the Hitler-Stalin Pact in 1939, he argues that 'the central stream of English literature was more or less directly under Communist control'. This 'Marxised literature' did not get any nearer to the masses. And it has occasioned serious problems for literature because the harsh reality is that the Communist Party is 'controlled by people who are mentally subservient to Russia and have no real aim except to manipulate British foreign policy in the Russian interest'. As he puts it, the more vocal Communist can best be seen as 'a Russian publicity agent posing as an international Socialist'. This pose can normally be sustained without too much difficulty, but in times of international crisis, when the Soviet Union shows itself to be 'no more scrupulous in its foreign policy than the rest of the Great Powers', it causes serious difficulties.[11] From this essential truth, he weaves a generalised indictment of the British intelligentsia that is both prejudiced and wrong-headed. A consideration of the impact of Popular Front politics in other countries which would have shown that while he might well be right in some specifics, his generalisations were neither sustainable nor helpful. Nevertheless, his indictment of the contortions willingly performed by British Communists was absolutely accurate.

From this he returns to Miller's 'quietism', his readiness, as he sees it to be a Jonah swallowed by the whale. For Miller, the whale's belly is 'simply a womb big enough for an adult. There you are, in the dark, cushioned space that exactly fits you, with yards of blubber between yourself and reality'. Is this where literature is going? In a world where progress and reaction 'have both turned out to be swindles . . . there is nothing left but quietism'. He had first met Miller in 1936 and had ignored his preaching of the virtues of 'quietism' then to go and fight in Spain, something Miller considered 'the act of an idiot'. Now Orwell leaves this question open, very much a reflection of his response at this time to the Hitler-Stalin Pact and to the 'Phoney War'. This moment of hesitation was to quickly pass with his whole-hearted embrace of the need for a revolutionary war to defeat the Nazis. Indeed, he was to revisit Miller in the pages of *Tribune* early in December 1942 where he adopted a completely different tone. Now, he assured his readers that 'No more that is of value will come out of Henry Miller'. In a period of history like the one they were living through, Miller seemed to be running away all the time, first from France to Greece and then from Greece back to the United States and if there was ever any fighting in the USA, 'one feels reasonably certain that he will be in Argentina'. What a book he might have written about everyday life in Paris under the Germans, but Miller's overriding concern was to escape danger. He was the poet of the 'unheroic', but 'we live in what is, however unwillingly, a heroic age'.[12]

'The Betrayal of the Left'

Between 1939 and 1942, the membership of the Left Book Club fell from 57,000 to only 15,000. It was harried relentlessly by the CP with Gollancz himself subjected to a vicious campaign of lies and slander. In response, Gollancz put together a volume, *The Betrayal of the Left*, from articles that had appeared in *Left News* and that provided a detailed critique of CP policy between October 1939 and January 1941. Harold Laski provided the 'Preface', John Strachey contributed four articles, Orwell contributed two, Konni Zilliacus contributed one under the pseudonym 'A Labour Candidate' and the rest of the volume, the bulk of it in fact, was made up of Gollancz's contributions. This was very much a mixed bag, in some respects devastating, in others positively embarrassing. Let us look at some of the contributions.

In his contribution, 'R Palme Dutt v. Harry Pollitt', Zilliacus compared the pro-war arguments in Pollitt's quickly withdrawn September 1939 pamphlet, 'How to Win the War' with Dutt's revolutionary defeatism in his 1941 pamphlet, 'We Fight for Life'. He wholeheartedly endorsed Pollitt's position:

> The correct policy remains in essentials that originally advocated by the Communist Party – the war on two fronts, i.e. supporting the country's war effort by every means in our power, while fighting reaction and plutocracy and pressing for the adoption of Labour's home, Imperial and foreign policy as necessary to enlist in our cause the revolutionary and democratic forces on the Continent and in the Colonies.[13]

Orwell would have agreed with this except, as we shall see, that he had no faith whatsoever in the Labour Party at this time, regarding it as very much part of the problem rather than contributing in any way to the solution.

Among John Strachey's contributions was a truly remarkable essay, 'Totalitarianism'. A former Labour MP, he had been one of the leading intellectual advocates of CP politics in the 1930s, faithfully following the party line, with his books and articles being regularly discussed with the party leadership before publication. He was a member in all but name and had actually applied to join but had been turned down. This was certainly because he was considered of more use as someone who appeared to be 'independent' arguing the party line than he would have been as a member arguing it. What we see in his contributions to *The Betrayal of the Left* is someone desperately trying to re-orient himself now that he has lost his intellectual anchor. In this contribution, he accused the CP of actually underestimating 'the vileness of fascism'. This 'vileness' derived from fascism's totalitarian character, from its practice of 'enforced conformity'. He had still not fully broken with his Stalinist dependency at this time though. As he somewhat apologetically acknowledged, using his completely inadequate definition of totalitarianism, 'it cannot be denied that the Soviet Union is a totalitarian society'. But, he went on quite incredibly, to argue that 'there would be no objection to mental uniformity in the Soviet Union if the doctrine enforced were completely true'. He proceeds to give his full support to the Moscow Trials which had absolutely proven that the likes of Trotsky, Radek and Bukharin had 'pushed their opposition to the point of plot, espionage and sabotage', indeed at a time when Stalin was looking forward to a period of 'liberalisation', they had provoked 'the new period of extreme Soviet totalitarianism', starting with 'the murder of Kiroff'. What had to be acknowledged, however, was that this totalitarianism, for which Trotsky and co were certainly responsible, had seriously damaged the Soviet Union. The problem, as he sees it, is that the 'mental uniformity' that is being enforced is not true enough although it is 'incomparably truer . . . than is Fascist doctrine'. Clearly, Strachey was feeling his way towards a rejection of totalitarianism per se, but was not completely there yet. Even so he concludes quite remarkably that while totalitarianism might be damaging the socialist cause at the moment, this might not always be the case! There might come a time when 'mental uniformity . . . will become not only harmless but immensely beneficial'.[14] It is worth making the point here that for all Orwell's weaknesses and confusions, his arguments stand up magnificently when compared to the appalling sophistries of a lapsed Stalinist, someone widely seen as one of the leading Marxist intellectuals of the day. Strachey was to rejoin the Labour Party in 1942, was once again elected a Labour MP in 1945, and went on to become Minister of Food in 1946 and Minister for War in 1950.

What of Gollancz? One of his contributions to the collection was his 'An Immediate Programme' where he proclaimed that 'We stand for victory – for the decisive defeat of Hitler. The alternative was 'enslavement to foreign fascism, or to native fascism acting as its puppet'. There was no other choice. And at the same time, the struggle for socialism had to continue. He called for 'a rapid growth in the militancy of the Labour movement' while recognising that 'on the political side, the Labour Party is the only possible spearhead for advance'. He looked forward to 'a Labour victory over Hitler-fascism, leading to a new Britain and a new world'. One of his key demands was the immediate release from prison of Gandhi, Nehru and other leaders of the Congress movement in India. He acknowledged that 'big business and the money power are still effectively in control, but insisted that with Labour in 'partnership or semi-partnership', capitalism had at least 'to some extent, mind its P's and Q's'. He singled out the effective end of the household means test as a great step forward. And this situation could and had to be built on. What he absolutely rejected was the argument that the CP was putting forward that it hardly mattered whether Hitler or Churchill won the war because there was so little difference between them, that 'the difference between a Churchill victory and a Hitler victory was merely the difference between a ninety per cent evil and a hundred per cent evil'. This contribution was followed by another, an 'Epilogue: On Political Morality', that focussed quite remarkably on the extent to which the Communists lied and, of course, at this time, he did not know the half of it. They lied without any apparent qualms. They even lied to themselves. One problem that Gollancz had, of course, was that throughout the Popular Front period, he had enthusiastically helped the Communists propagate their lies. He does attempt to explain this, arguing that he went along with their lies because they were allies in the fight against fascism which took priority over everything else. Even so, by the summer of 1938, he was finding working with the CP 'increasingly difficult'. He ended this 'Epilogue', however, by proclaiming that whatever the Communists did, he was still prepared to admit that they did it 'in the service of the greatest of all causes: the emancipation of the working class, and, through it, of humanity'.[15]

Once again, Orwell's contributions compare most favourably with those of his fellow contributors, not least, but not only, because he had already settled accounts with Stalinism, had grasped its enormity, the extent to which it was a brutal murderous travesty of socialism.

'The War and the Revolution are Inseparable'

The first of Orwell's contributions to *The Betrayal of the Left*, 'Fascism and Democracy' opens with a consideration of the meaning of 'Democracy'. As he points out, even if a government 'representing the poorer classes' gets into power, 'the rich can usually blackmail it by threatening to export capital'. They can use their almost complete control of 'the whole cultural and intellectual life of the community – newspapers, books, education, films, radio . . . to prevent the spread of certain ideas'. Indeed, he doubted whether it was actually possible for the power of the rich to be 'broken' by parliamentary means. They would rebel 'and probably with success, because they would have most of the permanent officials and the key men in the armed forces on their side'. Although he does not say it here, this was the lesson of the Popular Front government elected in Spain in 1936. He went on: 'There is no strong reason for thinking that any really fundamental change can ever be achieved peacefully'. Nevertheless, he absolutely insisted on the value of civil liberties in Britain. The country might well be dominated by the rich but pointing this out did not lead to arrest and imprisonment and this was important and had to be defended. Indeed, he effectively repudiated his pre-war pronouncements that war would inevitably lead to the fascisation of Britain. This had not happened. As far as he was concerned this demonstrated that even what he described as 'Chamberlain's England' was worth defending against the Nazis. But this was no longer what the war was about because now 'the choice is between Socialism and defeat'.

The problem was that while socialism was absolutely necessary if the Nazis were to be defeated, Britain has 'never possessed . . . a Socialist party which meant business'. The Labour Party was certainly not to be taken seriously as a vehicle for socialist transformation and much of the 'revolutionary feeling' that existed had ended up in the 'blind alley' that was Communism. Far from fighters for socialism, Communists were 'mere publicity agents for the Russian regime. What you had in Russia was 'oligarchical rule, rigid censorship of ideas and the slavish worship of a Fuehrer' and this, in effect, was what Communists advocated for Britain. He looked forward to the appearance of a 'real English Socialist movement . . . both revolutionary and democratic'. It would be committed to making 'the most fundamental changes and be perfectly willing to use violence if necessary'. For the time being though, it was necessary to recognise that even 'Bourgeois Democracy' was 'very much better than fascism'.[16]

His second contribution, 'Patriots and Revolutionaries', once again argued the necessity of fundamental change, of a 'revolution'. Indeed, Orwell was convinced that Britain was already 'on the road to revolution, a process that started, in my opinion, about the end of 1938'. There had been a revolutionary moment in May and June 1940 when the 'ruling class' stood discredited by defeat and disaster. 'Had any real leadership existed on the Left', he argued, 'there is little doubt that the return of the troops from Dunkirk could have been the beginning of the end of British capitalism'. No one could deny 'the leftward swing of public opinion' at the time. But the strategic moment passed and by October 1940, 'the forces of reaction' had recovered. It still remained the case though that, what he acknowledged as a Trotskyist slogan, 'The war and the revolution are inseparable', remained true. Only a socialist Britain could defeat the Nazis, enlisting 'the progressive forces of the world' in the struggle and therefore, as he put it, 'fighting against the sins of its own past'. And, returning to one of the themes of *The Road to Wigan Pier*, this revolution required the support of what he described as 'the indispensible middle class', of 'the technical middle class' or what today would be called white-collar-workers. Revolutionary patriotism was the key to winning these people over, 'the impulse to defend one's country and to make it a place worth living in' that had inspired 'the Paris workers in 1793, the Communards in 1871, the Madrid trade unionists in 1936'.[17]

The Betrayal of the Left was published early in 1941 and then on 22 June 1941, Nazi Germany invaded the Soviet Union and everything changed. Overnight the CP abandoned 'revolutionary defeatism', turning to enthusiastic support for the war effort, and Gollancz rushed into print his *Russia and Ourselves*, proclaiming 'our complete and uncompromising solidarity' with the Soviet Government. Britain, he wrote, was now allied with 'the only socialist state in the world'. His return to his earlier pro-Soviet stance was never to be as unquestioning as during the Popular Front years though. Now he argued that the reality was that the Soviet Union was only socialist 'in foundation and in ultimate intention but not in actual day-to-day practice'![18] But while he embraced the Soviet Union, with whatever qualifications, he was to never again trust the leadership of the British Communist Party. The abuse and slander they had heaped on him after the Hitler-Stalin Pact was never forgotten or forgiven. For Orwell, though, even this qualified embrace of the Soviet Union meant that his short-lived reconciliation with Gollancz was effectively over and when he came to write *Animal Farm* he had to look elsewhere for a publisher.

'Turning this War into a Revolutionary War'

Around the same time that *The Betrayal of the Left* was published, Orwell published his own *The Lion and the Unicorn*, part of the 'Searchlight' series of short books, published by Frederick Warburg, that he edited with Tosco Fyvel.[19] These volumes were intended to help prepare the way for the emergence of the new socialist movement that Orwell believed was urgently needed if the war was to be won. Here, he explored his understanding of 'Englishness', urged the importance of winning 'the technicians and the higher-paid skilled workers, the airmen and their mechanics, the radio experts, the film producers, popular journalists and industrial chemists' over to the socialist cause, emphasised the bankruptcy of the ruling class and put forward a political programme that would sweep away that ruling class. It is worth examining that programme, not least because it has recently been argued by Robert Colls that most of it was actually implemented by the Churchill and Attlee governments, and that it was this that ended Orwell's flirtation with revolution and reconciled him with British Labour Party. He was liberated from revolutionary politics, so to speak, by his involvement 'in the People's War' and became 'a Labour man'.[20] The reality was somewhat different. What Orwell proposed was not a programme of reforms that would improve the condition of the working class within capitalist society, but still leave the ruling class in place. What he proposed was a programme that was intended to strip the ruling class of their wealth, power and privilege once and for all. There would no longer be a ruling class in Britain. This was his intention. It was not a call for a Bolshevik-style Revolution with street barricades, the occupation of the factories and the establishment of workers' councils, but it certainly cannot be reduced to the politics of the Churchill and Attlee governments. As far as Orwell was concerned, in a country like Britain, the choice was not between an insurrectionary and a gradualist road to socialism, neither of which was viable. Instead, there was a third way, a centrist way between piecemeal reform and insurrection, whereby a Socialist Party would take power, legislate the abolition of the ruling class and be ready to put down any opposition by force if necessary, mobilising a mass popular movement such as had driven the revolutionary process in Spain. This might involve the workers taking over the factories and establishing workers' councils with the Home Guard playing the role of a revolutionary militia. In his own words, it was all intended to turn 'this war into a revolutionary war and England into a Socialist democracy'.[21]

The programme he put forward had six points, three domestic and three international. He called for the nationalisation of the land, mines, railways, banks and the major industries. This would not involve the payment of massive sums in compensation, but their confiscation. The power of the ruling class derived from the concentration of wealth in their hands and this wealth was to be taken from them. In this way, 'the dominance of a single class will have been broken'. With regards to land ownership, he proposed a maximum limit of 15 acres for the ownership of land in rural areas but no private ownership of land in the towns and cities. The likes of the Duke of Westminster would be no more.[22] He proposed both a minimum and a maximum income with the maximum set at no more than ten times whatever the minimum rate was. And the education system had to be democratised with the taking over of the public schools. Although not included as one of his six points, he went on to make clear that the socialist government he was calling for would certainly abolish the House of Lords, but he could imagine it keeping the monarchy! And this was just the beginning, of course. What could be absolutely guaranteed was 'the hatred which the surviving rich men of the world will feel for it'. As far as international policy was concerned, India would be immediately offered Dominion status with 'the unconditional right to secede' and similar terms would be offered 'to Burma, Malaya and most of our African possessions'. The important point was that there would be complete equality between nations. An Imperial General Council would be formed, in effect a Socialist Commonwealth, which would, under point six, ally itself with everyone fighting fascist aggression throughout the world. This was a far more radical programme than anything the Labour Party has ever put forward.

Far from Orwell's politics being changed by his involvement in any supposed 'People's War, his wartime writings are in fact one long protracted complaint that it was not a 'People's War' and a demand that it be transformed into one. In *The Lion and the Unicorn*, he describes wartime Britain as 'still the rich man's Paradise' with all talk of 'equality of sacrifice' just so much 'nonsense'. Inequality of wealth in Britain was still 'grosser than in any European country, and you only have to look down the nearest street to see it'. What, he asked, have 'people with £100,000 a year and people with £1 a week' got in common? When people in the East End of London are bombed out, they 'go hungry and homeless', while the rich 'simply step into their cars and flee to comfortable country houses'. All this had to end. While the means of production had to be taken over, it was even 'more urgently necessary that such monstrosities as butlers and "private incomes" should disappear'. And, moreover, Orwell absolutely insisted that nationalisation on its own, was not 'a sufficient definition of Socialism'. What was also required was 'approximate equality of incomes', 'political democracy' and the 'abolition of all hereditary privilege, especially in education'. Without this the class system would reappear, and, very much with the Soviet Union in mind, you could end up with 'a self-elected political party, and oligarchy and privilege . . . based on power rather than money'.

What was the vehicle for implementing this programme? He dismissed the Labour Party. Even if it 'meant business', he did not think a Labour government that attacked the ruling class 'could make itself obeyed'. Any attempt at socialist change carried the risk of upper class revolt which scared the Labour leadership off, leaving them with the option of continuing 'with the same policies as the Conservatives'. At best, Labour stood for 'a timid reformism'. As far as he could see, the Labour leadership no longer wanted radical change, but instead just wanted 'to go on and on, drawing their salaries and periodically swapping jobs with the Conservatives'. A new socialist movement was necessary to carry out his revolution, although he recognised that it would have at its core 'the old Labour Party and its mass following will be in the Trade Unions, but it will draw into it most of the middle class...skilled workers, technical experts, airmen, scientists, architects and journalists'. This winning over of the new technical middle class was crucial and he believed that the embrace of 'revolutionary patriotism' by the left was one of the ways that it could be accomplished. Of course, a socialist revolution would not go unopposed and the new socialist government would have to 'shoot traitors, but it will give them a solemn trial beforehand . . . It will crush any open revolt promptly and cruelly'.[23] Civil liberties would be maintained because, as far as Orwell was concerned, they were an essential part of what democratic socialism was all about. Socialism would extend liberty, not curtail it. Once again, it is important to emphasise that this programme was intended not to extract concessions from the ruling class, but to abolish them, to altogether strip them of their wealth, power and privilege. It is worth noticing here that the much vaunted Beveridge Report on Social Security that Labour was to embrace as the centre piece of its post-war reforms, was dismissed by Orwell as 'this very moderate measure of reform'.[24] His political programme was and was meant to be revolutionary. If Orwell's programme had actually been implemented by the Churchill and Attlee governments, as Colls argues, then Britain would look very different today.[25]

One last point worth making here is the importance of Orwell's belief, certainly a correct belief, that the ruling class would resist its abolition by some kind of rebellion and that this would have to be put down by force, in effect by the people in arms. As far as he was concerned, this was a commonsense truth, a truth that had been concretely demonstrated on numerous occasions throughout the world in the 1920s and 1930s with the rise of fascism and dictatorship, culminating in the Spanish Civil War. Indeed, so commonplace was his recognition of ruling class resistance to fundamental social change that he could even joke about it. In *Tribune* on 7 January 1944, he wrote of a possible future use for the air raid shelters that had been put up during the Blitz. They had been mainly built in the 'poorer streets' and would be 'useful . . . as block-houses in street fighting . . . It would amuse me if when the time came the higher-ups were unable to crush the populace because they had thought-lessly provided them with thousands of machine gun nests beforehand'.[26] And, as we shall see, just before the 1945 general election (see Chapter 7), he was to broadcast a warning on the BBC no less that 'the capitalist class would not just let itself be abolished', but 'would stop at nothing in defence of its possessions'.[27] At the same time, he thought full-scale civil war most unlikely because however deep the divide between the classes in Britain, there was not the same degree of class hatred as there was on the Continent.

'That Strange No Man's Land Where the Fascist and the Pacifist Join Forces'

As we have seen, before the outbreak of war in September 1939, Orwell had actively campaigned against war, very much involving himself with ILP and anarchist opposition to the coming conflict and actually briefly joining the Peace Pledge Union (PPU). Once war had begun, he radically changed his position and during the course of the war was to clash, often quite bitterly with his former fellow-thinkers. In one diary entry (17 June 1940), he rather unkindly dismissed his former ILP comrades as living 'almost entirely in a masturbation fantasy'.[28] One additional dimension to this clash was that the US journal, *Partisan Review*, to which he contributed his 'London Letter', was opposed to US involvement in the war and became one of the sites where his conflict with wartime pacifism was fought out. Essentially, Orwell's case against those opposed to the war was twofold: first that they were objectively aiding the Nazis by undermining the war effort and second that many of them were actually subjectively pro-Nazi, that is to say, they supported either a peace dictated by the Nazis or even a Nazi victory. This last proposition seemed to place Orwell very much in the position of slandering those he disagreed with; committing the very offence that he had so often condemned the CP for committing. As we shall see whatever one thinks of his argument that an anti-war stance objectively aided the Nazis, his second proposition was in some respects accurate. Not only were there pacifists who adopted a pro-German stance, but the pacifist movement had been very deliberately infiltrated by fascists and fascist sympathisers in the run up to the war.

His 'London Letter' that appeared in *Partisan Review* early in 1942 acknowledged that the anarchists were still following what he described as a revolutionary defeatist line and that the ILP position was similar to *Partisan Review's* own stance, but what was interesting, he argued, was the 'increasing overlap between Fascism and pacifism', an overlap often tainted with anti-Semitism. The anti-war far left was not altogether exempt from this either. He argued that Middleton Murray had taken the *Adelphi* down the pacifist road, even on occasions indulging in 'Jew-baiting of a mild kind' and portraying Nazi Germany as a socialist country fighting a defensive war against a plutocratic Britain. He specifically singled out George Woodcock's magazine, *NOW*, for censure, referring to the copy in front of him that contained contributions by an open fascist like Hugh Ross Williamson, by an unrepentant appeaser and covert fascist like the Duke of Bedford, by the Trotskyist, Julian Symons, who 'writes in a vaguely Fascist strain but is also given to quoting Lenin', and by the anarchist-pacifist Alex Comfort. This one issue of the magazine embodied the overlap he had identified.[29]

This provoked a fierce exchange, what David Goodway describes as 'a bad tempered brawl',[30] in the September-October issue of *Partisan*

Review with Woodcock himself, Alex Comfort and Derek Savage replying to Orwell's attack. Woodcock, an anarchist, defended his magazine, pointing out that only two of the fifty or so writers featured in the first seven numbers of NOW were 'even reputed to have Fascist tendencies', that Orwell was grossly unfair to Julian Symons, and that all his other contributors were either 'anarchists, Stalinists, Trotskyists, pacifists and New Statesmen moderates'. He went on to accuse Orwell of being a former colonial policeman who had returned to his 'old imperialist allegiances' by working for the BBC broadcasting war propaganda to India. Savage's contribution, where he described a Nazi victory as 'a profound justice', it must be said, went a long way towards substantiating Orwell's critique.[31] Orwell responded to Woodcock with a defence of his BBC work and indeed he invited Woodcock to participate in a broadcast which he agreed to do. He refused payment in case it was 'a trap of some kind'. In a private letter, Orwell confided to Woodcock that he was well aware that the 'British governing class' were using him, but that as far as he was concerned the only alternative was to 'remain outside the war', and he did hope that to some extent he had been able to 'deodorise' the BBC. Compared to some of the 'muck and filth . . . I consider I have kept our corner of it fairly clean'.[32] Orwell was to subsequently become friends with Julian Symons, Alex Comfort and most especially with George Woodcock (he was to contribute to NOW himself), and, of course, Woodcock was to go on to write one of the best books on Orwell, *The Crystal Spirit*.[33] Nevertheless, while Orwell was prepared to admit to intemperate language and to sometimes being unfair, as far as he was concerned there still remained 'that strange no man's land where the Fascist and the pacifist joined hands'.[34]

Was there any substance to Orwell's critique? Certainly, he was most unfair to Symons in this controversy.[35] He privately defended his characterisation of where the *Adelphi* had ended up to Comfort, however, pointing out that Max Plowman, who had taken over as editor of the *Adelphi* in 1938, 'hated Jews' and that John Middleton Murray on at least one occasion had 'referred with apparent approval to Hitler's "elimination" of the Jews'. Comfort, once again privately, acknowledged that 'on seeing the references', Orwell's comments on the *Adelphi* had been valid.[36] But what of the supposed overlap between pacifists and fascists? According to Richard Griffiths' recent study, *What Did You Do During The War?*, this began as early as 1939, before the actual outbreak of war, with the Peace Pledge Union (PPU) becoming involved with the anti-war campaigning of the Far Right. Pro-Nazi organisations were allowed to advertise their meetings and activities in *Peace News*. Even the anarchist pacifist Ethel Mannin became involved, warning against anti-Fascist propaganda as leading to war and engaging in some crude 'Jew-baiting'. She wrote quite shamefully in *Peace News*, complaining in August 1939 of the power of 'Jewish interests vested in Big Business and the Press', of how the 'racial feeling of the Jew . . . makes him prepared to plunge the world into mass-slaughter' and ridiculed 'stories of Nazi brutality' against the Jews. Her words were quoted approvingly by the Mosleyites. As late as the middle of 1942, she was still denying Nazi atrocities against the Jews. Her stance did not really improve after the war. In her post-war memoir, *Brief Voices*, she actually complains of her publisher objecting to her novel, *The Dark Forest*, for suggesting that being occupied by the Nazis was no worse than being occupied by the British. She wrote that '1945, with the talk all of Buchenwald and Belsen, was no time to suggest it' and she made the required deletions but only under protest.[37]

More generally, *Peace News*, in the words of Mark Gilbert became a 'consistent apologist . . . for Nazi Germany'. In 1940, the PPU published a pamphlet, *Money has Destroyed Your Peace* arguing that both Stalinist Russia and Nazi Germany were 'a progressive improvement over liberal capitalism'. This was a regular theme, at least up until June 1941, when support for the Soviet Union was curtailed because it was now allied with Britain. And John Middleton Murray who had taken over the editorship of *Peace News* in 1940 became increasingly openly pro-Nazi. According to Richard Rempel, Murray advocated acceptance of a 'Pax Germanica' on the Continent. Nazi Germany was championed as progressive and *Peace News* became an apologist for its actions. After the Nazis executed 100 French civilians in reprisal for the killing of two German soldiers by the Resistance, Murray condemned the reprisal, but also asked why 'nobody condemns the original murders'. He dismissed Chaplin's *The Great Dictator* as the 'worst Chaplin film I have ever seen'. On another occasion, Murray made clear that Vichy France was the direction Britain should have taken. Indeed, Rempel describes him as being almost alone in Britain in his defence of Petain. We are, as Gilbert puts it, confronted with the remarkable paradox that between 1938 and 1943, the PPU provided the spectacle of 'an avowedly pacifist movement whose public statements, more often than not, excused, or even exalted, the most ruthless user of military force known to man'. What changed in 1943 was that after initial scepticism, Murray became convinced, not least by Gollancz's pamphlet, *Let My People Go*, that the Nazis were exterminating Poland's Jews.[38] He was to personally find pacifism increasingly untenable as a philosophy and, according to Orwell, by 1948 was 'demanding a preventive war against the USSR'.[39]

'Bombing is Not Especially Inhumane'

On 19 May 1944, Orwell used his *Tribune* 'As I Please' column to review Vera Brittain's 'eloquent' pamphlet (in fact it was a short book), *Seed of Chaos*, that attacked the RAF's indiscriminate bombing of civilian targets, what she described as their 'obliteration bombing'. She was not a pacifist, but was instead opposed to what Orwell somewhat scornfully described as 'killing civilians', the 'massacre of women and children' and the 'destruction of our cultural heritage'. 'Why', he asked, 'is it worse to kill civilians than soldiers' and proceeded to dismiss any idea of 'humanising' war as 'sheer humbug'. While one should obviously not target children, he argued that bombing killed a cross-section of the community, indeed probably less children because of evacuation. In the Blitz, German bombing had killed 'between six and seven thousand children', which he assured his readers, was 'less than the number killed in road accidents in the same period'. And he went on to seriously argue that it 'does not seem to me a bad thing that others should be killed besides young men'. The suffering in this war has been 'shared out more evenly' because of bombing' and unlike Miss Brittain I don't regret that'.[40] She replied a month later and, with considerable restraint, accused Orwell of not having read her book with enough care, which seems to have certainly been the case.

Seed of Chaos was, in fact, a tremendously powerful indictment of the systematic bombardment of German cities to which Orwell hardly did justice. As Brittain wrote: 'as a Londoner who has been through about 600 raids and has spent 18 months as a volunteer fireguard I have seen and heard enough to know that I at least must vehemently protest when this obscenity of terror and mutilation is inflicted upon the helpless civilians of another country'. Indeed, she argued that polling had shown that in the parts of the country that had been most heavily bombed by the Nazis most people agreed with her! The book relentlessly chronicled the development of British bombardment, overwhelmingly using British sources to detail the damage done and the numbers killed. 40 per cent of Lubeck destroyed in March 1942 and 70 per cent of Rostock the following month and then in May the first 1,000 bomber raid on Cologne with – according to a report from a neutral source – 20,000 people killed in one night. She describes the raids on Hamburg between 24 July and the 2 August 1943 which saw some 10,000 tons of bombs dropped on the city. According to the *Daily Telegraph*, one RAF officer described the destruction as 'truly devastating. In comparison the enemy raids on London were child's play'. The *Telegraph* reported a death toll of some 50,000 or more. Her account of the destruction of much of Hamburg includes the testimony of neutral observers which are truly horrific. A Swiss correspondent reported on the effects of the fire storm the bombing had created: 'the majority of the victims are women and children. Numerous completely charred bodies of women and children were found . . . reports by survivors of burning women and children and of women throwing their children into canals'. It is difficult to believe that Orwell could have bothered to read this far. In terms of casualties, she argued that by the end of October 1943, British bombing had already inflicted '24 times the amount of suffering' that the Nazis had inflicted on Britain over the same period. And the worst was still to come. As for Orwell's argument regarding the futility of trying to 'humanise' war, she referred to her experience as a nurse on the Western Front during the First World War when she had treated the victims of mustard gas. As she wrote, 'I for one am thankful for the development of public opinion which has caused the belligerent nations to observe up to date the Poison Gas Convention of 1925'.[41] She returned to this point in her letter to *Tribune* on 23 June, prompting a particularly shabby and wholly inadequate reply from Orwell who not only dismissed her as a pacifist but went on to express doubt as to whether 'gas or bacterial warfare was worse than the ordinary kind' anyway.[42]

Orwell still held to his views on bombing when he journeyed to the Continent as a war correspondent for the *Observer*. On 8 April 1945, he wrote of how 'the scale of the Allied blitzing of Germany is even now not realised in this country'. Indeed, to walk through 'the ruined cities of Germany is to feel an actual doubt about the continuity of civilisation'. Nevertheless, he still insisted that 'Bombing is not especially inhumane'.[43]

'No Real Shift of Power'

What of the belief that the Second World War was, as far as Britain was concerned, a People's War? This was not something that Orwell would have agreed with at all. Indeed, as far as he was concerned the challenge from 'the People' had been successfully beaten off. He had done his best, in his own small way, to transform the conflict into a People's War, but the ruling class had won. Far from the war having produced democratic and progressive change on the Home Front, as far as he was concerned, since 1940 'we have suffered a long list of Thermidors'.[44] The decisive moment for Orwell was the failure to prevent the suppression of the Quit India movement with the arrest of Gandhi, Nehru and thousands of others. The repression unleashed in India had the full support of the Labour members of the Churchill Coalition; indeed, it was Attlee acting as Deputy Prime Minister, who ordered the crackdown.[45] The result was that the British ruling class emerged from the war with its wealth, privilege and power intact. He noted a small indication of this in April 1944 when he commented on how even the pretence of equal sacrifices was being abandoned with 'the bourgeoisie... .... coming more and more out of their holes, as one can see by the advertisements for servants quite in the old style'.[46] The reality was that the war had seen 'no real shift of power and no increase in genuine democracy' so that the 'same people still own all the property and usurp all the best jobs'. He admitted that looking back, he had 'exaggerated the social changes' that were taking place in Britain and had 'underrated the enormous strength of the forces of reaction'.[47] Orwell had hoped and believed that the war would bring the overthrow of British capitalism, the abolition of the British upper class and the establishment of democratic socialism. Instead the 'forces of reaction' had prevailed.

5

'It is Astonishing How Little Change Has Happened': Orwell, the Labour Party and the Attlee Government

The experience of the 1930s and early 1940s had left Orwell with a very low opinion of the Labour Party. As he had written in *Left News*, the monthly magazine of the Left Book Club, in February 1941, 'England has never possessed . . . a socialist party which meant business *and* took account of contemporary realities'. It was the Labour Party, as far as he was concerned, that never meant business, while it was the Communist Party, among other things, that never took account of contemporary realities. Indeed, as far as the Labour Party was concerned, he wrote dismissively that 'it has been difficult for ten years past to believe that its leaders expected or even wished to see any fundamental change in their own lifetime'. In *The Lion and the Unicorn*, published that same month, he condemned the Labour Party for its 'timid reformism' and as having become nothing more than 'a variant of Conservatism'. This he put down at least in part to the fact that it was 'a party of the Trade Unions' primarily interested in 'the prosperity of British capitalism', so that it had degenerated 'into a Permanent Opposition'.[1] Just over a year later, he could still refer, quite casually, without any apparent fear of contradiction, to the 'discredited Parliamentary Labour Party'.[2] As we have seen, at the time he wrote these words, he confidently expected the emergence of a new socialist movement that would mean business, was in tune with contemporary realities and would set about carrying through fundamental change, change that was not just necessary to establish a classless and egalitarian society but also, he insisted, to win the war. While he expected Labour Party members to make up an important part of this new socialist movement, the Labour Party itself was not a vehicle for fundamental change. This judgement was, of course, amply borne out by the Labour Party's performance since the moment of its foundation.

His hopes of a British revolution miscarried. Revolutionary opportunities, which, in retrospect, he admitted he had exaggerated anyway, had been missed, the forces of conservatism were too strong and the Soviet Union and the United States had saved the British Empire from military defeat. Once he reluctantly acknowledged that a revolution was not going to take place in Britain and that the war was going to be won regardless, he instead began looking towards the despised Labour Party as the best that was possible in Britain, at least for the immediate future, perhaps longer. Much of the thinking that informed these conclusions was laid out in the 'London Letters' that he wrote for *Partisan Review*. Emblematic of his new thinking was his decision to become the literary editor of the left-wing Labour Party newspaper *Tribune* at the end of November 1943.

Bernard Crick, in what is still the best biography of Orwell that we have, welcomed his turn to the Labour Party as a combination of him both coming to his senses and coming home. Orwell embraced '*Tribune* Socialism', something that Crick positively celebrates.[3] There is a much more careful discussion of Orwell's political trajectory in the collection of his *Tribune* contributions, edited and introduced by Paul Anderson, *Orwell in Tribune*. He acknowledges Orwell's continued engagement with the ideas of the revolutionary left, even though he saw the Labour Party as the only practical way forward, certainly after the 1945 general election.[4] The most enthusiastic and uncritical celebration of Orwell's supposed embrace of British Labourism, however, is in Robert Colls' *George Orwell English Rebel*. Here Colls pretty systematically downplays, denigrates and dismisses any connection between Orwell and revolutionary politics of any description. Indeed, one is left feeling that even Orwell's involvement with the Labour left is a bit suspect, a remnant of his early revolutionary contrariness, before he at last embraced what Colls describes as 'The English Road to Socialism'. According to Colls, by 1943, Orwell was a 'Labour man . . . because he saw it as a responsible party, attuned to real lives rather than ideological postures' and 'because Labour enjoyed an organic connection with the British working class'. From some sort of revolutionary romantic, he had turned into 'a pretty straightforward supporter of the Labour party' who thought that 'Attlee's government . . . was a socialist state and ought to be defended as such'. When it comes to what Orwell actually meant by socialism, Colls puts forward a number of possibilities, some of them positively grotesque, it has to be said. We are seriously told that for Orwell socialism was variously 'present society with the worst abuses left out', 'a form of upper-middle-class charity for the poor', 'liberty and justice . . . and more help for the unemployed' and even that he understood what Herbert Morrison meant when he proclaimed that socialism was whatever the Labour Party says and does.[5] The reality was very different. While Orwell certainly came to regard the Labour Party's reformism as the best that was possible in the context of British politics for the foreseeable future, at the same time he still engaged with more radical socialist ideas, principally in the pages of the US journal *Partisan Review* where he expressed dismay at the Attlee government's failure of radical nerve, and, on occasions, he even hoped that the Labour Party might actually take on the capitalist class.

'Both Progressive and Humane'

The *Tribune* newspaper had been established in January 1937 by Sir Stafford Cripps, a wealthy lawyer, and the effective leader of the Labour left, in the form of the Socialist League at that time. It was intended to champion a Unity Campaign that involved both the CP and the ILP. The attempt was stillborn, partly because what the CP wanted out of the campaign was affiliation to the Labour Party, whereas the ILP saw it as a way of launching a new Socialist Party that would involve a decisive break away from what they regarded as a Labour Party wholly discredited by its performance in office in 1929–31. More important though were the steps that the Labour Party leadership took to crush the Labour left, disaffiliating the Socialist League and making membership of the organisation incompatible with Labour Party membership. The Socialist League duly dissolved itself in April 1937 and the Unity Campaign collapsed. Even without this move by the Labour Party leadership, relations between the CP and the ILP became increasingly hostile owing to CP support for the suppression of the POUM in Spain and their relentless slandering of critics of the Soviet Union and its actions, both at home and abroad, as either little better than or as actual fascists. *Tribune*, it has to be said, reported that the suppression of the 'Catalonian rising' in which Orwell had participated, far from weakening Republican Spain, had left it 'definitely stronger'.[6]

Tribune survived the Unity Campaign debacle, even though it was losing money, kept afloat by Cripps' fortune.[7] The paper continued as a champion of CP calls for a Popular Front against fascism, a Popular Front open not only to Labour, but also the Liberals and even Conservatives. The ILP were very much excluded from this project for continuing to champion class politics and criticising the Soviet Union. These were, of course, as we have already seen (Chapter 2), factors in Orwell's decision to join the ILP. As for *Tribune*, the paper, as Paul Anderson puts it, 'took an unquestioningly pro-Soviet line . . . Through late 1938 and 1939, it published nothing even remotely critical of the Soviet Union'.[8] Trotsky's book, *The Revolution Betrayed,* was actually handed over to a loyal Stalinist, Pat Sloan, for review. This pro-Soviet line survived even the Hitler-Stalin Pact which was praised in the paper as 'a great reinforcement for peace in Eastern Europe' and condemned the idea that it left Nazi Germany 'with a free hand against Poland' as 'a lie'. Indeed, the Pact was described as a Soviet triumph successfully bringing the Nazis to terms without war. And when the Soviet Union joined its new ally in partitioning Poland, *Tribune* remained supportive. The Russian attack on Finland in November 1939 marked the beginning of a struggle to end the paper's effective subordination to the CP. The attack on Finland was condemned as owing more to *Mein Kampf* than to the *Communist Manifesto.* For the time being, *Tribune* continued parroting the CP line of opposition to the war, calling for a negotiated peace with Nazi Germany, in effect, for a Hitler-Chamberlain Pact, but there was growing opposition to this stance.[9] When Raymond Postgate took over as editor subordination to the CP line finally came to an end.[10] Needless to say at this stage of its political trajectory, *Tribune* would have been of no interest to Orwell, except as an example of the pernicious influence of Stalinism on the British left.

His first contribution, a review of the *Memoirs of Sergeant Bourgogne,* appeared in the paper within weeks of Postgate having taken over, on 29 March 1940, and thereafter he contributed a book review on average about every three weeks. On 20 December 1940, the paper published his article, 'The Home Guard and You' in which he advocated the 'Revolutionary Patriotism' that was his response to the crisis of 1940–41. Here he warned that the Home Guard was 'trembling in the balance, uncertain whether it wants to become a real People's Army' or not. This was what 'the rank and file want it to become', but a 'shove in the right direction was required'. He used the paper's pages to urge socialists to join the Home Guard and help turn it into a People's Army because 'the influence of even a few thousand men who were known to be good comrades *and* to hold left-wing views could be enormous'. We live, as he put it, 'in a strange period of history in which a revolutionary has to be a patriot and a patriot has to be a revolutionary'.[11] He did not contribute to the paper again until September 1942, contributing fairly regularly thereafter until he became literary editor. By this time, the left-wing Labour MP, Aneurin Bevan had replaced Postgate as editor.

Bevan, born in November 1897 in South Wales, had gone to work down the mines in 1911, aged 13. He became active in both the South Wales Miners' Federation and the Labour Party, winning election as both a union officer and local councillor, until in the June 1929 general election, he was elected MP for Ebbw Vale. Dissatisfaction with the appalling performance of the Labour government saw him align himself with the revolt of a prominent junior minister, Oswald Mosley. When Mosley broke away in February 1931 to launch his New Party, even though Bevan had helped write the party programme, he took the decision to stay with Labour. Mosley, of course, had started on the road to fascism. Although he identified himself with the Labour left in the 1930s, even his future wife, Jennie Lee, admitted to having had initial doubts about him. He was too fond of mixing with the rich and powerful, enjoying their company, their hospitality and their patronage. As she later put it: 'I did not like some of the company he kept. He delighted in the Beaverbrook ménage and talked exuberantly about slumming in the West End'.[12] She was not alone in noticing a contradiction between his leftism and his liking for the 'good life'. Max Aitken, better known as Lord Beaverbrook, was a right-wing press baron, who liked to cultivate amenable left-wing mavericks. At a dinner party, one of Beaverbrook's own circle, Brendan Bracken, actually ridiculed Bevan for his hypocrisy, denouncing him as a 'Bollinger Bolshevik . . . swilling Max's champagne and calling yourself a socialist'.[13] And Orwell himself, in a profile of Bevan that he wrote for the *Observer* both praised the man as someone who 'thinks and feels as a working man', as someone who knows 'how the scales are weighted against anyone with less than £5 a week', but also noted that 'he is remarkably free . . . from any feeling of personal grievance against society', was someone who 'shows no sign of ordinary class consciousness . . . equally at home in all kinds of company'.[14] Bevan was someone who could denounce the Tories as 'lower than vermin' at a Labour Party rally and then, apparently without any embarrassment whatsoever, go on to drink champagne at a dinner party in the company of those same Tories.

In the late 1930s, however, Bevan was a leading figure in the Socialist League and after it disbanded, continued to support Cripps in challenging the Labour Party leadership. When Cripps was expelled from the Labour Party towards the end of January 1939, Bevan stood by him and was himself duly expelled on 31 March. He applied for readmission the following day, but was not allowed back into the Party until the end of the year. Cripps himself was not to make his peace with the Labour Party until 1945. Meanwhile, Attlee took the Labour Party into coalition with the Conservatives in May 1940, and Bevan, as one biography of the man puts it, set himself up as the de facto leader of the parliamentary opposition to the Churchill Coalition.[15] The ferocity with which Bevan attacked the Coalition government, including both Churchill and Attlee, was wholly commendable. This was the man editing *Tribune* when Orwell joined its staff. The paper was busy playing 'a noisy oppositional role'.[16]

Looking back at the end of January 1947 on his involvement with *Tribune*, Orwell claimed that he did not even know of the paper's existence until 1939 and when he first started writing for it 'in the cold winter of 1939', he did not see it regularly and so did not have 'a clear idea of what kind of paper it was'. He knew it was left-wing but not much more. Then *Tribune* 'passed out of my consciousness for nearly two years'. His interest in the paper was renewed while he was working at the BBC where it was highly regarded among 'BBC personnel' because 'it was then the only paper of any standing which criticised the government'. Indeed, he concedes that criticism might not be a strong enough word considering the sometimes 'surprisingly violent attacks on Churchill'. According to Orwell, 'the fiery personality of Aneurin Bevan gave the paper its tone'. While the paper was not perfect, it was, he argued, 'the only existing weekly paper that makes a genuine effort to be both progressive and humane – that is to combine a radical Socialist policy with a respect for freedom of speech and a civilised attitude towards literature and the arts'.[17]

Orwell was literary editor of *Tribune* for fifteen months, responsible for the content of something like a third of the paper. This included his regular 'As I Please' column which, according to Paul Anderson, was 'conceived as a means of providing relief from a diet of political polemic and political analysis'. In practice, the column was often 'intensely political', but as Anderson points out, it never commented 'even in asides' on the 'political situation in Britain'.[18] Nevertheless Orwell ranged over a vast variety of topics in the column, discussing the press and journalism, V bombs, toads, racism and anti-Semitism, free speech, the BBC, nature, imperialism, roses, war crimes, the honours system, clothes rationing, the American Occupation of Britain and the bombing of Germany. George Woodcock describes the column as simply 'the best short essay writing of the Forties'.[19] In his recent discussion of the column, Richard Keeble not only argues that Orwell made a significant contribution 'to the survival of *Tribune*', but that in the process, he also defined 'a new kind of radical politics . . . reducing the power of press barons, facing up to racial intolerance, defending civil liberties'. He describes him somewhat ingeniously as a 'proto-blogger'.[20] Inevitably, the column proved controversial, attracting considerable correspondence, much of it provoked by Orwell's unashamed hostility to Stalinism at a time when the Red Army was widely seen as the West's saviour. One particular controversy worth noticing was the storm caused when *Tribune* reported the mass rape of Austrian women by Russian troops in Vienna. This was not something that Stalin's apologists were prepared to acknowledge, some not even today, and the report and the reporter were bitterly attacked. Orwell defended the report in his *Tribune* column, arguing that 'genuine progress can only happen through increasing enlightenment, which means the continuous destruction of myths'.[21]

As literary editor, Orwell published articles and reviews from across the broad spectrum of the left, many by people to the left of the Labour Party. As Woodcock puts it, he gave space in the paper's literary pages to 'writers far nearer in their views to the independent attitudes of the Anarchists, Trotskyists and Independent Labour Party than they were to the policy of the official Labor Party'. The only exception he made was with regard to members of and apologists for the Communist Party. They were not welcome. After all, as he put it, they would 'take the greatest delight in pushing me under a bus' if they thought they could get away with it.[22] In many ways, during his time as literary editor, he came to 'define *Tribune* socialism almost as much as Bevan'.[23] This was, of course, before the Labour Party took office and Attlee became Prime Minister.

He gave up being literary editor in mid-February 1945 when he became a war correspondent for the *Observer* newspaper,[24] and only returned as a columnist in October 1945 (in the meantime Tosco Fyvel had replaced him as literary editor). One reason for his absence from the paper's pages even after he gave up the *Observer* job was, Orwell himself believed, Bevan's worry that there might be 'a row' when *Animal Farm* was published.[25] And indeed, when the book was finally published in August 1945, Fyvel reviewed it in the pages of *Tribune* as if it were a harmless children's book ('one of the best and most simply written books for the child of today') without even mentioning that it was about the betrayal of the Russian Revolution![26]

'I Suppose the Drift is Towards Socialism'

Orwell did not expect the Labour Party to win the July 1945 general election. He predicted a narrow Conservative victory. He was not alone in this with Clement Attlee telling Churchill's private secretary, 'Jock' Colville that he hoped to reduce the Conservative majority in the Commons to double figures.[27] Instead, Labour was triumphantly elected on a manifesto, *Let Us Face the Future*, that proclaimed that it was 'a Socialist Party and proud of it' and that its ultimate aim was 'the establishment of the Socialist Commonwealth of Great Britain'. It went on to warn, of course, that 'Socialism cannot come overnight as the product of a weekend revolution' and that the Labour Party was made up of 'practical-minded men and women'. Whatever the left rhetoric, as far as actual proposals went, the manifesto was, in Ralph Miliband's words, certainly not 'a quasi-revolutionary document', but really only 'a mild and circumspect document'. The emphasis was very much on 'practical-minded' which absolutely excluded any attempt to confront the British capitalist class and to break their domination over British society once and for all. Instead, Labour was committed to using the resources of the state to restore the fortunes of British capitalism, to the safeguarding of Britain's international position and to preserving as much of the British Empire as was possible. Exploitation was not to be brought to an end, but the terms under which the working class were exploited were to be improved, not least by an extension of welfare provision. The position of the working class was to be improved within capitalism, although these improvements were to be kept within strict limits, no one wanted the working class getting carried away, and there was certainly no intention in the process of threatening in any sort of fundamental way the wealth and power of the capitalist class. Given the quite unjustified reputation for radicalism that the 1945–51 Labour government has today, it is very easy to mistake its nationalisation measures and its welfare reforms, most notably the setting up of the National Health Service, as some sort of fundamental challenge. Orwell, it has to be said, never made that mistake.

Orwell published a considered view of the general election and its significance in *Partisan Review* soon after the general election. Here, he emphasised that Labour's victory did not mean that 'Britain is on the verge of revolution'. There was 'discontent smouldering in the armed forces', but taken as a whole, 'the mood of the country seems to me less revolutionary . . . than it was in 1940 or 1942'. He told his American readers what to look out for to see if Labour meant business: first off it should nationalise 'land, coal mines, railways, public utilities and banks'; it should immediately offer India 'Dominion Status (this is a minimum); and it should purge 'the bureaucracy, the army, the Diplomatic Service etc'. He expected 'a battle with the House of Lords'. If this programme was not implemented, then 'it is a pretty good bet that no really radical economic change is intended'. He admitted that he did not know 'whether the government has any serious idea of introducing Socialism, but if it has, I don't see what there is to stop it'.[28] He reiterated many of these points a little while later in November 1945 in another US journal, *Commentary*. Here, he once again made the point that it would be 'absurd to imagine that Britain is on the verge of violent revolution, or even that the masses have been definitely converted to Socialism'. Most people did not know what socialism meant. For most people the Labour Party did not stand for 'red flags, barricades and reigns of terror', but for 'full employment, free milk for school-children, old-age pensions of thirty shillings a week and, in general, a fair deal for the working man'. This was certainly not socialism and he was not yet certain whether or not the Labour government 'will make a genuine effort to introduce Socialism'. He saw considerable problems ahead for the government internationally. Nevertheless, he was 'hopeful'.[29]

Despite his initial reservations concerning the meaning of the 1945 victory, he nevertheless seems to have convinced himself that some sort of full-scale attack on the position of the capitalist class was still possible. This was all part of the argument that he was still having in his own mind between the *Tribune* Labourism that he had embraced and the socialist ideas that he still adhered to and continued to rehearse in *Partisan Review*. It was also very likely the fact that Bevan had joined the government that led him to make the mistake of exaggerating its likely radicalism. Within a very short time, he realised that there was going to be no attack on the position of the upper class in society carried through by the Labour government, no confiscation of wealth, no takeover of the public schools, no purge of the civil, diplomatic and intelligence services. Tosco Fyvel later recalled Orwell coming in to the *Tribune* offices to discuss writing for the paper once again after Labour had taken power.

He was going to write 'non-political pieces' for the paper, but the first article he proposed was one arguing that 'the new Labour Government must make it its first socialist task to abolish all titles, the House of Lords and the Public Schools' and that welfare reform should come second to such measures. Fyvel took this as constituting an attack on Bevan's position and describes how he laughed Orwell out of such a ridiculous idea.[30] What Orwell was proposing, however, was that the Labour government should use its massive House of Commons majority and its strong support among service men and women to launch a full-scale political attack on the British upper class and those forces in British state and society that supported them. Orwell was certainly not opposed to welfare reforms, in fact he did not consider they went far enough, but his criticism was that they left the power of the capitalist class intact. The Labour government had no intention of making any such attack, indeed the very idea would never even have occurred to most Labour ministers or MPs. Denied access to *Tribune*, he turned once again to *Partisan Review* to give voice to his doubts and disappointments.

In the summer of 1946, *Partisan Review* published his last 'London Letter' in which he surveyed the contemporary British political scene. The Labour government was still popular even though there was a lot of moaning about how hard circumstances still were. There was resentment against 'long hours and bad working conditions' that had led to unofficial strikes, the housing situation had not improved, food shortages rankled and there had been a rise in unemployment. What he could not understand though was 'how little change seems to have happened as yet in the structure of society'. He supposed that in 'a purely economic sense . . . the drift is towards socialism, or at least towards state ownership'. But while the railways were being 'taken out of private hands', the shareholders were being exorbitantly compensated 'at prices they would hardly get in the private market'. What he found most astonishing though, was that so far as 'the social set-up' was concerned, 'there is no symptom by which one could infer that we are not living under a Conservative government'. He went on: 'No move has been made against the House of Lords, for example, there has been no talk of disestablishing the Church, there has been very little replacement of Tory ambassadors, service chiefs or other high officials, and if any effort is really being made to democratise education, it has borne no fruit as yet'. The upper classes 'dislike the Labour government (but) they don't appear to be frightened of it'. Of course, this might all be part of the British way of doing things slowly and without 'stirring up class hatred', but even so 'almost any observer would have expected a greater change in the social atmosphere when a Labour government with a crushing majority had been in power for eight months'.[31]

Orwell believed, quite correctly, that the capitalist class would resist any attempt to strip it of its wealth and power by any means necessary, including the use of force. This was true even of Britain, although he did not envisage a full-scale civil war because class hatred was not as sharp as on the Continent. The fact that the Labour government had excited no such response was precisely because it was not perceived as in any way constituting a fundamental threat to the capitalist class. They were not 'frightened' of it. Only bankrupt industries were being nationalised at very generous rates of compensation and while the upper class might not like the 'pandering' to the working class and the poor that Labour proposed, it did not threaten their domination over society. Where he had been naïve was in expecting anything different, after all Labour had been in coalition with the Conservatives for six years. The sort of political attack on the bastions of ruling class power in state and society that Orwell saw as crucial to the struggle for socialism, a political attack that would have certainly frightened them and provoked resistance, was never going to happen. Indeed, the Labour leadership itself would have been just as frightened by any such attack whatever the rhetoric it occasionally used when seeking votes. They wanted accommodation, not confrontation with the ruling class. Politics was what took place in the House of Commons and they wanted it kept there. And as for abolishing the public schools, Attlee, the Labour Prime Minister, was devoted to his old school, Haileybury, and quite unashamed about promoting other old boys, in his own word, 'all other things being equal'.[32] And as for abolishing the House of Lords, the future Lord Attlee, Earl of Walthamstow and Viscount Prestwood, was hardly the man to do that.[33]

Orwell went on in the same article to describe the Communist Party as the only serious threat the Labour government faced, because of its ability to exploit discontent. He thought they might do 'tremendous mischief' especially if allowed to affiliate to the Labour Party. They would certainly try and cause trouble over domestic failures and difficulties. He also thought that 'some calamity abroad', for example, such as 'large-scale fighting in India' might provide them with an opportunity to damage the government. Indeed, according to Orwell, many Tories were counting on the CP being able to splinter the Labour Party and force the Labour

Party right-wing 'to form another coalition'. He was also concerned about the number of Communist sympathisers elected on the Labour ticket. He thought there were probably between twenty and thirty and actually named the Labour MP, Konni Zillliacus, as an 'underground' Communist.[34] This wildly exaggerated fear of the CP was, as we shall see, to have a serious and debilitating influence on his political trajectory in this period.

'Where Does Tribune Stand?'

In December 1947, Orwell wrote to his by now good friend, the Trotskyist turned libertarian socialist, Julian Symons that *Tribune* was getting 'worse and worse'. He expanded on this a week later in another letter where he criticised the paper for its 'over-emphasis on Zionism' before going on to say that they should have come out and admitted that they were, in effect, 'a government organ . . . because in all major matters they are in agreement with the government'. He blamed the paper's decline on Richard Crossman MP, 'who influences it through Foot and Fyvel'. *Tribune* 'looks fearfully left' by criticising aspects of government foreign policy and 'attacking America', but in practice they come down 'on the side of the government whenever there is a major issue'.[35] Looking back from the vantage point of late 1963, Symons remembered more generally how they had joined together 'in lamenting the decline of *Tribune*, which with the Labour Party's access to power had become much less radical, particularly in relation to home affairs'.[36]

This hostility was reciprocated. Michael Foot was one of the dominant figures on the paper at this time, becoming editor in 1948. Looking back, he described how Orwell had in this period become 'detached from, if not hostile to his old *Tribune* associations'. Partly this was because 'he felt we were relapsing into the shameful pro-Stalinist sympathies from which he had done so much to rescue us', but also because of his opposition to the government's failure to make any sort of political assault on the power of the upper class. He was critical, as Foot puts it, of the Cabinet 'for its Fabian tastes'. As far as Foot was concerned, all this did was show 'his distance from practical politics' and in a disgraceful sleight of hand, he actually tries to suggest that Orwell, the author of 'How the Poor Die' that was published in George Woodcock's anarchist magazine, *Now*, in November 1946, was somehow disparaging of the establishment of the National Health Service![37] The difference was, of course, that the setting up of the NHS was not an attack on the upper class, however much they might have deplored free healthcare, whereas abolishing the public schools would have been.

One cannot help but wonder what Orwell would have made of the fact that in 1951, Foot was to secretly approach his good friend the ferociously anti-Labour reactionary Lord Beaverbrook, proprietor of the *Daily Express* and *Evening Standard*, for a subsidy to save *Tribune* from closure and himself from bankruptcy and the likely end of his political career. Beaverbrook, it is worth reminding ourselves, has been described in one of Foot's biographies as having had a wholly 'malign' influence on British journalism, while the *Daily Express* 'set an example of . . . unscrupulous content which has dogged Fleet Street ever since'.[38] During the 1945 general election campaign it had carried front page headlines such as 'GESTAPO IN BRITAIN IF LABOUR WIN and THE NATIONAL SOCIALISTS'. The paper focussed on the systematic slandering of Harold Laski or 'Gauleiter Laski' as he was called, arguing that this left-wing academic was the man who would really be running the country if Labour won. This hostility was sustained throughout the lifetime of the Labour government. In the 1950 general election, while Bevan became the main focus of Beaverbrook's attacks, the *Evening Standard* found time to smear John Strachey, the new Minister of War, as having links with Communist spies. Foot denounced this smear in the pages of *Tribune* as worse even than those carried in the Kelmsley press. Lord Kelmsley promptly sued the paper which found itself facing imminent bankruptcy.[39] Incredibly, Foot turned to Beaverbrook for a financial bail-out. The *Daily Express* secretly gave *Tribune* £3000 to keep it afloat, something that only came to light in 1972, when A J P Taylor published his biography of Beaverbrook. Beaverbrook also provided Foot and his wife with a cottage rent-free in the grounds of his Cherkley estate. Foot's devotion to the man was such that he described him on one occasion as a 'second father'.[40] Presumably this is what 'practical politics' was all about. It has to be said that if the viciously anti-Labour *Daily Express* subsidy to *Tribune* had come out at the time, Foot's political credibility on the Left would have been altogether destroyed.[41] He, on the other hand, later wrote that 'this story . . . reflects considerable merit on Beaverbrook and *Tribune*'.[42]

One of Orwell's criticisms of *Tribune* was its enthusiastic support for Zionism. This had, in fact, been official Labour Party policy since even before the Balfour Declaration of 1917, regularly reiterated at Party conferences. In the spring of 1944, the Party had issued a statement on 'The International Post-War Settlement' which had called both for the removal of the Arab population from Palestine and the possible extension of what would be the Zionist state's borders into Egypt, Transjordan and Syria. This document was adopted as Party policy at the December 1944 Party conference. Indeed the *Speaker's Notes* that the Party issued for the 1945 general election called for Zionist settlers to be allowed into Palestine 'in such numbers as to become a majority' while the Arabs should 'be encouraged to move out as the Jews moved in'. The Attlee government was to repudiate this policy once it took office for fear of its destabilising effect throughout the Middle East, but *Tribune* remained strongly in support of it. At one point, Bevan actually considered resigning over the issue. The most vehement and extreme advocate of the Zionist cause in Labour's ranks was Richard Crossman, the man who Orwell held primarily responsible for *Tribune's* decline. Among the grounds on which the Tribunites justified their support for Zionism was that a Zionist state would be a reliable military ally, providing Britain with military bases from which to safeguard the British Empire's Middle Eastern interests![43] Orwell was completely opposed to Zionism which he regarded, as we have seen, as an example of settler colonialism imposed on a native population. According to Tosco Fyvel, himself a staunch Zionist, as far as Orwell was concerned 'the Palestine Arabs were coloured Asians, the Palestine Jews the equivalent of the white rulers in India and Burma'. Orwell could 'not be budged' from this position.[44]

Orwell was also critical of *Tribune's* failure to pursue a determined enough anti-Communist and anti-Soviet line. This erupted into the paper's pages when the Labour MP Konni Zilliacus responded to Orwell's accusation in *Partisan Review* that he was a covert Communist. Zilliacus, with considerable justice, accused Orwell of peddling a 'silly and offensive falsehood', pointing out that he was not and never had been a Communist Party member, but had instead been a member of the Labour Party for 28 years. He had bitterly condemned the Hitler-Stalin Pact and the CP's refusal to support the war until the Nazi attack on the Soviet Union. What he was opposed to now was what he described as 'the Bevin-Churchill under-the-counter coalition in foreign policy'. What Zilliacus could also have pointed out was that he, albeit using a pseudonym, like Orwell had contributed to Victor Gollancz's volume *The Betrayal of the Left*, attacking CP policy back in early 1941. Zilliacus's letter appeared in *Tribune* on 17 January 1947, along with Orwell's reply.

Here Orwell shifted ground, calling Zilliacus a 'crypto-Communist' instead and, it has to be said, attempting to cover up the shaky ground he found himself on with a declaration that he would not be frightened 'into silence' and would 'continue my efforts to counter totalitarian propaganda in this country'.[45]

Orwell evidently recognised that his response had been inadequate and subsequently despatched a much more substantial critique of both Zilliacus and more importantly *Tribune* itself to the paper, a critique that it declined to publish. Here, he insisted that the big question today as far as world affairs were concerned was whether you were 'for Russia' or 'for America'. He praised Zilliacus for at least being consistent in his support for the Soviet Union and for turning Britain into a Soviet satellite state. He was being completely unfair to Zilliacus here at least regarding satellite status as Zilliacus was to show by his later support for Tito when he broke with the Soviet Union. As for *Tribune*, 'where does *Tribune* stand?' Orwell asked. He saw three components making up *Tribune's* position on foreign policy issues: first, opposing everything that Ernest Bevin supported almost as a matter of principle, even when they really agreed with him. Indeed, Orwell thought that 'broadly . . . he [Bevin] and *Tribune* stand for the same kind of policy'. Second, criticising the Soviet Union, but always finding 'extenuating circumstances' for their conduct. And third, 'insulting' the United States at every opportunity they could find. They had to recognise that there were only three alternatives open to Britain: subservience to the Soviet Union, subservience to the United States or membership of a 'federation of western European Socialist republics'. Incredibly, he thought Bevin actually supported the setting up of a European Socialist federation. And, even more incredibly, he also thought, at this time, that such a project not only needed US support, but might actually get it! As for *Tribune*, instead of coming out in support of a consistent policy, it was running scared of 'the Communists, the fellow-travellers and the fellow-travellers of the fellow-travellers'. He characterised its performance as one of 'endless equivocations: a paragraph of protest when this of our friends is shot – silence when that one is shot, denunciation of this one faked election – qualified approval of that one and so on'. And one consequence of this was that Zilliacus was allowed to 'infest' *Tribune's* correspondence columns 'like a perennial weed'.[46]

What we see here, once again is the debilitating effect of Orwell's exaggerated fear of the Soviet Union. He was absolutely and unequivocally right about the nature of the Soviet regime and about the nature of the regimes that were being imposed throughout Eastern Europe, but he was completely wrong about the threat that the Soviet Union, devastated as it was by war, posed. This led to him ignoring the realities of US Imperialism and was an important, although not the only, factor in sustaining his allegiance to the Labour government even while he was becoming increasingly disillusioned by the limitations of its domestic programme.

As we have seen, Orwell's discussions of British politics tended to appear in left-wing US journals, *Partisan Review*, *Politics* and *Commentary*. In the July-August edition of *Partisan Review*, he published his contribution to their important 'The Future of Socialism' series,[47] 'Towards European Unity'. The first point to notice is that he does not champion British Labourism as the way forward. This is no paean of praise for the achievements of the Attlee government. Indeed, at the very moment that British Labourism supposedly reaches its high point, Orwell actually writes that for a socialist today the situation is all but 'hopeless'. Hardly a ringing endorsement! Indeed, the whole article is pretty bleak, not to say pessimistic, but not completely so. 'Socialism', he told his readers, 'does not exist anywhere'. In the USA, as far as he could see, 'the masses are contented with capitalism, and one cannot tell what turn they will take when capitalism begins to collapse'. As for the Soviet Union, 'a sort of oligarchical collectivism' prevails. In Asia, 'even the word "socialism" has barely penetrated'. This leaves Western Europe (and Australia and New Zealand) as the only place where the tradition of democratic socialism can be said to really exist. And even here, he explicitly includes Britain in this, 'it only exists precariously'. Obviously, 'socialism cannot properly be said to be established until it is world-wide', so in the prevailing circumstances, 'I cannot imagine it beginning except through the federation of the western European states, transformed into socialist republics without colonial dependencies'. Indeed, 'a socialist United States of Europe seems to me the only worth-while political objective today'. It might have been possible to have turned the British Empire into 'a federation of socialist republics', but even if such an idea had been possible, 'we lost it by failing to liberate India and by our attitude toward the coloured peoples generally'. But, he admitted, even the possibility of establishing a United Socialist States of Europe seemed 'to me a very unlikely event'. Interestingly one of the obstacles that he identifies is that the 'forces of imperialism will turn out to be extremely strong' and that British workers might decide 'that it is better to remain an imperial power at the expense of playing second fiddle to America'. Substitute Labour Party leadership for British workers and this is, of course, what happened. Indeed, he specifically identifies the fact that since 1940 Britain has become 'almost a dependency of the USA' with its global interests 'all hostages in American hands' as a massive problem. There was, he wrote, 'always the danger that the United States will break up any European coalition by drawing Britain out of it'.

'Towards European Unity' was written around much the same time as his rejected and unpublished article on Zilliacus and *Tribune*. Looked at together, they show the extent to which Orwell was still debating the issues himself. The piece for *Tribune* comes out in favour of choosing America while the *Partisan Review* article identifies the United States very much as an obstacle to socialism. These were clearly issues that he was still wrestling with. One last point worth making here is that while he thought prospects for the future were grim, with nuclear war likely to destroy civilisation altogether or the domination of the world by totalitarian empires a possibility, he also did not rule out the eventual emergence of a socialist movement in the United States and argued that by 1960 there was likely to be 'millions of young Russians who are bored by dictatorship and loyalty parades, eager for more freedom'.[48] This was a very different prospect from that imagined in *Nineteen Eighty-Four*.

'The Main Objective is National Survival'

Why did Orwell continue to support the Labour Party? Certainly, part of the reason was the international situation and his exaggerated view of the Soviet threat. But this was not all. In an article that he wrote for the US journal, *Commentary*, and that they published under the title, 'Britain's Struggle for Survival: The Labor Government After Three Years' in October 1948, he made his position clear. For the time being the struggle for socialism had to be put to one side. As he put it, 'in Britain the struggle between collectivism and laissez-faire is secondary. The main objective is national survival'. Britain faced an economic crisis on a scale that made every other consideration seem secondary. The Labour government responded to the crisis by imposing its own regime of Austerity with a programme of cuts, including to the food ration, and a freeze on wages agreed by the TUC. From 1948 on, the share of wages as a proportion of national income began to fall.[49] The Labour government proceeded to use troops to break strikes and there was an attack, with suspensions and expulsions, mounted against opponents of the wage freeze in both the Labour Party and the trade unions. On one occasion, Bevan himself was to urge that troops be used to break a bus drivers' strike so that miners could get to work.[50] And when he became Minister of Labour in January 1951, in the words of one biographer, he found himself 'bringing down the might of the law on working people'.[51]

Orwell absolutely accepted the Labour government's position. As he put it, the immediate problem the government faced was 'to make Britain's exports balance her imports'. And this had to be achieved with worn-out industrial equipment, continued high levels of military expenditure and a working class that looked to the government to improve their lives. The government could not afford to altogether disappoint its supporters. They might not want socialism, but they did want 'shorter working hours, a free health service, day nurseries, free milk for school children'. As it was, he thought that ordinary people were actually materially worse off than when Labour had come to power. Nevertheless, in the circumstances, he supported a Labour government attacking working class living standards and even using troops to break strikes.

What we see here is Orwell's support for the Labour government pulling him very much to the right. Criticism of the government's lack of radicalism was put on hold. When confronted by the wartime crisis of 1940–41, he had called for socialist revolution; now with a Labour government confronting an economic crisis, all talk of socialism went out the window and instead he embraced 'austerity' and the need for the working class to continue to make greater sacrifices into the indefinite future. His discussion of the situation on the shop floor in industry is positively reactionary with him embracing arguments that up until then he would have rejected as viciously anti-working class. He wrote:

If wages are evened out, labour drifts away from the more disagreeable jobs; if especially high rates are paid for those jobs, absenteeism increases, because it is then possible to earn enough to live on by working only three or four shifts a week. Not only individual absenteeism, but the innumerable stoppages and unofficial strikes of the past few years have probably been due to sheer exhaustion quite as much as to any economic grievance . . . Today, when the main problem is how to produce a bare sufficiency of goods, a strike is in effect a blow against the community as a whole, including the strikers themselves, and its net effect is inflationary.

This rehearsal of conventional right-wing thinking is bad enough, but he goes on to seriously argue that the socialist movement had to face up to some uncomfortable realities:

> One is that certain jobs which are vitally necessary are never done except under some sort of compulsion. As soon as you have full employment, therefore, you have to make use of forced labour for the dirtier kinds of work. (You can call it by some more soothing name, of course).

To have George Orwell of all people advocating disguising forced labour by means of a soothing euphemism certainly takes one by surprise. And it was no good people being resentful of the fact that 'the country houses and the smart hotels are still full of rich people', because even if they 'were wiped out', there would still be hardship. Once again, he had come a long way from 1940–1. Now he believed that it was vital that Labour remained in power, because only Labour could persuade the working class to make the necessary sacrifices. If a Conservative government had tried to do what Labour was doing the result would have been 'a disaster'. The TUC would never have agreed to a wage freeze if the Conservatives had been in power. It was gratitude for Labour's welfare reforms that enabled the government to get agreement for the sacrifices necessary to save British capitalism in its hour of need. If the Conservatives came to power, the country would be plunged into open class warfare and the only beneficiaries would be the Communist Party.

He went on to imagine a possible scenario where the country might even move down the road towards *Nineteen Eighty-Four*. He thought Britain would survive, but 'the question is whether we can survive as a democratic country . . . the main problem will be to induce people to work harder . . . without forced labor, terrorism, and a secret police force'.[52] He did, of course, exaggerate the scale of the crisis and his fears of the collapse of democracy were misplaced, but all this justified his supporting a Labour government imposing austerity rather than introducing socialism. Of course, it is important not to see this particular article as in some way summing up or concluding Orwell's thinking on the subject. He continued debating with himself and others right up until his death, pulled in different directions by different concerns. Clearly when he wrote this article, the working class were seen as very much the problem, rather than the solution. Moreover, one can be reasonably sure that if it had been a Conservative government in power and confronted with this crisis, then the likelihood is that Orwell would have been condemning the timidity of the Labour Party in opposing them, calling for a new Socialist Party and advocating socialist revolution. Having embraced the Labour Party, with whatever reservations, when they were confronted with this crisis, he found himself pulled sharply, indeed, on this occasion, grotesquely, to the right. More generally, of course, this is the perennial Labour dilemma that derives from the decision to run capitalism rather than abolish it. Even at this time though there was still a continuing debate taking place in his own mind between his support for Labourism and his commitment to socialism. He never abandoned this libertarian commitment and his belief in a classless society.

6

'Ceaseless Espionage':
Orwell and the Secret States

The revelation that towards the end of his life, George Orwell had collaborated with the secret British government propaganda agency, the Information Research Department (IRD), provided conclusive proof as far as his political critics were concerned that he and his politics had always been flawed; that he had never been a reliable adherent of the socialist cause and that he had certainly abandoned that cause in his last years. The eminent Marxist historian, Christopher Hill, a former Communist, could piously remark that 'I always knew he was two-faced' and that there was always 'something fishy about Orwell'.[1] And this from someone who was still, as we shall see, a faithful Stalinist at the time of Orwell's death! For another of his critics, Scott Lucas, Orwell's 'list' was merely 'the culmination of his response to the left from the 1930s onwards' and indeed, he could actually be seen as having provided a kind of template for betrayal with Christopher Hitchins the most recent example of this history of treachery.[2] Certainly, Orwell's relationship with the IRD has to be seen as a serious mistake, but it is necessary to both be absolutely clear about what exactly that relationship was and also to put it into a broader context, to get the relationship into some sort of perspective. What is necessary is an examination of Orwell's relationship with the British secret state throughout his life, and indeed, not just with the British secret state, but with the Soviet and US secret states as well.

'Some Connection With Literary Work'

One can safely assume that Orwell had his earliest encounter with spies, informers and the world of intelligence while serving as a police officer in Burma. John Sutherland has gone so far as to describe him as having worked as 'a competent spy in a policeman's uniform'. And on his return to England, he even speculates that some sort of attempt was likely made to recruit him to MI5.[3] Whatever the truth of this, and it seems most unlikely, it nevertheless comes as no surprise to discover that once back home Orwell was kept under episodic surveillance by British intelligence, both Special Branch and MI5. According to James Smith, in his path-breaking study of the British secret state's surveillance of writers, 'governmental surveillance of George Orwell during the 1930s was at times paranoid but, from a security standpoint, sporadic and largely peripheral'. His Special Branch and MI5 files are 'slim' and, he argues, not too much should be made of it. He was certainly not any sort of prime target and was 'one of least monitored of the writers' that he looked at (the others were the Auden Circle, Ewan MacColl, Joan Littlewood and Arthur Koestler). This was almost certainly due to the fact that he never joined the Communist Party, indeed always kept his distance from them. It was the CP that was the main target on the left as far as Special Branch and MI5 were concerned and Orwell, at least initially, only came under scrutiny when he strayed into the CP's orbit. Even so, Smith can still write of 'the often-comical difficulty the police had in categorising this gruffly independent left-wing writer'. Another authority on Orwell and the British secret state, Richard Lance Keeble is, it has to be said, more impressed with the level of surveillance that was devoted to Orwell 'with his every career and life move being recorded'.

Orwell first came to the attention of the secret state as early as 1929. Captain H M Miller of Special Branch received information that a certain E A Blair, residing in Paris, had approached the Communist newspaper, *Worker's Weekly*, hoping to become their Paris correspondent. The prospect of 'a renegade colonial policeman' working for the Communists certainly required further attention and MI6 accordingly checked him out. A report dated 8 February 1929 recorded:

He is a single man and lodges at 6, Rue du Pot de Fer, Paris, having arrived in France on 7.6.28...wrote three articles in the 'Progress Civique' of 29.12.28., 5th and 12th January, 1929, entitled 'La Grande Misere de L'Ouvrier Britannique'...he spends his time reading various news papers, among which is 'L'Humanite', but he has not so far been seen to mix with Communists in Paris and until he does (name redacted) consider that the French will not interfere with him.

This was, of course, also Orwell's own opinion: if he kept away from the French CP then the French police would leave him alone.

Orwell did not come under 'sustained security investigation' again until he travelled up to Wigan in 1936. Here his activities drew the attention of the police with a report noting that he was staying 'at an apartment house in a working-class district, that this accommodation had been found for him by 'a member of the local Communist Party' and that he had attended a Communist meeting in this town addressed by Wal Hannington'. With rare perception, the report's author tentatively concluded that it was likely from his 'mode of living that he is an author, or has some connection with literary work as he devotes most of his time to writing'. He spent a lot of time collecting 'local data' and received a suspicious amount of mail, including letters from France! He suggested further enquiries to establish this man's identity.

This probably prompted a four-page MI5 background report, chronicling his life so far. He had resigned from the Burmese police reportedly because 'he could not bring himself to arrest persons for committing acts which he did not think were wrong'. In Paris, 'he took an interest in the activities of the French Communist Party', but there was not enough information available 'to show whether he was an active supporter of the revolutionary movement'. The report went on to note the publication of *Burmese Days* by Gollancz, 'a firm which specialises in left-wing literature', his time as a 'down and out', his teaching career and the fact that he had worked in a left-wing bookshop, 'Booklover's Corner', which was apparently suspected of 'handling correspondence of a revolutionary character'.

One interesting indication of the episodic nature of the surveillance that Orwell was subjected to is that the fact that once he had finished writing *The Road to Wigan Pier* and had gone to fight in Spain, Special Branch only became aware of his volunteering by reading about it in the ILP newspaper, the *New Leader*. His file contains a clipping of Ethel Mannin's review of *The Road* in which she reported that the book's author had gone to Spain as part of an ILP contingent fighting with the POUM.[4]

'They Are Our Worst Enemies'

In Spain, Orwell was to encounter the Russian secret police, an encounter that was to almost cost him his life and that understandably played a decisive role in informing his attitude towards Stalinism. He had first-hand experience of the Stalinist campaign against the POUM and the anarchists, something that was as important in the development of his politics as his experience of workers' power in Barcelona. What was the reason for this hostility? Comintern policy was dictated by the perceived foreign policy needs of the Soviet State. Any idea that the Stalin leadership had some sort of sentimental attachment to internationalism or solidarity is seriously mistaken. Similarly, the Stalin regime had no interest whatsoever in supporting the socialist cause or socialist revolution in other countries. The successful establishment of workers' power in other countries was rather perceived as a threat to Soviet interests, first because it would inevitably expose the Soviet regime for the murderous tyranny that it was and this would weaken, perhaps even destroy, Soviet control over foreign Communist Parties as their rank and file rebelled against the travesty that had been foisted on them. This in turn would weaken the Soviet Union's international influence by undermining the ability of national CPs to exert pressure on their governments. And moreover, successful socialist revolutions would inevitably lead to improved relations, perhaps even an alliance between capitalist states, whether bourgeois democracies or fascist, that would threaten the Soviet Union. The domestic impact of successful workers' revolutions abroad was also a worry of the Stalin leadership that had still not completely eradicated the legacy of the Russian Revolution at home.

There is still considerable resistance to recognising the realities of great power politics as practiced by the Stalin regime, in particular with regard to Russian support for the Spanish Republic and the Popular Front more generally. Because the thousands of rank and file Communists and Communist sympathisers who rallied to the Spanish cause were sincere idealists, genuinely committed to the fight for democracy and with many of them dying in the struggle, it is somehow assumed that at least on some level the Stalin regime must have shared these sentiments. Nothing could be further from the truth. One does not have to wait for the Hitler-Stalin Pact for the regime to show its true colours. In September 1933, Stalin had concluded a little-known Pact of Friendship, Neutrality and Non-aggression with Mussolini, the culmination of years of friendly relations, and intended to buttress both governments against a resurgent Nazi Germany. As well as a trade deal, there was improved military collaboration between the fascist and Communist regimes with Italian submarines visiting Russia and Russian warships visiting Italy (the ships' captains were personally welcomed by Mussolini). The two countries established cooperation in the field of chemical warfare and in August 1934 a high-powered Soviet delegation, including five generals visited Italy and met with Mussolini. In the winter, 'Moscow and Rome exchanged observers to their annual manoeuvres'.[5] This alliance broke down in 1935.

When it came to the military coup in Spain, the Soviet stance was determined by the perceived interests of Russia as a great power. By now the alliance with Fascist Italy had effectively collapsed and the regime looked to France as an ally against Nazi Germany. The overriding fear that the Russians had regarding events in Spain was that a military regime aligned with Nazi Germany and Fascist Italy would seriously weaken the French. A subsidiary fear was that the international Communist movement would be seriously weakened if it was left up to others on the Left to champion the cause of democracy in Spain or that there might even be a successful Socialist Revolution. One recent account has suggested that the regime was worried that there might be a proletarian Revolution in Spain which would involve 'the successful realisation of Trotskyist theories and predictions', and that this 'was not something that could be contemplated with equanimity at the Kremlin'.[6] Initially though, the Soviet Union tried to have it both ways by officially supporting non-intervention while at the same time having the government-controlled trade unions deduct a supposedly voluntary donation from Russian workers wages to aid the Spanish cause. With it looking increasingly likely that Franco was going to take over the whole country, the decision was taken to begin the covert supply of arms to the Republic. The first shipment was despatched on 18 September 1936. With Soviet military aid came the NKVD.[7]

Once the decision was taken to support the Spanish Republic, the decision to rollback and liquidate the revolutionary gains made by the working class inevitably followed and this necessitated the destruction of the revolutionary left, starting with the POUM and then moving on to the anarchists, who were a more difficult proposition because they had mass support. When the first Soviet consul, Vladimir Antonov-Ovseenko, one of the organisers of the October Revolution in Petrograd, arrived in revolutionary Barcelona in September 1936, he made clear from the very start that the destruction of the POUM was a Soviet priority. As he told the city's chief of police, 'They are our worst enemies. We shall treat them as such'. The POUM proposal that Trotsky should be offered asylum in revolutionary Catalonia would certainly have increased the Soviet determination to destroy them. The Russian Communist newspaper, *Pravda*, was soon able to report that 'the elimination of the Trotskyites and anarchosyndicalists' in Catalonia had begun and that 'it will be carried to its conclusion with the same energy with which it has been done in the USSR.'[8] On 27 December, the Comintern executive instructed the Spanish Communist Party that it had to complete 'the final destruction of the Trotskyists . . . exposing them to the masses as a Fascist secret service carrying out provocations in the interests of Hitler and General Franco.'[9] Having gone to Spain to fight the fascists, Orwell was to find himself embroiled in this struggle.

Communist hostility towards the POUM was, as we have already seen, extended to the ILP. The British CP regarded the ILP as an enemy to be fought and this included spying on their volunteers in Spain. At this time, Orwell still regarded the CP as being on the same side and while he had disagreements with them he was still, on his own testimony, more sympathetic towards what he understood as the Popular Front strategy than he was towards the POUM position. It seems clear that he had no idea about the extent of Communist surveillance that he and his comrades were subject to. The head of the NKVD operation in Spain was Alexander Orlov, charged with both the elimination of foreign Trotskyists' and the destruction of the POUM.[10] While individual 'Trotskyists' were kidnapped, tortured and killed, the actual destruction of the POUM was to be accomplished by deliberately provoking an outbreak in Barcelona and using this as an opportunity to crush them once and for all. In the build-up to the May 1937 uprising, the ILP was kept under surveillance by Communist agents, most notably David Crook, who was charged with keeping a particular eye on John McNair, Georges Kopp, and both Orwell and his wife Eileen. Crook was working undercover for the NKVD, posing as a sympathetic left-wing journalist who was a Labour Party member and had been secretary to a Labour MP. Together with his controller, Hugh O'Donnell, Crook was to be later involved in the kidnapping of Andres Nin and the Austrian, Kurt Landau, both subsequently tortured and killed. Meanwhile, Crook 'had the run of the ILP offices, so much so that during lunch breaks . . . he slipped into the empty office, stole files, took them to the Russian Embassy, had them photographed and returned before anyone got back'. Operating more openly was Wally Tapsell, a leading member of the British CP, who was trying to persuade ILP volunteers to come over to the International Brigades, with Orwell as one of his prime targets. In a report he wrote early in 1937, Tapsell referred to Orwell as 'the leading personality and most respected man in the contingent' and noted that Orwell had decided to join International Brigades 'in a few days'.[11] Even though Orwell was warned by Bob Edwards of the ILP that, with his views, he would be putting his life in danger by transferring to the International Brigades, he was determined to go ahead.[12] The May events intervened.

'Known Trotskyists'

After the May uprising, Orwell returned to the front where he was shot in the throat. It was while he was recovering from his wound that the POUM was banned and a general round-up began with a number of ILP volunteers swept up. Crook was one of those arrested, but only as part of his undercover work, still pretending sympathy for the ILP and the POUM. For a while he was even put in the same cell as Georges Kopp, still fishing for intelligence. Eileen Blair, even though she figured as a 'known Trotskyist' in secret police reports,[13] was left at large in the hope that she could be used as bait to capture Orwell as well. She successfully warned Orwell off. Even before the POUM was banned and the crackdown began, when Richard Rees of the *Adelphi* visited her on his way to serve as an ambulance driver, he found her 'in a state of numb terror of the Communist political police'. She refused to have lunch with him, warning him that it was 'too dangerous', something he did not take seriously until that evening when the leader of the ambulance convoy he was attached to told him he had been seen 'entering the POUM office and that he was advised to discourage such visits'.[14] Orwell and his wife successfully escaped, of course. If they had been arrested, as 'known Trotskyists' they would certainly have been imprisoned, perhaps for months and subjected to interrogation, which Orwell, given his state of health, would have been most unlikely to survive, even if the decision had been taken not to shoot him. As it was, his papers and diaries were seized and are presumably still in the Russian archives.

Less fortunate were Georges Kopp and another ILP volunteer, Bob Smillie. Kopp was arrested, held in prison for eighteen months during which he was starved, deprived of sleep, beaten and repeatedly interrogated. By the time he was released he had lost seven stone in weight and could only walk with the use of a stick.[15] This treatment has not stopped suggestions that he was a Communist agent![16] Smillie was not so lucky, although there is some controversy regarding his fate. He was only 21 years old, chair of the ILP Guild of Youth and was getting ready to return to Britain for an ILP speaking tour when he was arrested.

The generally accepted view is that he died from appendicitis while in custody through neglect, most likely deliberate. This was the view accepted by the ILP at the time and by most historians today. What was not so widely known is that according to Kopp the story of appendicitis was 'absolutely imaginary' and that Smillie had, in fact, been brutally kicked to death while being 'persuaded' to implicate the ILP leadership in the supposed Trotsky Fascist plot in Spain. According to Kopp, he had seen the original doctor's report on Smillie that stated that Smillie's belly had been perforated by a kick so powerful that his 'intestines were partly hanging outside' and that his jaw had been partially dislocated. This report had been suppressed and replaced by the report of death from appendicitis that the ILP, with some reservations, accepted.[17] Certainly Orwell seems to have found Kopp credible enough to sarcastically remark when told that Andres Nin's body had been found that presumably it 'will be suicide or perhaps appendicitis again'.[18] There is, of course, nothing intrinsically unlikely about Smillie being killed in this way by the Communist secret police, and no reason has ever really been suggested as to why Kopp would invent the story. It is not unfair to say that Kopp's allegation has provoked attempts to discredit him, attempts assisted by the way he seems to have lied pretty regularly about his own past. As Peter Davison puts it, he was 'to put it politely . . . a man of mystery'.[19] Nevertheless he was Bob Smillie's commander, trusted enough to be elected to the position by his men, among them George Orwell, and had, moreover, won their respect on the front line. This alone, leaving aside the Communist record of torture and murder, should entitle his testimony to more attention than it has received.[20] Certainly, Smillie's death had a tremendous impact on Orwell. According to Gordon Bowker, 'If anything tipped Orwell finally from a simple hostility to Stalinist Communism into a deep-dyed loathing of it, it was the death of Smillie'.[21]

And then, of course, there is the question of whether Orwell himself was working for one or other of the intelligence agencies operating in Republican Spain at this time. Peter Davison has raised this question in the *Facing Unpleasant Facts 1937-1938* volume of the *Complete Works of George Orwell* where he reports a British member of the Republican secret police, the SIM, involved in the censorship of letters, telling him that they suspected Orwell of sending coded correspondence back to Britain. This claim from a member of an organisation that framed, tortured and murdered dissident leftists barely deserves acknowledgement though and serves rather as a distraction from what the Communists actually were doing at the time.[22]

Back in Britain, the CP did everything it could to discredit and silence the critics of Popular Front politics as they were being implemented in Spain. One of their manoeuvres was the use of perjured testimony from a British volunteer who had served with the POUM, Frank Frankford, who was persuaded by a *Daily Worker* correspondent, Sam Lesser, to testify that both the POUM and the ILP contingent had been in league with the fascists at the front with Kopp instrumental in managing the arrangement. His allegations first appeared in the *Daily Worker* on 14 September 1937, occasioning outrage, not least because they might well have contributed to Kopp and others being killed.[23] A statement in reply to Frankford's slander, written by Orwell and signed by another 14 members of the ILP contingent, appeared in the *New Leader* on 24 September. Frankford, they pointed out, had deserted and then been arrested with every likelihood of being shot. He had saved himself from this fate by allowing his name to be put to lies invented by others in order to discredit the POUM and the ILP. They had not even bothered to send their response to the *Daily Worker* because it was not a paper 'likely to let its opponents have a fair hearing'.[24] Relations between the ILP and the CP became increasingly embittered with the *Daily Worker*, for example, first refusing an advert for an ILP pamphlet, written by Fenner Brockway, *The Truth About Barcelona*, and then imposing a blanket ban on advertising any ILP literature. The CP continued to attack the ILP as 'Trotskyists and fascist agents' while the ILP attacked the CP for having 'ceased to be revolutionary'.[25] And, of course, as far as Orwell was concerned, his experience of the Spanish War which had started so hopefully with him seeing the working class actually in power in Barcelona had ended with 'a richer crop of lies than any event since the Great War' and 'a reign of terror – forcible suppression of political parties, a stifling censorship of the press, ceaseless espionage and mass imprisonment without trial'.[26]

'Dresses in a Bohemian Fashion'

What of Orwell's relationship with the British secret state during the Second World War? Certainly, while he was working at the BBC, he attracted the attention of Special Branch who considered him a security risk. A report submitted to MI5 early in 1942 described him as having 'advanced communist views' as having been seen 'at communist meetings' and as being someone who 'dresses in a bohemian fashion both at his office and in his leisure hours'. The MI5 response to this report was somewhat more sophisticated, pointing out that while he had been 'a bit of an anarchist in his day and in touch with extremist elements', it 'is evident from his recent writings – "The Lion and the Unicorn" and his contribution to Gollancz's symposium "The Betrayal of the Left" – that he does not hold with the Communist Party nor they with him'. He has 'strong Left Wing views but he is a long way from orthodox Communism'.[27] Orwell was left in place at the BBC, presumably in the belief that any harm he might do was outweighed by the use that could be made of him regardless of his 'bohemian' attire. As W J West has pointed out, Orwell was bitterly opposed to the British suppression of the Quit India movement in 1942 and to the constraints imposed on reporting but any attempt to violate the guidelines 'would have been immediately silenced by the switch censor'.[28] One interesting footnote to this discussion is that Orwell's colleagues at the BBC at this time did actually include two NKVD agents, Guy Burgess and Peter Smollett, formerly Peter Smolka. Burgess, of course, was to be later revealed as one of the Cambridge spies alongside Kim Philby and Donald Maclean. Smollett, however, was not 'uncovered' until after his death in 1980, although, as we shall see, he was to figure in the notorious list that Orwell was to later give to the Information Research Department in 1949.[29]

While Orwell certainly worked as a propagandist for the British war effort at the BBC, what of the time he was employed as a war correspondent by the *Observer* and the *Manchester Evening News*? This particular period of his life has been somewhat neglected with only Richard Keeble really giving it the attention it deserves. And as he asks of this Continental excursion: 'Could he have been on an intelligence mission?' He was employed as a war correspondent from February until May 1945 during which time he provided the *Observer* with 14 articles (two actually written after he had returned home) and wrote for the *Manchester Evening News*. Certainly, his friend, David Astor, the *Observer*'s proprietor, had intelligence connections, and while on the Continent Orwell met with people involved in intelligence work, but that is really as far as the evidence goes.[30] Of course, even if he was on an intelligence mission, while this would be of considerable biographical interest, its significance as far as insight into the development of his political thinking, of his hostility to Stalinism, is of much less moment. The Second World War saw many on the Left, including Communist

Party members, working for British intelligence agencies, among them, for example, James Klugman, the future editor of *Marxism Today*. Klugman, we now know, was also a somewhat reluctant agent for the NKVD.[31] Much more problematic was Orwell's later involvement with the Information Research Department (IRD).

'A Moral Lead to the Forces of Anti-Communism in Europe and Asia'

The revelation in 1996 that George Orwell had not only collaborated with the IRD with regard to allowing their use of his work for anti-Communist propaganda but had also provided them with a list of supposed pro-Communists writers and artists came as a complete shock to those on the left who admired the man, and as a welcome vindication to those who had always been opposed to him. According to Paul Lashmar and James Oliver, whose 1998 book, *Britain's Secret Propaganda War 1948-1977*, really brought the IRD's activities out into the open, Orwell's 'reputation as a left-wing icon took a body-blow from which it may never recover'.[32] It is, of course, never healthy to accord anyone iconic status, but there was more at stake than this. What Orwell's critics and enemies (not too strong a word) hoped to do with these revelations was to undermine his credibility as an opponent of Stalinism. His years of determined opposition to Stalinism from a committed socialist stance were at last shown to be compromised by his arrangement with the British secret state. In the end, he stood revealed as just another McCarthyite-style informer, giving names, including the names of people almost universally admired. He was just another Cold Warrior, nothing more and nothing less. His reputation for integrity had been dealt a fatal blow. At best he was no better than his Communist opponents and at worst his anti-Communist testimony had now been exposed as completely unreliable and his socialist credentials as false. How valid was this particular response to the revelations?

What will be argued here is that while Orwell's association with the IRD was a serious mistake on his part, indeed inexcusable, it was not what his critics have made it out to be. And, moreover, both his handing over of the blacklist to the IRD and his allowing his writings to be used as anti-Communist propaganda have to be put into the context of the time. At the time, the IRD was a propaganda organisation set up by and working for the Attlee Labour government, a government that, with whatever reservations, Orwell supported. Orwell was not alone at the time in thinking that it was engaged in combating Stalinism from a reformist Labourite position, rather than already beginning to develop into a covert propaganda organisation supporting US and British imperialism in their confrontation not just with the Soviet Union but with national liberation movements and 'Third World' governments that defied western hegemony throughout the world. As we have already seen, he was certainly ready to support the United States as the 'lesser evil' in a confrontation with the Soviet Union, but how far this support would have gone we have no way of knowing because of his premature death. What we can establish though is how far it went during his lifetime and it is on this that he has to be judged, not on his posthumous conscription as a fully-fledged Cold Warrior.

The IRD was set-up by the Attlee government in 1948 with the intention of countering the international Communist movement's anti-Western propaganda in Britain and throughout the British Empire, Europe and indeed the world, not least by exposing the realities of Communist rule both in the Soviet Union itself and throughout Eastern Europe. The intention was also to put forward British Labourism as an alternative model whereby the remedying of grievances could be secured. When Foreign Secretary Ernest Bevin proposed establishing an organisation to wage a propaganda offensive against Communism to the Labour Cabinet in January 1948, it was to be charged with giving 'a moral lead to the forces of anti-Communism in Europe and Asia', with going 'over to the offensive' and with forcing the Communists to 'defend themselves'.[33] It is worth making the point here that the IRD hardly had to invent material and evidence that showed the Soviet Union in a bad light. Telling the truth about the regime was bad enough, indeed, sometimes even the truth about the Gulag had to be toned down because of the fear that no one would believe it.

The proposal was certainly acceptable to Aneurin Bevan who was in the Cabinet at the time, and to the likes of Michael Foot, Richard Crossman and the Labour left more generally because they were assured that Communism would not be countered with pro-capitalist propaganda but by the advocacy of a reformist social democratic alternative. That this was not merely just so much camouflage at the time was shown by the fact that the IRD was actively involved in ensuring that *Tribune* was distributed abroad and indeed set out very deliberately to recruit people on the left. In Bevin's words, the IRD would advocate 'a positive rival ideology . . . the broad principle of social democracy which, in fact, has its basis in the value of civil liberties and human rights'. The architect of the initiative who was also charged with putting it into effect was a junior minister, Christopher Mayhew. According to Paul Lashmar and James Oliver, in its first year of operation, the IRD produced 'twenty-two briefing papers on different aspects of Stalinism which were circulated not only to British diplomats abroad but also to selected journalists, politicians and trade unionists at home'. Particular attention was paid to placing anti-Communist material in the Italian press and to combating Communism in Egypt, Malaya and Burma. By October 1949, Mayhew was claiming with considerable justice that the IRD 'has had an impact out of all proportion to its size and cost'.[34] A recent authoritative study of 'Cold War Secret Intelligence' has concluded that 'The importance of the IRD is difficult to overestimate'.[35] It was to go on to play a significant role in the Cold War, in the protection of British imperial interests and in the class struggle at home in Britain. The IRD was, for example, to be actively involved in the judicial frame-up of the Shrewsbury building pickets in 1972, something that was certainly not contemplated when it was first set up.[36]

'This List is Very Libellous'

What was the nature of Orwell's involvement? First of all, it is worth making the general point that at this time he regarded both the Soviet Union and the international Communist movement more generally as a threat, but a threat to what. As far as he was concerned, he was not involved in defending capitalism or imperialism, but in defending the future possibility of democratic socialism from a totalitarian tyranny that would altogether extinguish that possibility unless defeated. This has to be absolutely insisted upon. He can certainly be accused of naivete but this derived from his support for the Attlee government and his failure to recognise both that government's determination to hold on to as much of the British Empire as it could by whatever methods necessary and to protect Britain's great power status, something which had placed it in a position of subordination to the United States.[37] As we have seen, he had some understanding of these developments, but had not fully grasped the implications. Indeed, Hugh Wilford actually goes so far as to argue that the fact was that at the time 'Orwell was given no reason to doubt IRD's socialist credentials'.[38] The bottom line was, however, that in the event of war breaking out between Britain and the Soviet Union, something

that seemed quite possible at the time, Orwell would have supported the
Attlee government. Indeed, a good case can be made that he regarded his
association with the IRD as no different from his working for the BBC
during the Second World War and that if he had been in better health he
would have become more involved in its propaganda work. As well as his
loyalty to the Labour government affecting his judgement, in retrospect
it is clear that he also accepted an exaggerated view of the Soviet threat.

His first involvement was to recommend people who were on the left
to the IRD and likely to want to assist it in its propaganda efforts, among
them Franz Borkenau, for example, but at the same time he offered
them a list of people too unreliable to approach. It was this list that he
gave to the IRD on 2 May 1949; people on the left who he advised them
not to try and enlist the services of because they were, as far as he was
concerned, in some way or other apologists for Stalinism.[39] The list was
extracted from a much larger list of 'fellow travellers' that he and Richard
Rees had compiled for their own information. This was at a time when
the IRD was, as we have seen, deliberately trying to recruit people on the
left who were opposed to Stalinism. Among those enlisted was Tosco
Fyvel for example.

The list was clearly not some sort of great McCarthyite betrayal on
Orwell's part, indeed in practical terms it is of no great significance at
all. There is no credible evidence that it ever damaged anyone's career,
although this is not to say that it would not have been used in that way
if the Cold War had become more intense than it did. Indeed, the only
serious damage done has been to Orwell's reputation. And, of course, at
the very same time as he handed his list over, he was actively involved in
opposing any curtailment of the civil liberties of CP members and others
on the left. Nevertheless, it was certainly a serious mistake on his part,
not least because the IRD was even at this time not what he believed it
to be, seeking to further as it did a foreign and imperial policy that had
nothing in common with any socialist principles for all that there was a
Labour government in power. Once the Conservatives were returned to
office in 1951 any pretence of propagandising for democratic socialism
was abandoned. And, of course, the nature of the list itself was pretty
unsavoury; certainly something he should have been ashamed of. He
identified one of those listed as 'occasionally Homosexual' (illegal at the
time) and a number of others were singled out for being Jewish.[40] As he
himself put it to Celia Kirwan, the go-between in his dealings with the
IRD, 'this list is very libellous, or slanderous, or whatever the term is,

so will you please see that it is returned to me without fail'.[41] The only person on the list who was any sort of real security danger was Peter Smollett, who had used his position at the Ministry of Information to try and block publication of *Animal Farm* while at the same time assisting with the publication of K E Hulme's pro-Stalinist *Two Commonwealths*. Smollett was awarded the OBE for his wartime services and he very nearly went on to become editor of the *Observer*. Orwell describes him in the list as giving a 'strong impression of being some kind of Russian agent' and as a 'very slimy person'. He told Kirwan that he felt his list was justified if it helped stop 'people like Peter Smollett worming their way into important propaganda jobs where they were probably able to do us a lot of harm'.[42] Regardless of Smollett, the list is still indefensible and the arguments sometimes advanced in Orwell's defence that he was seriously ill (which he was) and enamoured with Celia Kirwan (which he was) do not really stand up. The likelihood is that if he had not been ill, he would have got more involved with the IRD rather than less.

While Orwell can be accused of serious naïveté regarding the Labour government and its foreign and imperial policies, he cannot be seriously accused of mistaking the realities of Stalinist rule in the Soviet Union and Eastern Europe: that people on the left apologised for it, or of the threat that the continued grip of Stalinism on much of the European Left posed for any hope of democratic socialism. The continued support that much of the left gave to the Soviet Union is clearly of considerably more importance than his list, but it has received nothing like the attention that his involvement with the IRD has received. If Orwell can quite correctly be called to account for his list then his critics cannot object to similar scrutiny. The Marxist historian Christopher Hill, for example, in his short 1945 book, *Two Commonwealths* (published under the name K E Hulme), glibly covers up mass murder in the Soviet Union: 'when public opinion decides that a thing is necessary it gets done. To the reply that this has been achieved at the cost of disregarding the wishes of a minority, sometimes (as in the case of collectivisation) of a considerable minority, the Russian would shrug his shoulders and say he was building a new social order and you can't have an omelette without breaking eggs'. As for 'the purge of the fifth column' during the Great Terror? Well, he turns to Sir John Maynard for support, quoting his belief that the Stalin regime 'did not lose the support of the masses by the drastic proceedings of 1936–38, for the masses believed that the punishments have been deserved: as – in general – they probably were'. What of the role of the Communist Party in the Soviet Union? For Hill, the Russian CP governed by 'persuasion', it was 'organized on democratic lines' with 'free and positive discussion of party policy'. The CP was, he goes on, in intimate contact with the masses, functioning like a 'permanent "Gallop poll"' with the party able to register 'trends of opinion in the USSR more rapidly and effectively than the ballot-box' and immediately acts to implement them. Just as 'the British Empire is united by the symbol of the Crown' so the Soviet Union is 'united by the very real presence of the ubiquitous party'. And so on.[43] This book was published the same year as *Animal Farm*. As for Hill criticising Orwell's involvement with the British State, this would have more credibility if it did not come from someone who, even while a CP member, had also been a major in the British Army Intelligence Corps before going on to become head of the Russia desk at the Foreign Office during the War. And as late as 1953, Hill was in print in full 'squealer' mode, celebrating the recently deceased Stalin's credentials as a historian, intellectual and humanitarian in the most fulsome terms: 'Stalin's dicta on history . . . are regarded . . . as worthy of the most serious consideration . . . he was a very great and penetrating thinker, who on any subject was apt to break through the cobwebs of academic argument to the heart of the matter . . . His statements, therefore, approximate to the highest wisdom of the collective thought of the USSR'. 'Humanity', Hill concluded, 'will always be deeply in his debt'.[44]

Orwell's willingness to make his writings available for use as anti-Communist propaganda was by far the most important aspect of his relationship with the IRD. This began before his death, but increased dramatically afterwards. The scale of this operation was enormous with both *Animal Farm* and *Nineteen Eighty Four* being widely translated and distributed. By the end of 1950, *Animal Farm* had even been turned into a comic-strip, courtesy of the IRD, that was to appear in newspapers 'in New Delhi, Rangoon, Eritrea, Bangkok, Saigon, Caracas, Lima, Mexico City, Karachi, Ankara, Cyprus, Bogota, Reykjavik, Rio de Janeiro, Singapore, Colombo, Ceylon, Benghazi and Montevideo'. And it must be acknowledged that Orwell himself was not always terribly scrupulous about where his books were published. As early as November 1945, he made clear to his agent, Leonard Moore, that while he could not allow *Animal Farm* to be published by any publisher with links to the 'Spanish fascists', not least because 'it could do me a great deal of harm . . . if it got out, as it would', he was not so concerned about it being published in a 'semi-fascist' country like Portugal![45]

'They Appear to Have Considerable Funds at Their Disposal'

The propaganda value of Orwell's work was recognised not just by the IRD but by various US agencies as well. US intelligence agencies were very concerned with waging a propaganda war against the Soviet Union, a propaganda war that had an important cultural dimension. This has come under increasing scrutiny, not least since the publication of Frances Stonor Saunders' path-breaking *Who Paid the Piper?* Orwell was certainly involved with this US dimension, not least because some of those involved were people associated in some way or other with *Partisan Review* and the broader New York intellectual milieu. He had dealings with Melvin Lasky and the West German magazine he edited *Der Monat*, which later became a mainstay of the CIA funded Congress for Cultural Freedom. Less well-known is the approach he received from a US intelligence front, the International Rescue and Relief Committee (IRRC). In March 1946, he wrote to his good friend and fellow anti-Stalinist Arthur Koestler that he had been approached by Francis Henson about becoming involved with the IRRC. Henson had assured him that that the organisation had no Communist links, that it had been set up to aid 'the victims of total-itarianism' and was, in fact, strongly 'anti-Stalinist to the extent that the people they assist are largely Trotskyists etc'. Henson told him that the IRRC wanted to establish contact with 'various people in the Labour Party'. As Orwell observed, 'They appear to have considerable funds at their disposal'. As he told Koestler, 'these are the sort of people we should keep in close touch with, as it is all more or less up the same street'.[46] While nothing seems to come of this particular contact, it certainly shows Orwell's readiness to cooperate with US organisations. The IRRC was, at this time, controlled by the 'Lovestoneites', former US supporters of Nikolai Bukharin and followers of Jay Lovestone, the onetime leader of the American CP, expelled as long ago as 1929. Their anti-Stalinism had eventually led them into the arms of US intelligence.[47] While the IRRC did undoubtedly engage in 'Relief and Rescue', it was also in the process of becoming 'fully integrated into the foreign policy establish-ment as a vital member of the CIA's covert network'. It was to eventually become the International Rescue Committee (IRC). As its historian, Eric Thomas Chester writes, throughout the Cold War, the IRC was 'to act as an essential component of the covert network, the interconnected set of organisations helping the US intelligence community to implement a variety of clandestine operations to destabilise the Soviet Union and its dependent allies'. What particularly marked it out was that 'it unstintingly cultivated its ties to European social democracy'. And since the end of the Cold War, it has continued to 'operate in close conformity with the policy mandates of US foreign policy'.[48] At the time of writing (August 2017) the President and CEO of the IRC is the former New Labour Foreign Secretary David Miliband.

While Orwell was wholly on board the propaganda campaign against the Soviet Union, the fact remains that both *Animal Farm* and *Nineteen Eighty-Four* were always intended as critiques of Soviet Communism from the left. His overriding concerns was to destroy the illusions that many socialists still had in the Soviet Union, something that he regarded as an essential first step on the way to the achievement of democratic socialism. With the onset of the Cold War, he was ready; indeed, eager to put these books at the service of the Attlee government and its US ally, but nevertheless up until his premature death, his longer-term concern was still with the establishment of a United Socialist States of Europe. He mistakenly regarded these two concerns as compatible. What we do not know is whether as the Cold War continued he would have eventually recognised the contradiction between these two concerns and once he recognised the contradiction if he would have remained true to the cause of democratic socialism or, as many others did, continue a remorseless trajectory to the right. The conclusion that commentators come to regarding his political trajectory if he had lived a longer life tells us more about them, about their politics, than it does about Orwell. Once he was dead, attempts to insist that he had remained a democratic socialist came to an end and his own previous efforts at making this clear were increasingly suppressed as he was made more and more use of in the propaganda war. Both sides in the Cold War united in suppressing his socialist credentials for their very different reasons.

One telling piece of evidence that is worth considering that points towards the contradiction between his democratic socialism and the priorities of the Cold War is provided by the British animated film of *Animal Farm* that we now know was financed by the CIA. According to Scott Lucas, the film was a 'reward' for Orwell's assistance in the propaganda war, a somewhat posthumous reward.[49] What distinguishes the film as far as Tony Shaw is concerned is 'its political distortion of

Orwell's book'.[50] The CIA insisted that Joy Batchelor's original script that had been faithful to the book be changed to reflect their propaganda concerns. The 'investors' objected to Snowball being portrayed as 'intelligent, courageous, dynamic' because this suggested that if he had defeated Napoleon then he might have succeeded in 'creating a benevolent successful state . . . this implication we cannot permit'. Instead he had to be shown as a 'fanatic intellectual whose plans if carried through would have led to disaster'. It had to be made clear that not all farmers were bad and that there were well-run farms with contented animals. And that the film had to end not with pigs and men becoming indistinguishable but with a meeting with just pigs present and with the other animals rising in revolt.[51] This, in a backhanded way, is testimony to the contradiction between Orwell's concerns and those of both the British and US secret states.

'When a Labour Government Takes over, I Wonder What Happens to Scotland Yard Special Branch? To Military Intelligence?'

As we have seen, while Orwell did not consider the Labour election victory in 1945 as a vote for socialism, he still hoped and expected that the incoming Labour government would launch an attack on the ruling class and its domination over society. He expected the abolition of the House of Lords and the taking over of the public schools as necessary first steps along with a great purge of upper-class military officers, senior civil servants, senior police officers, diplomats, people whose loyalty could not be relied on, the potential supporters of a Spanish-style coup in fact. This seriously overestimated the Attlee government's radicalism. As early as December 1945, he wrote in *Tribune* about how a few weeks before five people were arrested outside Hyde Park selling *Peace News* and the Anarchist magazine, *Freedom*. Four of them were bound over and the fifth sentenced to a fine or a month in prison. He had opted for prison and as far as Orwell knew was still inside. Now while no one would compare the British police to the Gestapo, it was no secret that they 'have been unfriendly to Left-wing activities' and he recalled police conduct at the BUF meeting he had attended back in 1936. It was, he observed, always the seller of the *Daily Worker* who was harassed, never the seller of the *Daily Telegraph*. He was somewhat surprised to find that this was still the situation 'under a Labour government'.

From this starting point, he went on to ask 'When a Labour Government takes over, I wonder what happens to Scotland Yard Special Branch? To Military Intelligence? To the Consular service? To the various colonial administrations – and so on and so forth?' As far as he could see no 'extensive reshuffling' was taking place. Even the BBC still had 'the same subtly reactionary colour that it always had'. Surely, he thought, 'no government can afford to leave its enemies in key positions, and when Labour is in undisputed power for the first time . . . it clearly must make sufficient changes to prevent sabotage'. What we see here is that he still thought the Labour government might pose a threat to the fundamental interests of the ruling class, a threat serious enough to provoke unconstitutional resistance rather than constitutional opposition. Having asked the big question, he returned to the persecution of newspaper sellers at Hyde Park. Freedom of the press in Britain was actually overrated because, as he pointed out, 'most of the press is owned by a few people' and this results in a system of censorship that 'operates in much the same way as State censorship'. What was crucial was Freedom of Speech and this was why the people arrested at Hyde Park, whether they were selling anarchist, Communist, Trotskyist or pacifist newspapers had to be defended.[52]

But what did happen to Special Branch and MI5 when the Labour Party was in office? The short answer is that they continued spying on the Left but for a Labour government rather than a Conservative government. Meanwhile Orwell was involved in setting up the Freedom Defence Committee (he was vice-chairman) together with Herbert Read (chairman), Michael Tippett, E M Forster, Henry Moore, Bertrand Russell, George Woodcock and others to defend civil liberties and free speech. He gave the organisation 'quite substantial donations' and made one of his rare contributions as a public speaker at a Freedom Defence Committee public meeting at the Conway Hall in Red Lion Square in London. Woodcock remembered how his voice, 'weakened by the throat wound he had received during the Spanish Civil War, did not carry very well'. The Committee remained active until the end of 1949, although Orwell's involvement had already been curtailed by his poor health.[53] As for the Labour government, it carried on spying.

According to Daniel Lomas, when Labour took office, far from regarding MI5 as any sort of threat, they saw the agency as 'an important instrument of government' and 'fully appreciated MI5's value'. The 'Zinoviev Letter' was very much in the past as far as Attlee and his colleagues were concerned. Indeed, the extent to which Attlee was personally comfortable with MI5 and its activities is perhaps best shown by the fact that he was the first Prime Minister to visit MI5 headquarters and actually wrote a 'Preface' to the memoirs, *Cloak without Dagger*, of MI5's Director-General, Percy Sillitoe. Once in office, Attlee relied on MI5 to spy on those Labour MPs suspected of being 'crypto-Communists' as well as on CP activities in the trade unions. In November 1947, he was particularly worried about supposedly Communist-instigated strikes disrupting the Royal wedding and was considerably reassured when told that MI5 'had quite a number of agents in the Communist Party who were well placed'.[54] By 1949, Attlee had been convinced by MI5 that the Communists were behind the increasing industrial unrest that the Labour government's 'Austerity' regime was provoking and that they were trying 'to overturn social democracy'.[55] In July of that year, a general lockout on the London docks where dockers were refusing to unload two Canadian ships crewed by scabs saw the government send in over 12,000 troops to try and break this tremendous display of international solidarity which was predictably condemned as Communist-inspired. Bevan, of all people, condemned the dockers' action as 'a betrayal of the labour movement' and the Transport and General Workers Union subsequently expelled or suspended the dockers' unofficial leaders from the union.[56]

The Attlee government introduced negative vetting which saw suspect civil servants sacked, forced to resign or transferred, but resisted proposals to support the setting up of a House of Commons Un-British Activities Committee in 1947. The opposition to an Un-British Committee was more to do with the government keeping control over what was going on and avoiding it either getting out of hand or actually being used by the Conservatives to smear the Labour Party itself than with concern with civil liberties. That this was a very real danger was to be shown by the campaign spearheaded by the Beaverbrook press to smear John Strachey in 1950, and, of course, Senator Joseph McCarthy was to denounce the 'long and odious career' of 'Comrade' Attlee himself in May 1953.[57] There was also a government determination to keep as much of what it was doing out of the public eye as possible so as to minimise opposition. The purge that took place in Britain was not a 'full-blown Great Fear' on the US model but rather what Rhodri Jeffreys-Jones has described as 'a kind of "silent McCarthyism"', what he calls the 'Great British Silence'. He argues that the low profile of this British purge meant that it lasted considerably longer than McCarthyism.[58] The government was also involved in encouraging sackings and blacklisting in private industry with MI5 providing employers with secret information. Various union leaders cooperated in this up to and including Vincent Tewson, general secretary of the TUC. Lomas describes it as 'the industrial purge'.[59]

The scale of all this never approached that of the sackings and victimisations conducted in the United States, a purge that swept up many people who in Britain would have been considered part of the 'moderate' left, mainstream Labour supporters, liberals even, and no security threat whatsoever. But while the number directly affected by sacking and transfer was, in the words of one study, 'minimal', it is impossible to calculate the scale of blacklisting and there was also the deterrent effect, encouraging people to steer clear of dangerous affiliations.[60] There were also people sacked on other pretexts, the most high-profile example being Monica Felton, chair of the Stevenage Development Corporation, a long-standing Labour Party member and town planning expert. She was sacked by Hugh Dalton, then Minister of Local Government, on 12 June 1951 ostensibly for being four hours late for a meeting at the House of Commons. The real reason was that she had been part of a pacifist delegation that had visited North Korea and had publicly condemned British and American conduct of the war. She was also expelled from the Labour Party. There were Conservative demands that she should be put on trial for treason and hanged but the Labour Attorney General ruled that there was not enough evidence.[61] There were clear indications that if the Labour government had not lost office in 1951, it was seriously considering intensifying the 'purge' and extending it to schools and universities very much in response to the war in Korea.[62]

How did Orwell respond to all this? He was certainly opposed to people being victimised for their beliefs, although he accepted that genuine security considerations had to be taken into account. As far as he was concerned the fight against domestic Communism was a battle of ideas that had to win the CP's rank and file and sympathisers over from Stalinism by exposing its true nature. In early March 1949, he wrote to Richard Rees that what had to be avoided was becoming 'a fanatic oneself' in the fight against Stalinism.[63] A year earlier he had written to George Woodcock urging that the Freedom Defence Committee had to take a stand on the civil service purge. It was a difficult question because one had to recognise the right of government 'to govern . . . to choose suitable agents', (he had, of course, advocated a dramatic purge of the agents of the ruling class from the machinery of State himself) but nevertheless 'the whole phenomenon seems to me part of the general breakdown of the democratic outlook'.[64] Orwell was, of course, to publish *Nineteen Eighty-Four* in June 1949, with its great indictment of the ultimate Secret Police State together with its powers of total surveillance and ability to manufacture the 'truth'. It is a supreme irony that this book was to be 'weaponised' by the British and US secret states in their Cold War against the Soviet Union and its satellites, while for their part the Communist secret police proscribed the book, hunted its readers down and imprisoned them.[65]

'2+2=5': Orwell, *Nineteen Eighty-Four*, and the New Left

George Orwell died from a massive haemorrhage of the lungs in a private room at University College Hospital in London on 21 January 1950. He was only 46 and had been seriously ill for some time. His dream of a life on Jura had to all intents and purposes been abandoned when he went into the Cranham sanatorium in Gloucestershire on 6 January 1949. His condition deteriorated and he went into UCH on 3 September. He did not expect to die but was reconciled to spending the rest of a necessarily short life as an invalid, hopefully still capable of at least some writing. Even towards the very end, his socialist politics were very much intact. On 17 April, he had complained in his diary about all the 'upper class English voices' at Cranham. In Scotland, he had got used to 'working-class or lower-middle-class Scottish voices', but now it was like hearing the English upper class 'for the first time. And what voices! A sort of over-fedness, a fatuous self-confidence . . . above all a sort of heaviness and richness combined with a fundamental ill-will'. These people were 'the enemies of anything intelligent or sensitive or beautiful. No wonder everyone hates us so'.[1]

Among those visiting Orwell in hospital was Stephen Spender. He was to record that both of them had 'expected something more spectacular than Attlee's England of the Beveridge Plan and the Welfare State', indeed Orwell had hoped for a 'manifest revolution'. Still people seemed content with welfarism rather than socialism. He saw Orwell, for the last time, a couple of weeks before his death when he complained 'that despite there being a Labour government there were far too many visible signs of wealth in London. There were all these Rolls Royces'. This was at a time when the Labour government was imposing a regime of austerity on the working class. Even when Spender told him that most of them belonged to foreigners or foreign embassies, Orwell still felt that 'such visible signs of one class being much better off than another' were wrong, not least because 'It is bad for morale'.[2] On another occasion, Spender discussed how to reply to Communist attacks with Orwell, who responded somewhat typically that there 'are certain people like vegetarians and communists whom one cannot answer'.[3]

'NOT INTENDED as an Attack on Socialism'

Nineteen Eighty-Four was the great British novel of twentieth-century tyranny. Orwell had finished typing the final draft on 4 December 1948 and it was published on 8 June 1949 in Britain and on 13 June in the United States. Even while he was effectively fighting for his life, he was already worried by the way that the novel had been received, indeed positively welcomed as an attack on the left, especially in the US. He had expected the Communists to portray it as such, but the response was more general with people on the right praising the book as anti-socialist as well. To some extent this was his own fault, a product of his intentions when he wrote it. When he wrote *Animal Farm*, it had been very much a book intended to combat support for the Soviet Union on the left. There had been a dramatic increase in support and admiration for Stalin and the Soviet Union in Britain across the political spectrum occasioned by the importance of the Russian war effort in the defeat of Nazism. What *Animal Farm* set out to do was to tell the story of the betrayal of the Russian Revolution and to make the point that Stalin's Russia was no different in its conduct from the other Great Powers. The final scene of the novel when the farm animals cannot tell the pigs from the men was not a satire targeted at the Hitler-Stalin Pact, but rather a satire of the November 1943 Tehran Conference where, as far as Orwell was concerned Stalin, Churchill and Roosevelt were intent on dividing the world between them. At the time he wrote *Animal Farm*, he expected the alliance between the Soviet Union and the United States and Britain to continue into the post-war period, not without difficulty or conflict, but nevertheless the Cold War was not something he predicted at this time. By the time the book was published in August 1945, the situation was already changing. Nevertheless, *Animal Farm* was clearly intended as a contribution to the fight against Stalinism and for democratic socialism within the left. And it was certainly not a repudiation of revolution, as has been sometimes argued, but a warning against the 'revolution betrayed'. When he came to write the 'Preface' to the Ukrainian edition of the book in 1947, he still made clear that his intention was to help 'destroy the Soviet myth' which he believed had contributed massively 'to the corruption of the original idea of Socialism' so that every act of the Soviet leadership 'must be excused, if not imitated'. The destruction of this myth 'was essential if we want a revival of the Socialist movement'.[4]

When he wrote *Nineteen Eighty-Four*, he had two objectives in mind. He certainly intended the book to be another, much grimmer, contribution to the fight against Stalinism, indeed totalitarianism in general. While he was still wholly committed to the cause of democratic socialism, as we have seen, he was also pessimistic about the immediate prospects for advance in that direction, something that is certainly reflected in the novel. His *Partisan Review* article, 'Towards European Unity', published in July 1947, was, as we have seen, a good indication of his thinking at this time: the situation as far as a socialist was concerned was all but, but not quite hopeless, But *Nineteen Eighty-Four* was also intended as a contribution to the propaganda war against the Soviet Union, as a contribution to the Cold War. It is important to remember that this was as far as he was concerned still a Cold War waged by a Labour government, albeit allied with the United States, a Labour government that with whatever reservations he supported. And, of course, he was unaware of how far removed its foreign and imperial policies actually were from any kind of socialist politics. It was this second objective that was responsible for the book being of such use to the right, both in Britain and in the United States, in their propaganda war against the Soviet Union. When it comes to the book's usefulness against the left more generally, however, another important factor has to be taken into account, that is, the extent to which much of the left, Communists and fellow travellers of one kind or another, continued to embrace the very Soviet myth that Orwell sought to destroy. This section of the left effectively surrendered the book to the right to be used against them all the while complaining of the fact.

Orwell was very much aware of the hijacking of the book in the months before he died and did his best to counter the development. The process was most advanced in the United States and Orwell told his publisher, Frederick Warburg that he was 'very worried' about it.[5] Through his agent, Leonard Moore, Orwell issued statements to the United Automobile Workers and to the New York newspaper, the *Socialist Call* on 22 July 1949. As he made absolutely clear, *Nineteen Eighty-Four* was 'NOT INTENDED as an attack on Socialism'. It is difficult to see how he could have possibly made the point clearer. Neither was it an attack on 'the British Labor Party [sic] (of which I am a supporter)'. It was instead intended to expose 'the perversions to which a centralized economy is liable and which have already been partly realised in Communism and Fascism'. The book was intended to combat 'totalitarian ideas' and was set in England to show that English-speaking countries were not exempt from this contagion.[6]

His attempt to stop the book falling into the hands of the right was cut short by his untimely death and there can be no doubt that but for this his efforts would have continued and the book's reputation and indeed the uses to which it was subsequently put would have been radically different. And if his health had recovered enough for him to begin serious writing again, then instead of appearing to be his last testament, the book would without any doubt be judged in the light of subsequent writings, novels he had planned, major essays on Evelyn Waugh, Joseph Conrad and on nineteenth-century anarchism, but also essays, articles and reviews that advocated socialism, defended the integrity of the socialist cause and discussed contemporary issues. As Fyvel insists, *Nineteen Eighty-Four* was 'not meant by him to be his own personal literary farewell'.[7]

Instead the book was seized upon by both the United States and the British governments as a potent propaganda tool in their Cold War conflict with the Soviet Union and in defence of their global imperial interests. Indeed, this great exposé of the Secret Police State, of the systematic lies continually reinvented by the Ministry of Truth, became itself a weapon in the hands of the US and British secret states, used for purposes that its author would never have sanctioned had he lived. According to David Caute, *Nineteen Eighty-Four* 'exercised a greater impact on the culture of the Cold War than any work of history, political science or reportage'. It had been broadcast as a serial by the Voice of America and the CIA sponsored its translation into over thirty languages.[8] It provided a whole ready-made vocabulary for the cultural battle with the Soviet Union that was waged across the world. And it was not just the CIA and the IRD that found a potent propaganda use for Orwell and his work. As John Rossi has pointed out, even while he was still alive, Orwell had become 'virtually a saint for the American Right' with the Luce press, in particular, engaged in the process of canonization. He goes on:

> *1984* was not only reviewed favourably by *Time* but also a special editorial in *Life* called the American public's attention to it. *1984*, they argued, pointed up the dangers confronting the free world with special impact because 'it comes from a leftwinger who is cautioning

his fellow intellectuals of the left to beware lest their desire to help the common man wind up in trapping him in hopeless misery'.

This was categorically not what Orwell had intended but his attempts to counter it were, of course, completely ignored.[9] What of the response from the left?

'No Slander is Too Gross'

The response of British Communists to *Nineteen Eighty-Four* was absolute fury. The party was completely devoted to Stalin, to the myth of a Stalinist utopia, and to the destruction of its enemies and critics on the left. A L Morton, the CP historian, author of the excellent *A People's History of England*, was typical in the way that he tried to portray the book as an attack on socialism, as deliberately intended to undermine the struggle for socialism and to strengthen the right. In his in many respects outstanding book, *The English Utopia*, published in 1952, he condemns *Nineteen Eighty-Four* as a 'degraded' book that embraces 'the frankest reaction, a determination to resist the "actual realisation" of Utopia'. Orwell urged that 'we must cling to all existing institutions, however corrupt, since any change can only be for the worse'. His intention was to show that 'any attempt to realise socialism must lead to a world of corruption, torture and insecurity' and to achieve this purpose 'no slander is too gross, no device too filthy'. The book was 'the last word . . . in counter-revolutionary apologetics'. It was a degenerate book that was 'beneath contempt'. And just in case anyone had missed the point, Orwell, he assured his readers, found 'the power of the working class . . . terrifying'[10] This fury is still evident as late as 1984 when *Inside the Myth*, edited by Christopher Norris, was published by the CP publisher, Lawrence and Wishart. Norris put together a truly disgraceful collection of essays with the sole intention of discrediting George Orwell. Here Alaric Jacob, a fellow travelling journalist, for example, condemned *Nineteen Eighty-Four* as 'one of the most disgusting books ever written', a book that put the works of the Marquis de Sade in the shade so full of 'fear, hatred, lies and self-disgust' was it.[11] If only the realities of Stalinism or the years of covering them up had inspired such fury! And this hostility continues to this day in some shape or form among parts of the left, still concerned to discredit Orwell's attempt to 'destroy the Soviet myth'.

It is useful, at this point, to provide some context for the CP response to the publication of *Nineteen Eighty-Four*. When the book came out, Eastern Europe was in the grip of a ferocious wave of purges that was intended to root out any potential Titoites from the various satellite Communist Parties. The great split with Tito saw the Stalin regime move to make sure that the same revolt against Russian domination did not take place anywhere else. Across Eastern Europe, lifelong Communists, including men and women who had often suffered tremendous hardship in the Communist cause, were arrested, tortured and forced to confess to crimes that they were clearly innocent of. There can be no serious doubt whatsoever that the leadership of Communist Parties throughout Western Europe knew that the crimes charged against these people were false, manufactured, and yet they enthusiastically supported the purge, just as they had in the late 1930s.

The post-war purges came in two waves, the first in 1948–49 and principally affecting Albania, Hungary and Bulgaria and the second in 1950–53 affecting Romania, East Germany and Czechoslovakia, presaging a great purge in the Soviet Union itself that only Stalin's death forestalled. The second wave also had a distinct anti-Semitic dimension. According to one of the most recent academic accounts, 'hundreds of thousands of supposed "enemies of the people" were arrested, deported to labour camps, sacked from their jobs or expelled from schools and universities. Several thousands of those arrested and tried were executed or suffered extrajudicial murder'. The numbers varied from country to country. In Romania between 1948 and 1953, 'a highly conservative estimate is that 60,000 were arrested ... in Bulgaria, about 40,000 were imprisoned ... in Czechoslovakia, around 90,000 were prosecuted for political crimes'. In Hungary, 'a staggering 750,000 people were convicted between 1948 and 1953'.[12] East European Communist Parties were ruthlessly purged with well over 2 million members expelled, up to a quarter of their collective membership, many of them long-standing members, veterans of the years of Nazi occupation, and now many of these people were among those arrested and imprisoned, perhaps as many as 250,000 CP and former CP members rounded up.[13] But while hundreds of thousands of ordinary people, both CP members and non-members were swept up, the Party leaderships and security apparatuses were also purged on Stalin's orders, with the subsequent interrogations and 'show trials' supervised by the NKVD. In Bulgaria, a former deputy prime minister, Traicho Kostov, a man who had been a party member for 30 years and had spent some ten years in prison in Bulgaria, was arrested on 20 June 1949, charged with 'Titoism' and executed on 16 December. In Hungary, Laszlo Rajk, the former interior minister and himself 'a diehard Stalinist', was arrested in a sweep that eventually produced 141 defendants who were to appear in a number of show trials. Rajk was a veteran of the International Brigades, had been active in the Communist underground during the War and had ended up in a concentration camp in Germany. This record was no protection. Far from it. It only made him more suspect of 'Titoism' as far as the Russians were concerned. The Hungarian trials were staged under Russian supervision with Stalin himself reading through and agreeing to Rajk's final indictment. The prisoners were routinely tortured, a process which some of them did not survive, beaten to death, hunger saw them 'even eating excrement', and, of course, their families were threatened, often arrested and held as hostages. Rajk's wife, Julia, had been one of those imprisoned and their son was taken away. At their trials, they all confessed to 'the most absurd crimes'. Rajk himself was executed on 16 October 1949.[14] His wife was forced to watch him hang and even after she was released in 1955 she was still not told the fate of her son.[15]

In Czechoslovakia, Rudolf Slansky, the CP general secretary, was arrested on Stalin's orders on 23 November 1951. Slansky's wife Josefa was also among those arrested and she later wrote of how her interrogators had 'threatened that they would kill both our children'. They played recordings of her husband's interrogations to her in her cell and told her that her own confession had already been written and how they could even add her signature to it for her if she refused to sign.[16] After months of torture, both physical and mental, 14 defendants were eventually put on trial, eleven of them Jews, charged with 'Trotskyism-Zionism' and with working for French, British and US intelligence. This was as Kevin McDermott and Matthew Stibbe argue 'a major anti-Semitic show trial'.[17] Eleven of the accused were sentenced to death and executed on 3 December 1952. Among those hanged was Ludwig Frejka, who had worked on the *Daily Worker* in London during the war. His wife was among those demanding the death penalty. Another victim was Otto Katz, who was well-known to many British Communists. He had been involved in establishing the Left Book Club and in January 1937 it had published his *The Nazi Conspiracy in Spain*. He was also to be actively involved in the repression of the 'Trotskyist-Fascists' in Spain. In his 1952 confession, he implicated, among others, both Noel Coward and Claud Cockburn as British agents. Another individual named as a British double agent was Peter Smollett and there were plans to kidnap him and smuggle him to the Soviet Union for interrogation and almost certain execution. The trial did have one brief moment of grotesque 'humour' when Otto Sling was reciting his painfully memorised confession. He had been starved as part of the interrogation process, and now deprived of belt and braces to prevent any suicide attempt, his trousers fell down around his ankles mid-confession, briefly interrupting the proceedings.[18]

At the very same time that Orwell was being attacked for slandering Communism, the CP was celebrating these East European Show Trials. Who one is entitled to ask did the greatest damage to the socialist cause? James Klugman, for example, produced his *From Trotsky to Tito,* using the 'evidence' presented at the Moscow Trials to establish that the Trotskyists were fascist agents and that the Titoites were in many cases Trotskyists who had avoided detection in the 1930s. He also used 'evidence' from the more recent trials. Klugman quoted from Traicho Kostov's confession the fact that Tito had personally told him of 'his Trotskyist ideas' as early as 1934. He quoted Rajk's confession about how he had been a Trotskyist while in the International Brigades, working for a fascist victory, how afterwards when interned in France, he and the Yugoslav Trotskyists from the International Brigades had first worked for French intelligence before transferring their allegiance to the Gestapo. The Trotskyist group in the Yugoslav CP, was, according to Klugman, led by 'Tito, Kardelj, Djilas and Rankovic'. And so on for a relentless 204 pages. Klugman certainly knew that everything he wrote was lies, not everyday lies, but lies written in blood and pain. He knew personally many of the men he was slandering from the 1930s and yet put aside any scruples he might have had about quoting from confessions that he must have known were extracted by torture. According to his biographer, writing the book actually made him physically ill. People like him, far from being in a position to criticise *Nineteen Eighty-Four*, actually behaved as if they were characters from the book. One interesting point that Klugman made concerned the nefarious role that the British Special Operations Executive (SOE) had played in bringing Tito to power. He had worked for SOE during the war and had been personally involved in this, as he thought, furthering the Communist cause at the time. It would certainly have signed his death warrant if a Stalinist regime had ever taken power in Britain. As far as Klugman was concerned '2+2=5' whenever and as often as 'Big Brother' thought it necessary.[19]

To return briefly to A L Morton's *The English Utopia*, as well as condemning *Nineteen Eighty-Four*, he also espoused the virtues of Stalin's Russia. As far as he was concerned, the English Utopian tradition was in the process of being realised in the Soviet Union, 'translated into facts in the Stalin Plans which are now changing the face and the climate of the USSR'.[20] There is something particularly obscene about associating William Morris among others with Stalinism, but Morton was not alone in this. Even someone of the calibre of historian Edward Thompson parroted the line at this time. In an article he published in *Arena* in June 1951, 'William Morris and the Moral Issues Today', he quite grotesquely quoted Morris in endorsement of the Stalin tyranny before condemning Orwell, Koestler and others by name as 'defenders of American capitalism', covering up with their fine words a reality that consisted of 'napalm, the Hell Bomb and the butchers of Syngman Rhee'. It was a matter of great regret that the 'American capitalists and their British apologists' seemed to have gained 'the initiative in the field of morality'. It was 'under cover of . . . talk about "human rights"' that they were turning opinion against the Soviet Union. And his response was to ignore any allegations of abuse because of 'the very enormity of the lie. It is the Big Lie technique of Goebbels over again. The Lie is so monstrous that we cannot be troubled with it, we turn our backs on it, and divert the argument on to more practical questions'.[21]

'The Last Traces of Illusion'

Among those swept up in the East European purges was a member of the British CP, Edith Bone. She had been born in Hungary in 1889, became involved with the revolutionary left at the end of the First World War, joined the Bolshevik Party in Petrograd and in 1918 had been recruited by Victor Serge to edit the English language edition of the monthly magazine, *Communist International*, before going to work as a courier for the Comintern. She was in Germany during the rise to power of the Nazis and when they took over, she moved to Britain. In 1936, she was in Catalonia when the military staged their coup and was involved with the Catalan Communists, before returning once again to Britain. After more than twenty years in the Communist movement, she resigned in 1939, but rejoined the British CP in 1942. By now, in her fifties, she was not particularly active, but was rather, in her own words, 'marking time'. In 1949 though, she agreed to return to Hungary as a special correspondent for the *Daily Worker*. She was arrested soon after her arrival, effectively repudiated by the *Daily Worker* and spent the next seven years in solitary confinement. Even though she had been in the movement for some thirty years and was well-known to many in the British CP, her arrest and overnight disappearance turned her into a nonperson, someone not to be mentioned or inquired after.

As she recalled in her memoir, *Seven Years Solitary*, at first, as a good Communist, she still regarded 'the secret police at this time as an organ of the party of which I was a member . . . I still regarded them as acting in good faith although in my case they had made a mistake'. This error of judgement on her part was soon rectified. She was held in a tiny cell, 'a dirty coal cellar', with no window, no heating, the light on day and night, the only furniture a plank bed and kept half-starved. Her interrogators threatened her with considerably worse unless she confessed to being a British spy. One problem she had was coming to terms with the very fact that she had been imprisoned by her own side. If she had been in fascist hands, she would have known how to fight back, but now she found herself 'a prisoner in my own camp' and with 'my long service in the same organisation as that which they claimed to serve' counting for nothing. She quickly reoriented herself and came to regard her interrogators with 'an attitude of uncompromising hostility', as 'a cross between Teddy boy and spiv' to be regarded with complete contempt. Deprived of sleep, starved, cold (she was sometimes placed in a refrigerated cell), threatened with violence and subjected to repeated interrogation, she put her 'comparatively mild treatment' down to her British citizenship.

Once she realised that they were not going to actually use physical violence against her and without any family members they could threaten, she began what she describes as a succession of 'little wars' against her jailers. One can almost feel sorry for them, confronted with this exceptionally tough and resourceful woman, who treated them with open contempt and consistently refused to confess to her mission of recruiting saboteurs 'to cause accidents in factories'. They even had the names of the factories all ready for her. On one occasion, she was even told that it was her duty as a good Communist to confess, for the good of the Party. Her reply was, she writes, 'not fit to print'. She eventually received a farce of a trial without any evidence being presented or witnesses questioned and after a matter of minutes she was found guilty and sentenced without even being told either the charge or the sentence. Only on her release did she find out that she had been sentenced to 15 years for espionage. The first six months of her sentence was served in a tiny cell kept in complete darkness all the time. She managed to maintain her sanity against all the odds by reciting poetry, composing her own doggerel, memory exercises (remembering as many Dickens characters as she could – she got to four hundred!) and setting out to walk the distance to Britain in her four feet nine by ten feet cell. She made the journey four times. A succession of prison protests wore her jailers down over the years. Her language strike in 1951 saw her refuse to speak Hungarian, responding to their threats with abuse in the other five languages in which she was fluent, on one occasion giving the governor 'a blast of good Billingsgate' which he got the gist of even if he could not understand the specific insults. After one humiliation of the governor, a grinning guard, who had thoroughly enjoyed the episode, remarked in defiance of the no talking to prisoners regulation that he was glad 'you're not my mother-in-law'.

Eventually, the prison authorities gave up trying to break her and her situation improved so that even though still in solitary from January 1952 she had access to books. This remarkable woman taught herself to read Greek from German language books in the prison library. Not until 1952 did she finally cease to be a Communist though. As she puts it, 'my revolt against inhumanity had brought me into the Communist Party' but now, at last, she recognised the 'deeply rooted inhumanity' of Soviet Communism, putting an end 'at last to my infatuation', destroying 'the last traces of illusion' and lifting 'off my back the incubus I had carried for thirty years'. As far as she was now concerned, the Russian regime 'was a new type of aggressive imperialism' and the Hungarian regime merely 'a new type of colonialism'. She still had no expectation of ever being released and was resigned to dying, forgotten and un-mourned, in prison. She was eventually released by the Hungarian Revolution in October 1956.[22] She returned to Britain, ignored by the Party that had repudiated her and had effectively left her to die in prison.

Malcolm MacEwen, a journalist on the *Daily Worker* at the time, remembered how appalled he was by the dismissively cynical response of one of the veterans on the paper, Allen Hutt, who remarked on hearing of her release, 'So old woman Bone's turned up again'. Once he ascertained the facts of her case, he could not believe 'that we had allowed our correspondent to be jailed without lifting a finger to help her'. About half of the paper's journalists, 16 of them he recalls, signed a letter to the CP Executive Committee complaining that Edith Bone had been held 'in solitary confinement without trial for seven years, without any public inquiry or protest even after the exposure of the Rajk trial had shown that such injustices were taking place'. This failure to protest against the conduct of the Hungarian regime 'involves us in its crimes'.[23]

Why rehearse the almost forgotten story of Edith Bone? There were, after all, many more Hungarians, including Hungarian Communists, in prison at the same time as her who had suffered considerably worse treatment, protected as she was by her British passport. The point is that while Orwell's IRD list is to be absolutely condemned, it was of no real significance especially when compared to what many of his critics on the left had, at the time, either turned a blind eye to, knowingly lied about, or been actually complicit in. There can be no serious doubt that if Orwell had known of Bone's imprisonment and had been asked to support demands for her release, he would have done so, regardless of her long-standing Communist Party membership. Whether any member of the Communist Party would have been prepared to is another matter. Orwell was opposed to the persecution of Communists by fascist, democratic and Stalinist governments, whereas British Communists only opposed their persecution by fascist and democratic governments and actively supported their persecution by Stalinist governments. He supported the civil liberties of people who would quite cheerfully have seen him arrested, forced to confess by whatever means necessary, put on trial and shot.

'A Simple-Minded Anarchist'

The Communist Party's response to *Nineteen Eighty-Four* was, of course, completely predictable. More surprising perhaps was that of the biographer of Trotsky no less, Isaac Deutscher. In December 1954, he wrote his essay '1984 – The Mysticism of Cruelty', very much a response to the death of Stalin and hopes for 'liberalisation' in the Soviet Union and Eastern Europe. The essay appeared in a collection of his writings, *Heretics and Renegades*, published the following year. He considered himself a 'heretic' and placed Orwell very much among the 'renegades'. It is worth making the point here that while *Nineteen Eighty-Four* certainly left no space for any liberalisation in Oceania, this was not Orwell's finished position regarding the Soviet Union. He had acknowledged in 1947, for example, that while it was difficult to imagine the 'oligarchical collectivism' that existed in the Soviet Union undergoing 'radical change' there was still the hope that 'millions of young Russians' would by 1960 or thereabouts be 'eager for more freedom' despite the efforts of the NKVD. There is every reason to believe that if he had lived into the early 1950s, however sceptically or critically, he would have welcomed developments in the Soviet Union after Stalin's death, even as limited as they were, and urged a struggle for democratisation in both the Soviet Union and its satellites. And there is also every reason to believe that he would have welcomed events in East Germany in 1953 and even more so in Hungary in 1956 as demonstrating that 'hope' did indeed lie with the 'proles'. *Nineteen Eighty-Four* would certainly not have been his last word on the question of the Soviet Union. What Deutscher does, however, is unleash a full-scale assault on Orwell and his attitude towards the Soviet Union that in many ways prefigures the stance taken by much of the 'New Left' that was to emerge in the late 1950s.

As far as Deutscher was concerned the problem was that Orwell was not a Marxist and had no understanding of 'dialectical-materialist philosophy'. He was instead a rationalist with anarchist leanings, indeed, at one point he describes him as 'a simpleminded anarchist', who just could not 'get away from the Purges'. He had, according to Deutscher, been disillusioned by 'the spectacle of the Stalinist Great Purges of 1936–38, the repercussions of which he experienced in Catalonia'. The Purges 'supplied the subject matter for nearly all that he wrote after his Spanish experience'. Even though he had looked to Trotsky's writings for an explanation of the Soviet regime and its murderous savagery (my words, not Deutscher's), he never succeeded in breaking down the 'barrier between Trotsky's thought and himself'. The result was that he had 'projected the spectacle of the Great Purges on to the future . . . fixed there for ever'. His lack of a Marxist understanding meant that he was unable to grasp the Purges 'realistically, in their complex historical context'. The result was that he eventually abandoned rationalism for 'a quasi-mystical pessimism' so that *Nineteen Eighty-Four* stands as 'a document of dark disillusionment not only with Stalinism but with every form and shade of socialism'.[24]

Deutscher's account of Orwell is, of course, a complete travesty. Moreover, for all his criticism of Orwell for having his thinking about the Soviet Union determined by the Great Purges, something completely untrue as it happens, ignoring as it does not only Orwell's own inquiries into social conditions and social relations in the Soviet Union but also the impact of Spain and of subsequent events such as the Hitler-Stalin

Pact, the Katyn massacre and so on, it was his own thinking that was dogmatically static. Deutscher never moved beyond Trotsky's *The Revolution Betrayed*, first published in 1937. As far as Deutscher was concerned the Soviet Union was a 'workers' state' regardless of the character of the regime exercising power, the actual position of the working class in the social order and any such minor questions as slave labour, mass murder or whatever. There were certainly things to be deplored but a state-owned planned economy was by definition a workers' state and had to be supported. Orwell had certainly considered this proposition but recognised it for the exercise in sophistry posing as Marxism that it was before briefly considering the theory of state capitalism and then settling on the characterisation of the Soviet Union as a kind of 'oligarchical collectivism' as the most convincing account, embracing a Trotskyist heresy that he had encountered, as we have seen, in *Partisan Review*. The crucial point is that as far as Orwell was concerned, the Soviet Union was not socialist and indeed the belief that it was positively damaged the socialist cause and had to be fought if it was ever to revive. Hence, both *Animal Farm* and *Nineteen Eighty-Four*. Deutscher's understanding of the Soviet Union was to see him actually supporting the Russian invasion of Hungary in 1956! Having said this, there can be no excuse for either Orwell's IRD list or his inclusion of Deutscher on it as a 'Polish Jew' who had been 'previously' a Trotskyist but was now a Stalinist 'sympathiser', although he did concede that his biography of Stalin was 'moderately objective'.[25]

'Orwell Was Right After All'

The 1956 Hungarian Revolution was a decisive moment in the history of the post-war Communist movement. A working-class uprising against a brutal corrupt Stalinist regime that saw dual power established in the country with the reformist Imre Nagy government sharing authority with the workers' councils. In many parts of the country, the workers' councils effectively took over. Peter Fryer, the then *Daily Worker* correspondent in the country, wrote of their 'striking resemblance to the workers, peasants and soldiers councils which sprang up in Russia in the 1905 revolution and in February 1917'. They formed 'a network . . . which now extended over the whole of Hungary . . . They were at once organs of insurrection – the coming together of delegates elected by factories and universities, mines and army units – and organs of popular self-government which the armed people trusted'. The Russians finally moved to crush this revolution on 4 November with tanks and troops moving into Budapest, shelling working-class districts of the city, leaving some 20,000 people dead. In some parts of the city, resistance continued for up to a week. And even once the Russians were in control, they found themselves confronted by a general strike, 'one of the most prolonged and most solid general strikes in working class history'. The continued working-class resistance to the re-imposition of Communist control even after the successful occupation of the country by 200,000 Russian troops is one of the great unknown stories of international working-class history. On 15 December 1956, a Communist government actually introduced the death penalty for 'inciting strikes'. The great strike movement was finally worn down with any surviving independent working-class organisations suppressed amid widespread arrests.[26]

Events in Hungary plunged the international Communist movement into crisis, nowhere more so than in Britain. First in February 1956 came Khrushchev's revelations regarding the nature of the Stalin regime which led to the resignation of Harry Pollitt (for the second time) as general secretary and the establishment of a Commission on Inner Party Democracy. One interesting detail is that some twenty years after her execution, Pollitt took the opportunity of the Soviet regime's apparent 'liberalisation' to make a fresh inquiry about the fate of his old friend Rose Cohen. He wrote to the Central Committee of the Russian CP warning them, quite untruthfully, that there was press interest in her case and that the British Party needed to know if she was still alive. As Francis Beckett and Tony Russell put it, it was as if he 'still clung to some sort of hope that Rose might one day walk out of one of those terrible labour camps, old, bent and ill'.[27] He had continued faithfully supporting the Stalin regime for the twenty years since she had been shot, never knowing her fate, and not enquiring after her until now. And then in October came the Hungarian Revolution and loyal Communists had to support Russian tanks crushing a working-class revolt. The CP lost nearly a third of its members, over 9,000, as the Soviet regime stood revealed in its true colours.

The revolt in Hungary had an impact elsewhere in Eastern Europe. The artist Paul Hogarth, a loyal CP member who had briefly served in the International Brigades in Spain, arrived for a celebratory Congress of the International Brigades in Warsaw on 25 October 1956. He was confronted by demonstrations in support of the Hungarian Revolution.

'Trucks roared along the Marzalkowska jammed with workers and students waving Polish and Hungarian flags'. By mid-afternoon, there were 150,000 people in front of the Palace of Culture and Science, chanting slogans. Rather than take on the suppression of another mass movement, the Russians installed a 'reformist' Communist government under Wladyslaw Gomulka in power. This successfully divided the movement with those demanding 'complete democratisation' being eventually dispersed by the riot police who launched a 'series of savage and brutal attacks' driving people off the streets. The Congress went ahead however. Hogarth records the remarkable scene with Russian observers 'being challenged by Polish and Hungarian delegates to produce their heroes of the Spanish Civil War'. According to one embittered Polish delegate, they had all been executed on the orders of Stalin. Only in Warsaw, at this conference, 'did I realise that the destructive activities of the Communist Party reported by . . . George Orwell in *Homage to Catalonia* were, in fact, all too true'.[28]

'The Negations of 1984'

For many of those who broke away from the CP at this time, however, Orwell remained an enemy. The 'New Left' that emerged out of the CP's crisis never embraced Orwell. Edward Thompson, John Saville, Raymond Williams and other New Left luminaries remained determinedly hostile and this hostility undoubtedly affected the whole of the New Left.[29] Why was there this continued hostility on their part? Writing of John Saville, John McIlroy quite rightly celebrates him as 'an indefatigable organiser of socialist scholarship and a tireless pioneer of the history of the working class'. He goes on to put his post-1956 'antipathy to Orwell' down to his remaining 'a man of the 1930s who retained a defensive pride in the role of a party he never completely left behind'.[30] He never made a comprehensive enough break 'with the entire tradition of Stalinism'. This is true as far as it goes, but it does not go far enough. Orwell's anti-Stalinism was far more radical than anything that Saville was prepared to contemplate. Similarly with Edward Thompson, certainly the most celebrated Marxist historian since the 1950s.

Thompson's hostility towards Orwell derives from the partial nature of his eventual rejection of Stalinism. In his 'Through the Smoke of Budapest', that appeared in the journal, *The Reasoner* in November 1956, Thompson certainly supported the working-class revolt, condemned the

Russian invasion and the British CP's response to that invasion, but he saw Stalinism as primarily a question of theory. As he wrote: 'Stalinism is socialist theory and practice which has lost the ingredient of humanity'. Instead of dialectical materialism, 'the Stalinist mode of thought is . . . mechanical materialism'. Indeed, Stalinism, according to Thompson was all about 'distorted theories and degenerate practice, in which the British and other Communist Parties had been complicit, even though, as he insisted, 'it was our rank and file that was tainted least with these things and our leadership most'.[31] As far as Thompson was concerned whatever criticisms he might have of Stalinism, the Soviet Union remained socialist, whereas Orwell believed that not only was the Soviet Union not socialist but that it had been developing away from socialism since the 1920s, indeed since the Kronstadt Revolt. Instead, there had emerged a new kind of ruling class in Russia that, as he showed in *Animal Farm* in a way a child could understand, had reshaped the slogans of the revolution to fit a new regime of exploitation, oppression, police terror and tyranny. The irony is that Thompson the Marxist responded to the events of 1956 from an idealist standpoint, whereas it was Orwell who had embraced a materialist understanding of the Soviet Union as long ago as the 1930s. It was this that made Orwell unacceptable to the New Left. His critique of the Soviet Union was too radical. Indeed, paradoxically, they felt more comfortable with those on the Left who had drawn similar conclusions to Orwell and in response had begun a trajectory to the right, than they did with Orwell who remained a democratic socialist until his death. It was not that Orwell was a 'premature anti-Stalinist', but more to do with the fundamental nature of his rejection of Soviet Communism as having anything to do with socialism.

Thompson was particularly put out by Orwell and was quite concerned to settle accounts with him, publishing a substantial essay, 'Outside the Whale' that has appeared in a number of versions starting with the collection *Out of Apathy*, the publication of which in 1960 was an important event in the history of the New Left. This essay has been described as recently as 2004, by Andy Croft, writing very much from a position sympathetic to the CP tradition as 'still arguably the best essay on Orwell'.[32] What is interesting is that he does not confront *Nineteen Eighty-Four* as a pillar of what Thompson describes as 'Natopolitan culture' but rather focuses in on an essay, 'Inside the Whale' that Orwell had published back in 1940. He describes the piece as 'an apology for quietism' and identifies it as pointing the way 'the negations of 1984'.

Indeed, he quite seriously argues that it was 'in this essay, more than any other, that the aspirations of a generation were buried'. According to Thompson, after the Second World War, it was to 'Inside the Whale' that people turned 'back to' to excuse their passivity, their lack of engagement and hope, only to find themselves trapped inside 'the *real* whale of Natopolis', abandoning all prospect for progressive change. The whole of Thompson's essay is pretty dire stuff, probably the worst thing he ever wrote, and its inflated reputation shows a certain desperation on the part of Orwell's critics. First of all, Thompson focuses on a brief moment of 'quietism' after the outbreak of the war, treats it as the mainspring of Orwell's development, and proceeds to ignore all of Orwell's political activity during the rest of that conflict, including his writings for *Left News*, the Searchlight series of books, including his own *The Lion and the Unicorn*, his 'London Letters' in *Partisan Review*, his BBC broadcasts and his *Tribune* contributions. These clearly tell us more about Orwell's political development than 'Inside the Whale' but they do not assist Thompson's argument so they are completely ignored. More revealingly, Thompson also censures Orwell in the 1930s for criticising 'the deformities' of the Communist movement without appreciating 'the nature and function of the movement itself'. Here he is engaged in an attempt to rescue the politics of the Popular Front from Stalinism. Why did Orwell not recognise the 'profoundly democratic content' of Communist politics in 1930s Britain? Did he not believe 'that the heartland of Socialism must be defended' or that Litvinov's foreign policy did actually 'deserve to command the support of Western socialists'? Orwell was 'blind to all such discriminations and in this he anticipated the wholesale rejection of Communism which became a central feature of Natopolitan ideology'.[33] Once again what we come back to is that for all his criticisms of Stalinism, as far as Thompson was concerned the Soviet Union even under the Stalin regime was Socialist whereas Orwell's more fundamental critique was that it was not Socialist but a new kind of exploitative society with a new kind of ruling class that had successfully corrupted 'the original idea of Socialism'.[34]

To some extent, Thompson's mention of Litvinov's foreign policy gives the game away. You would never know from Thompson's essay that when Orwell wrote 'Inside the Whale', Litvinov had already been dismissed to be replaced by Molotov in preparation for the signing of the Hitler-Stalin Pact. And that when the essay was published the Soviet Union was allied with Nazi Germany. This was part of the essential context for Orwell's brief, repeat brief, flirtation with 'quietism'. One can, of course, understand why Thompson and others would rather forget the Hitler-Stalin Pact and move on. Part of their objection to Orwell was that he would not let them. Moreover, when we actually turn to 'Inside the Whale', we find that it contains a considerably more persuasive account of British Communist politics in the 1930s than we can decipher from Thompson's shabby apologetics. Here Orwell discusses how Communism throughout Western Europe 'began as a movement for the violent overthrow of capitalism and degenerated within a few years into an instrument of Russian foreign policy'. The committed Communist found him or herself behaving like 'a Russian publicity agent posing as an international Socialist'. This pose was easily maintained in 'normal times' but became considerably harder 'in moments of crisis, because of the fact that the USSR is no more scrupulous in its foreign policy than the rest of the Great Powers'. One consequence of this was that every time Russian foreign policy shifted, '"Marxism" has to be hammered into a new shape', involving 'sudden and violent changes of line, purges, denunciations, systematic destruction of party literature etc., etc.'. Indeed, this, Orwell pointed out, had happened 'at least three times in the last ten years'. And within a year it was to happen a fourth time with the Nazi invasion of the Soviet Union.[35]

This understanding derived, in part from Orwell's reading but also from events that he both participated in and saw taking place around him. His lack of appreciation for 'the profoundly democratic content' of Communist politics was at least in part informed by his experiences in Spain and the fact that he was lucky to escape with his life, by the determined attempts by the CP to suppress the truth about what had gone on and the systematic slandering of Orwell himself and others as 'Trotsky-Fascists' who either wittingly or unwittingly had been aiding the fascists. And unlike Thompson, he was not prepared to turn his back on the Great Terror and the Show Trials and move the argument onto 'more practical matters'. There is, of course, no intention here to try and define Thompson by his attitude towards George Orwell. The author of *The Making of the English Working Class* was, of course, much more than that, but rather to argue that his discussion of Orwell was deeply flawed, that this affected the attitude of the New Left more generally and that the cause of this was Orwell's fundamental rejection of the idea that the Soviet Union and similar societies were socialist.

'That Valiant Figure'

One other body of criticism of Orwell that emerged in the 1980s looked at him from a feminist perspective. The essential text here was Daphne Patai's *The Orwell Mystique: A Study in Male Ideology*, without doubt one of the most important books ever written on Orwell. This is not so much because of the answers it provided, but because of the questions it asked, questions that, in fact, need to be asked about any male writer.[36] As far as Patai was concerned Orwell was a misogynist, something that I would argue is not supported by the evidence. The evidence that he was sexist, however, is so overwhelming as to be completely irrefutable and there undoubtedly were occasions when his sexism was expressed in misogynistic terms. And, indeed, it does seem that there is now a general recognition that this was the case with whatever excuses, provisos or qualifications are put forward. As Gordon Bowker puts it in his 2003 biography: 'There is no doubt that Orwell had a poor attitude to women . . . The many shrewd women who knew him, even while being deeply fond of him and recognising his brilliance, almost invariably referred to his sadism, his seeing women as inferior, or his seeing them as sexually necessary but of little worth beyond that'.[37] 'Poor attitude' hardly seems adequate here. Reactionary attitude seems much more appropriate. And while it can be legitimately argued that these prejudices were what he had been bought up to hold and that they were arguably held by most men and many women during his times, the fact remains that there were men who did not share these prejudices and there were women, including women friends, fighting against them and for women's equality who he did not support in their struggles. He regularly dismissed both 'feminists' and 'feminism'. He was unfortunately one of those male socialists who were opposed to every oppression, except that of women. And, it is, of course, not good enough to defend him for having been raised with these attitudes or that they were the dominant attitudes within society, because the interest he excites is precisely because of all the other areas where he defied or broke with the attitudes he was bought up with and that were the dominant attitudes within society at the time.

To what extent were his views on the oppression of women changing during the Second World War? There is evidence of at least some shift in his attitudes. In August 1945, he wrote a short sympathetic review of Virginia Woolf's *A Room of One's Own*, 'a discussion of the handicaps which have prevented women, as compared with men, from producing literature of the first order'. Woolf argues that to produce good work a writer needs £500 a year and a room of their own and that 'far fewer women than men have enjoyed these advantages'. Somewhat inevitably, he thinks that she overstates the difficulties that confront women but nevertheless ends by remarking that 'almost anyone of the male sex could read it with advantage'.[38] In some respects, at least, he was becoming more sensitive in his arguments regarding gender issues. One of his 'As I Please' columns in *Tribune* (28 July 1944), included discussion of a letter he had received from a woman who had worked on a number of 'women's papers . . . the *Lucky Star*, the *Golden Star*, *Peg's Paper*, *Secrets*, the *Oracle* and a number of kindred papers'. He had dismissed them as telling reactionary 'Cinderella stories' in his famous essay on 'Boys' Weeklies' and she had put him straight. She told him the stories in these papers often mentioned unemployment, but never trade unions which she put down to the publishers being 'non-union'. No criticism of the 'system' was allowed and the word socialism was never mentioned but, she insisted, 'class feeling is not altogether absent'. The rich were often portrayed as villains, trying to take advantage of poor women, offering 'marriage without a ring', from which the woman was rescued by 'her strong, hard-working garage hand'. Orwell goes on to argue that making a poor man the hero and a rich man the villain has become a formula whereby film magnates and publishers both sublimate the class struggle and at the same time make a lot of money. Where reality does enter these magazines is through the correspondence columns where women are given space to discuss real problems. The contrast between the 'love' stories and the letters shows how important 'day-dreaming' is in modern life.[39] What is perhaps significant is that while 'Boys' Weeklies' was published in 1940, he did not address his unnamed correspondent's concerns until 1944.

Other columns he wrote for *Tribune* (28 April 1944) around this same time also addressed the right of women to wear make-up. He was responding to a juvenile magistrate in the East End complaining about 'Modern Girls', in particular the fact that 'Girls of 14 now dress and talk like those of 18 and 19, and put the same filth and muck on their faces'. As Orwell points out, there is a long history of attempts to discourage the use of cosmetics, but they have always failed. Indeed, he describes it is 'one of the big failures in human history'. He does not believe that 'sex attraction' is the reason why women have defied all these attempts, whether it was by the Romans, the Puritans, the Bolsheviks or the Nazis, but they have. He leaves the question why unanswered.[40] And, once again in *Tribune* (8 November 1946), he devoted something like half of his 'As I Please' column to a savage discussion of American fashion magazines.[41]

Before we get too excited by even this limited breakthrough, however, it is important to consider his unchanging attitude toward contraception, birth control and abortion. According to Christopher Hollis, one of Orwell's deepest beliefs had always been with 'the profound evil of contraception'. He thought that even the views of the Catholic Church on this issue were too weak and that 'people who desired intercourse without children were guilty of a profound lack of faith in life'.[42] In his *The English People*, published in 1947, but written in 1944, he put forward proposals that were as George Woodcock observes 'probably the most reactionary he ever made'.[43] In order to counter a declining birth rate, he advocated the punitive taxation of the childless ('taxation will have to be graded so as to encourage child-bearing') and more active action to stop abortion, which he complained was today looked on as little more than 'a peccadillo'. The idea that women having abortions, and the abortions procured by working-class women would have been dangerous 'back street' abortions, regarded it as in any way 'a peccadillo' is positively obscene. He even complained about the increase in the keeping of pets as affecting the birth rate![44]

What of *Nineteen Eighty-Four*? I have argued elsewhere that there has been a neglect in discussion of the book, by both feminist critics and others, of the powerful stand it takes in favour of the sexual liberation of women, that Orwell attacks the double-standard in his portrayal of the relationship between Winston Smith and Julia.[45] For Anne Mellor, Julia, 'sexually liberated, healthy, a creature of emotion but not intellect', is, 'a man-identified woman', in fact 'the stereotype of the ideal woman in a patriarchal society'.[46] This is certainly how she might appear in the early 1980s, but the battles being fought in the late 1940s were different battles. Placed back in the context of the time he wrote, Orwell's defence of Julia's defiant and subversive stand in favour of promiscuity and women's sexual pleasure as demonstrated by Winston Smith's endorsement of that stand is pretty much unique in the literature of the time. As Smith tells Julia, 'Listen, the more men you've had, the more I love you'.[47] There is still an argument around whether or not and to what extent Julia was based on Sonia Brownell, who a very ill Orwell married on 13 October 1949. Sonia was by all accounts very much an intellectual whereas Julia famously falls asleep when Winston is reading *The Theory of Oligarchical*

Collectivism to her. Nevertheless, Sonia's treatment in both Kingsley Amis's novel *The Anti-Death League* and in his later *Memoirs* certainly reveals that the double-standard was still very much alive. His account of a miserable failed attempt at group sex involving himself, Malcolm Muggeridge and Sonia has achieved a certain notoriety.[48] Indeed, to some extent, this episode has quite shamefully come to almost define Sonia Orwell.[49] Even John Sutherland in his book on Orwell published as late as 2016 can still quite incredibly refer to Sonia as 'a gratifyingly easy lay' who Cyril Connolly would 'allegedly' pimp out to potential financial backers when she worked on *Horizon*, and as 'a living vagina dentata'.[50] All this makes Hilary Spurling's biography of Sonia Orwell, *The Girl from the Fiction Department* essential reading.[51]

Just before his arrest in *Ninety Eighty-Four*, Smith convinces himself that 'the future belonged to the proles'. What gives him hope is watching a working-class woman singing while hanging out the washing. She was 'a solid unconquerable figure', 'that valiant figure' and there were 'hundreds of thousands of millions of people' just like her all over the world. They were held apart 'by walls of hatred and lies', but one day 'their awakening would come'. The woman who inspires Smith is not one of the women industrial workers whose strike action brought down the Tsarist regime in February 1917 or one of the women who fought on the barricades against the military in revolutionary Barcelona in 1936. She is the working-class woman as wife, mother and grandmother. Nevertheless, for all his undoubted sexism, in the end Orwell chooses a working-class woman, hanging out the washing, as the symbol of the working-class power that was to overthrow the world, of the hope that 'the future belonged to the proles'.[52]

Conclusion: 'Capitalism has manifestly no future' – Orwell Today

There has been an almost irresistible tendency to enlist George Orwell in fights, protests and disputes since his death. Would he have supported the Korean War? Would he have supported the Campaign for Nuclear Disarmament? Would he have opposed the Vietnam War? Would he have supported the Miners' Strike in 1984? Would he have embraced neo-conservativism? Would he have supported the invasion of Iraq? Would he have been pro- or anti-Brexit? Would he have believed Donald Trump was for real? Most recently, whether or not he would be a supporter of Jeremy Corbyn? The list is endless. The only thing we can say with any degree of certainty is that if he was still around to ask today, he would be extremely old and probably not too pleased to be bothered with such questions. The exercise has never been very productive because we can have no idea how his politics would have developed if he had lived into the 1950s and 1960s let alone longer. We cannot even be certain about how he would have responded to the Korean War. There is evidence from his political record pointing both to support and opposition. The strength of his anti-Communism might have led him to support British involvement, but by the same token he had opposed British troops being used to put down the Communist-led Greek resistance in 1945–46 and might have decided the war was an example of imperialist interference in Korea's internal affairs. He would certainly not have supported North Korea but he might well have believed that Britain should keep out of the war. We just do not know.

Generally, these exercises tell us considerably more about the views of the contemporary protagonists than they do about Orwell. Whether or not he would support Jeremy Corbyn, for example, inevitably reflects the views taken by those involved in the argument today. Interestingly, there are three possible positions here: in the main people who support Corbyn think Orwell would also have supported him, people who oppose Corbyn think Orwell would also have opposed him, but there are also people on the left who consider Orwell to be a traitor and a renegade, who support Corbyn and who consequently think Orwell would have opposed him!

This is not to say that considering some of the dilemmas that Orwell was going to have to confront if he had lived longer is not a useful exercise. He would inevitably have had to take a position on the Korean War. How much more involved would he have become with the IRD if he had lived? Would he have become a stalwart of the Congress of Cultural Freedom? Would he have retreated from political engagement altogether, or at least for a while, in response to the Conservative general election victory in 1951? Nothing can be said for certain, but the very questions throw light on the difficult times he lived through and the choices that he was having to make while still alive. One particular question should dominate these considerations, however, something that Orwell never imagined possible: the survival, indeed expansion of capitalism. As far as he was concerned, 'Capitalism manifestly has no future'.[1] This firm conviction was to be falsified as the system expanded to an extent that he would have considered impossible, unimaginable. His socialist politics would have had to grapple with this new reality. Would he have decided that the capitalist system could now be safely left to emancipate the working class and have moved to the right? Or would he have concluded that the dramatic expansion in the forces of production meant that everyone, right across the world, could now have 'fully human lives' if only the rich were expropriated, abolished? We do not know, but this would certainly have been the most important development that he would have had to explain, understand the significance of and draw conclusions from if he had lived.

But while the question of what Orwell would think if he was still alive is fruitless, this is not to say that Orwell's writings are not relevant today. Certainly, at the time of my first encounter with *Homage to Catalonia* in the late 1960s, I was convinced that the Orwell of 1936–37 would have been marching with us against the Vietnam War, would have shared our disappointment at the politics of the Wilson Labour government, and would have joined in our opposition to the Soviet invasion of Czechoslovakia in 1968. But this was really the wrong way to approach the issue. The point was that I was inspired by his support for and involvement in workers' revolution, by his taking up arms against fascism and by his opposition to Stalinism, an opposition that seemed absolutely vindicated by events in Czechoslovakia. It did not matter what he would have thought in 1968, when he would have been in his mid-sixties if he had lived. What mattered was the way that his writings from the 1930s and 1940s still spoke to me and others, were still relevant to our concerns in the modern world. Others might well draw different conclusions from what they read, but as far as I was concerned, Orwell showed that you could be both a real socialist, not a Labour reformist, but a real socialist, and an opponent of Stalinism. This was important. And it is this remarkable ability to write in language that still resonates about a wide range of issues that are still relevant that accounts for the remarkable interest in George Orwell, his life and writings today.

'How the Poor Die'

Let us start with *The Road to Wigan Pier*. While there are undoubtedly those who respond with hostility and distaste to the book, an Old Etonian writing about the working class, most readers are more likely to be amazed at how contemporary the conditions that Orwell describes and condemns still are. What this reflects is the fact that Orwell wrote the book in the aftermath of series of great working-class defeats, the General Strike and Miners' Lockout, the Great Depression and the collapse of the 1929–31 Labour government. The defection of the Labour leadership to the Conservatives in 1931 was the climactic blow. These defeats left working-class men and women in a weak position where any fight back was difficult and employers, local authorities and central government were able to treat them with contempt. The reason the book resonates so much today is that we are living through a similar period. The defeats of the trade union movement at the hands of Margaret Thatcher in the 1980s, the consolidation of the Thatcher counter-revolution in place by New Labour and the imposition of 'austerity' by the Conservative-LibDem Coalition have decisively rolled back the historic gains made by working-class people in the post-World War period. Whereas only a section of the Labour leadership defected to the Tories in 1931, in the 1990s virtually the entire Parliamentary Labour Party followed Tony Blair in defecting to neo-liberalism. What this has left is a world of low wages, long hours, bad working conditions, insecure work, bad and worsening housing conditions and massive cuts in welfare and education provision. The enormous scandal of student loans and the accompanying crushing debt levels for young people, first introduced by a Labour government are a hugely socially regressive step in a low-wage economy. For many people there has been a return to the slum and the slum landlord. And there is clearly much more still to come with the privatisation of healthcare, the effective abolition of the NHS, the great prize, neo-liberalism's 'Final Frontier' still to be completed. And this has become the reality not just for the manual working class, but for millions of white-collar workers as well. The zero hours contract, pseudo-self-employment and casual labour are all things that most contemporary readers of *The Road* just know that Orwell would instantly recognise. They are the hallmarks of helplessness in the face of the increased power of employers.[2] This Cowardly New World was, of course, all made possible by the scale of trade union defeat in the 1980s and the subsequent failure to successfully rebuild the movement. And while the working class has been ground down, the rich and super rich, 'the rich swine' as Orwell described them, have prospered as never before. All this history has been dramatically and dreadfully summed up by the Grenfell Tower fire, the history of cuts and neglect that led up to it and the subsequent treatment of the survivors. This, to steal the title of one of Orwell's articles, is 'how the poor die' in twenty-first century Britain.

In the middle of the Blitz, Orwell wrote in his diary (17 September 1940), complaining of how working-class people who had been bombed out were being treated by the authorities. 'Everyone I have talked to agrees', he wrote, that the empty furnished houses in the West End should be used for the homeless; but I suppose the rich swine still have enough pull to prevent this from happening'. The bitterness and resentment that wartime inequalities, together with the treatment of the victims of the bombing, created made him 'think of St Petersburg in 1916'.[3] The following year, one of the books that Orwell and Tosco Fyvel published in their Searchlight series was Ritchie Calder's *The Lesson of London*. He looked at the effective abandonment by the authorities of working-class families who were bombed out during the Blitz, made homeless by 'the deluge of bombs and the holocaust of fire'. As far as the authorities were concerned these people 'were just units in arid calculations and even the calculations were outrageously inadequate'. He describes the treatment that many people received reminded him of how people were treated in John Steinbeck's *The Grapes of Wrath*, like 'Dust Bowl refugees'. There were working-class survivors who were just left to sleep rough in Epping Forest. And while the working-class homeless were treated like poor law claimants, as 'casuals', middle-class victims were taken by taxi to be put up in hotels before being sent to the country to recover from their ordeal.[4] Not much has changed over the nearly eighty intervening years.

Orwell's writing still has a great deal of contemporary resonance because it addresses so many of our concerns today. The reason is, of course, obvious. While much had changed we still live in a capitalist society, indeed in a capitalist society where the rich and super rich have more power than at any time in the last ninety or more years.

'Big Brother'

One thing that is perhaps surprising is the continued resonance of *Nineteen Eighty-Four*. With the collapse of the Soviet Union and its Empire in Eastern Europe and 'Communist' China's embrace of capitalism, *Nineteen Eighty-Four* might have been expected to become of merely historical interest. As we have seen the novel had been weaponised during the Cold War, enlisted as propaganda in the struggle against the Soviet Union. Today, all that really remains of that enemy is the North Korean regime, a sort of grotesque caricature of the world of 'Big Brother', where Stalinism has mutated into a hereditary absolute monarchy. But the book still resonates. Why? First it is worth making the point that it was always directed against totalitarianism whether of the left or the right. When Orwell began writing the novel, Nazism was as much in his sights as Stalinism. We are certainly seeing a revival of the fascist right in parts of Eastern Europe and elsewhere today, but it is not this that resonates. What the novel speaks to is a widespread feeling of helplessness in the face of a 'Big Brother' who can manifest himself in many guises, corporate as well as State. The degree of surveillance in contemporary society would have both astonished and dismayed Orwell one feels. And as for the 'Truth'! Orwell's Ministry of Truth is often seen as being inspired by his time working as a propagandist at the BBC, but his first real encounter with what might today be called 'fake news' were the efforts of the international Communist movement to celebrate the Soviet Union as some sort of 'workers' state', to slander its enemies on the left and, of course, to change what constituted 'the truth' at a moment's notice, literally overnight, so that one day the Nazis are sworn enemies and the very next day they are close allies. What is new today though is the extent to which politicians and much of the media seem to have abandoned even the pretence of having a meaningful relationship with the truth. While US President Donald Trump is the most extreme instance of this phenomenon, much the same can be seen on a smaller scale with many of the leading politicians of the last thirty years or so. The likes of Tony Blair and Boris Johnson are obvious British examples. And the Murdoch press in Britain with all of its grimy criminality is another. Trump, though, is a special case. Whereas conventional politicians lie to cover up the truth for political advantage, with Trump lying appears to be a pathological condition, a symptom of a chronic psychological malaise, a serious personality disorder that with the immense power of the US State at his disposal threatens the whole world. With Donald Trump we are on our own. Nothing in Orwell's writings prepares us for the Trump phenomenon.

Notes

Introduction

1. It has been reprinted in Paul Flewers, ed., *George Orwell: Enigmatic Socialist*, London 2005.

Chapter 1

1. George Orwell, *Nineteen Eighty-Four*, London 1987 , pp 74, 89.
2. George Orwell, *The Road to Wigan Pier*, London 1987, pp 123, 128, 129, 130.
3. Ibid.
4. Orwell, *Nineteen Eighty-Four*, p 229.
5. Gordon Bowker, *George Orwell*, London 2003, p 105.
6. 'Save Sacco and Vanzetti'. They were two US anarchists who had been framed for murder and who despite an international campaign were executed on 23 August 1927.
7. Peter Davison, ed., *Complete Works of George Orwell*, California, 1998, 10, pp 244–245. Please note that hereafter this title shall be referred to as 'CWGO'. One point worth making here is that Orwell had been out of the country during the General Strike and the six-months-long Miners' Lockout that followed. One can only speculate on how these events would have impacted him if he had experienced them first-hand.
8. This refers to a dishwasher; see George Orwell, *Down and Out in Paris and London*, London 1984, p 45.
9. Orwell, *Down and Out*, p 130.
10. Bodil Folke Frederiksen, 'The Adelphi and Working Class Literature in Britain in the 1930s', *Middlesex Polytechnic History Journal*, 11, 1 (Spring 1985), pp 83, 86–87.
11. Orwell, *CWGO 10*, pp 458, 469.
12 Orwell, *CWGO 10*, p 471.
13. Orwell, *The Road*, pp 19, 31, 43–44, 74–75, 80–81, 116–117.
14. Orwell, *CWGO 10*, pp 424, 426–427, 430–431. His diary of his time in the North is an essential accompaniment to *The Road to Wigan Pier*. And for a much more generous assessment of Wal Hannington see CWGO 11, p 98.
15. Bernard Crick, *George Orwell: A Life*, London 1992, pp 343–345, George Orwell, *The Road*, p 115.
16. Orwell, *The Road*, pp 151, 154–155, 190.
17. George Orwell, *Homage to Catalonia*, London 1985, pp 8–9.

18. Orwell, *Homage,*, pp 48–49.
19. Orwell, *CWGO 11*, p 93.
20. Orwell, *Homage*, pp 28–29.
21. Orwell, *CWGO 11*, p 28.
22. Orwell, *CWGO 11*, pp 506.
23. Orwell, *CWGO 11*, pp 510–511.
24. For the Searchlight series see John Newsinger, *Orwell's Politic*, Basingstoke 1999, pp 70–86.
25. Orwell, *CWGO 12*, pp 407, 427.
26. Scott Lucas, *Orwell*, London 2003, pp 63–64, 105.
27. Beatrix Campbell, 'Orwell – Paterfamilias or Big Brother?', in Christopher Norris, ed., *Inside the Myth: Orwell – Views From the Left*, London pp 126, 127, 135.
28. George Woodcock, *Letter to the Past*, Don Mills 1982, pp 285–286.
29. Alfred Kazin, *New York Jew*, London 1978, pp 123, 126–127. According to Richard Cook in his biography of Kazin, in his Rockefeller report, he argued that whereas the coming of war had dampened down the class struggle in the USA, in Britain, the war had 'took the roof off', there was 'a social bitterness dangerous to ignore' and the country was going 'to go left with the troops'. See Richard M Cook, *Alfred Kazin*, New Haven 2007, pp 100–101.
30. Orwell, *The Road*, pp 139–140.
31. Orwell, *CWGO 11*, p 360.
32. Orwell, *CWGO 11*, p 260.
33. Orwell, *CWGO 17*, pp 247–248.
34. Orwell, *CWGO 19*, p 165.
35. Eric Hobsbawm, *Age of Extremes: The Short Twentieth Century 1914–1991*, London 1994, p 393. See also my unpublished paper, 'Orwell and Science Fiction'.
36. Orwell, *Nineteen Eighty-Four*, p 31.
37. Ibid., pp 72–3.
38. Ibid., p 74–5.
39. Ibid., p 85.
40. Ibid., p 89.
41. Ibid., p 172.
42. Ibid., p 198.
43. Ibid., pp 229–230.

Chapter 2

1. Ralph Miliband, *Parliamentary Socialism*, London 1972. See Chapter 7.
2. R E Dowse, *Left in the Centre*, London 1966, p 113.
3. John McNair, *James Maxton: The Beloved Rebel*, London 1955, p 190.
4. John McGovern, *Neither Fear Nor Favour*, London 1960, p 70.
5. Dowse, *Left in the Centre*, p 176.
6. McGovern, *Neither Fear*, p 75.
7. Orwell, *CWGO 12*, p 101.

8. There has been over recent years a lively debate over the extent of CP sub-ordination to Moscow with a number of historians pointing to a degree of latitude in the implementing of the various turns, but singularly unable to explain either the in-step performance of the various turns or the absolutely obligatory celebration of the Moscow Trials. See John Newsinger, 'Some Recent Controversies in the History of British Communism', *Journal of Contemporary History* 41, 3, 2006.

9. Richard Rees, *For Love or Money*, London 1960, p 152.

10. Bernard Crick, *George Orwell*, London 1992, p 241.

11. Rees, *For Love* p 152. Bernard Crick has questioned the extent of Orwell's understanding of Marxism at this time, pointing to the fact that no such understanding is demonstrated in *The Road to Wigan Pier*. This is not altogether convincing because Orwell believed that Marxist terminology put off the very people he wanted to win over to the socialist cause and so avoided it. See Crick, *George Orwell*, pp 305–306.

12. Francis Beckett, *The Enemy Within: The Rise and Fall of the British Communist Party*, London 1995, p 72.

13. Freda Utley, *The Dream We Lost*, New York 1940, p 30. The book was only published in the USA and there is no evidence that Orwell ever read it, although he does list her later *Lost Illusions* in his record of books he had read in 1949 (CWGO 20, p 222). And he does refer to Utley in an article, 'What is Socialism?', that appeared in the *Manchester Evening News* on 31 January 1946, as someone who had not 'reverted towards Conservatism' despite her disillusion with Stalinism. This was to soon change it has to be said. See CWGO 18, p 63.

14 John Lewis, *The Left Book Club*, London 1970, pp 45–46.

15. Isaac Kramnick and Barry Sheerman, *Harold Laski: A Life on the Left*, London 1993, p 365.

16. Orwell, *CWGO 11*, p 39.

17. Ruth Dudley Edwards, *Victor Gollancz*, London 1987, p 238. For his part, in a letter to Jack Common, Orwell described Gollancz as certainly 'very enterprising about "left" stuff', but 'he is not too bright intellectually' so that he does not 'necessarily see Trotskyist or other heretical implications if they are not on the surface'. See *CWGO 11*, p 122.

18. Sheila Hodges, *Gollancz: The Story of a Publishing House*, London 1978, p 141.

19. Edwards, *Victor Gollancz*, p 267.

20. Orwell, *CWGO 11*, pp 159–160. This review appeared in the *New English Weekly* on 9 June 1938.

21. Orwell, *CWGO 11*, p 87. For an interesting discussion of Orwell and James see Christian Hogsbjerg, 'C L R James, George Orwell and "Literary Trotskyism"', *George Orwell Studies* 1, 2 (2017).

22. Orwell, *CWGO 11*, pp 202–204.

23. C H Rolph, *Kingsley: The Life, Letters and Diaries of Kingsley Martin*, London 1973, p 228.

24. Orwell, *CWGO 11*, pp 41–42, 46.

25. Orwell, *CWGO 11*, pp 39–40.

26. Orwell, *CWGO 11*, pp 167–169. Orwell criticised Brockway for neglecting the importance of winning over white collar workers.

27. Fenner Brockway, *Workers' Front*, London, p 85. For Brockway at this time, the ILP was an unambiguously 'Revolutionary Socialist' organisation. *CWGO 11*, pp 123–124.

28. Orwell, *CWGO 11*, pp 153–154.

29. The scale of Nazi mass murder with the Holocaust as its centre was the crime that has come quite correctly to define the Second World War, but even so it is important to remember those episodes that have been almost completely written out of British history such as the Bengal Famine of 1943–1944 with perhaps as many as 5 million dead from starvation, disease and exposure. Towards the end of the war, Orwell complained of those Daily Telegraph readers who complained about doodle-bugs 'while not caring a damn for the starvation of millions of Indians'. See *CWGO 16*, p 330.

30. Orwell, *CWGO 11*, pp 358–361.

31. John Newsinger, *The Blood Never Dried: A People's History of the British Empire*, London 2013, pp 150–152.

32. Reg Reynolds, *My Life and Crimes*, London 1956, pp 70, 61–62. He writes that one of the problems Gandhi posed for the police was, as one superintendent complained, that everyone detailed to watch him 'goes over to his side' (p 60).

33. Ethel Mannin, *Privileged Spectator*, London 1939, pp 24, 74, 121. In this memoir, she describes how she was attracted to Trotskyism because they 'were revolutionaries who at least had no illusions about Russia', only to find that they could be 'as doctrinaire as the most rigid Communist' (p 303). Ethel Mannin, *Cactus*, London 1934, pp 75–76.

34. Ethel Mannin, *Women and the Revolution*, London 1938, pp 183, 184–185. Mannin's neglect is really quite shameful and needs urgent remedying. She seems to have been a victim of both the general neglect of women and also of the extent to which the left historiography of the 1930s is still viewed through the lens of the 'Popular Front', a double whammy so to speak. A notable exception to this neglect is Andy Croft, 'Ethel Mannin: The Red Rose of Love and the Red Flower of Liberty', in Angela Ingram and Daphne Patai, eds, *Rediscovering Forgotten Radicals: British Women Writers 1889–1939*, Chapel Hill 1993.

35. Reynolds, *My Life*, p 211.

36. Crick, *George Orwell*, p 343.

37. Reynolds, *My Life*, pp 212–213.

38. *CWGO 11*, pp 313, 340–341. According to Crick, the anarchists thought Read's basement was the best place to hide an underground printing press. See Crick, p 365.

39. Read thought the war 'would inevitably lead to revolution – that it would be neither won nor lost without a social upheaval'. See George Woodcock, *Herbert Read: The Stream and the Source*, London 1972, p 235.

40. Gordon Bowker, *George Orwell*, London 2003, p 256. Mannin still dedicated her novel, *Rolling in the Dew*, London 1940, to Orwell. In her *Stories from My Life* published in 1973, when she was in her early seventies, she could still write: 'I have been a socialist all my adult life, from the age of fifteen, and now, at close of play, in the seventies, am more than ever convinced of the necessity for social revolution'. She took her stand 'with the anarchists, opposed to all forms of centralised government, and profoundly mistrusting all political parties'. Daniel Cohn Bendit's book, *Obsolete Communism*, she tells the reader, had just joined Che Guevara's *Bolivian Diaries* on her bookshelves (pp 215–216).

Chapter 3

1. T R Fyvel, *George Orwell: A Personal Memoir*, London 1983, pp 180–182.
2. George Orwell, *The Road to Wigan Pier*, London 1986, p 159.
3. CWGO 10, pp 456–457, 466, 473.
4. George Orwell, *Collected Works of George Orwell* (CWGO) – 17, p 417.
5. Orwell, *CWGO11*, p 98.
6. George Orwell, *The Road to Wigan Pier*, pp 187–188.
7. Ibid.
8. Orwell, *The Road*, pp 191, 193, 201, 205–206.
9. Fenner Brockway, *Towards Tomorrow*, London 1977, p 120.
10. Bill Alexander, 'George Orwell and Spain' in Christopher Norris, ed., *Inside The Myth*, London 1984, pp 89–90, 96.
11. Fred Copeman, a veteran of the British battalion, remembered that the ordinary ranks in the International Brigade subsisted on 'beans, lentils, bread and coffee', while the staff sat down to 'bread fried in olive oil, a fried egg and lamb chops', followed by 'cherries and cream'. See James K Hopkins, *Into The Heart of the Fire: The British in the Spanish Civil War*, Stanford 1998, p 231.
12. According to Francis Beckett, Rust had a 'reputation of being the coldest Stalinist apparatchik Britain ever produced'. He was sent to Spain in 1937 to enforce 'the party line' and 'certainly maintained records on the soldiers, in which he frequently denounced their political heresies'. He also had the remarkable distinction of having abandoned his daughter Rosa in the Soviet Union where she was deported along with the Volga Germans after the Nazi attack in 1941. She was not allowed out of the country until March 1944. One *Daily Worker* journalist later remarked that if what she had been through and what she had seen had become known, Rust 'would have denounced these anti-Soviet lies and slanders'. See Francis Beckett. *Stalin's British Victims*, Stroud 2004, p 5, 103, 115. See also Andrew Flinn, 'William Rust: the Comintern's Blue-Eyed Boy' in John McIlroy, Kevin Morgan and Alan Campbell, eds, *Party People, Communist Lives*, London 2001. Flinn remarks that Rust's family were 'lucky to survive their brushes with Stalin's Russia' and that their experiences meant that he 'was intimately aware of the

true nature of that society. However, he elected to keep that knowledge to himself' (p 96).

13. Hopkins, *Into the Heart*, pp 273, 283–285, 288. Interestingly, there was the odd Trotskyist and Anarchist in the British battalion and according to Hopkins there may even have been a group of 'twenty-five or thirty anarcho-syndicalists' which he suggests 'could well have made the battalion's response to the POUM uprising in Barcelona in May 1937 more complex than heretofore thought' (p 140). Regarding Nan Green, her posthumous memoirs were published in 2004 and here she acknowledges that 'the Soviet-inspired hatred of "Trotskyism" . . . spilled over into the Communist movement everywhere and made heresy-hunting a righteous crusade for many members'. She admits that she fell foul of this herself and had no idea of 'what allegations about me' had been made 'some of which followed me round to my later jobs though I did not know it until much later'. On one occasion she was even accused of not really being Nan Green, but of being an imposter! See Nan Green, *A Chronicle of Small Beer*, Nottingham 2004, pp 80–81.

14. John McGovern, *Neither Fear nor Favour*, London 1960, p 109.

15. Orwell, *CWGO 11*, p 81.

16. George Orwell, *Homage to Catalonia*, London , pp 173, 174.

17. Orwell, *CWGO 11*, p 80.

18. Bernard Crick, *George Orwell*, London 1992, p 388.

19. Franz Borkenau, *The Spanish Cockpit*, London 1986. For his encounter with the Communist secret police see pages 236–251. As he put it: 'the communists have got into the habit of denouncing as a Trotskyist everybody who disagrees with them about anything...A Trotskyist in communist vocabulary, is synonymous with a man who deserves to be killed...the communists know no mercy where pretended Trotskyists are concerned'. His Trotskyism remained unproven because fortunately, friends had managed to hide the manuscript he was working on, part of what was to become *The Spanish Cockpit*, before the police could seize it otherwise 'things probably would have been even more unpleasant for me'. Among those who had denounced him was his 'English secretary' and he was shown 'the written protocol of her denunciation' (pp 240–241, 250).

20. Orwell, *CWGO 11*, pp 51–52, 202–204.

21. Orwell, *CWGO 12*, pp 158–159.

22. Orwell, *CWGO 15*, p 243.

23. See John Newsinger, *Orwell's Politics*, Basingstoke 1999, pp 124–127 and Chapter 7 of the present book.

24. Orwell, *CWGO 12*, pp 117–118; *CWGO 11*, p 160; Fyvel, *A Personal Memoir*, p 177.

25. Orwell, *CWGO 12*, p 236.

26. Orwell, *CWGO 12*, p 314–315.

27. Orwell, *CWGO 16*, pp 190–191.

28. Orwell, *CWGO 12*, p 417.

29. Orwell, *CWGO 16*, p 330.

30. Fyvel, *A Personal Memoir*, pp 177–178. The collected works to which Fyvel refers is the four volume *The Collected Essays, Journalism and Letters* edited by Sonia Orwell and Ian Angus and published in 1968.

31. George Orwell, *Down and Out in Paris and London*, London 1984, pp 18, 33, 65.

32. Salo W Baron, *The Russian Jew under the Tsars and the Soviets*, New York 1987, pp 184–185.

33. Orwell, *CWGO 19*, pp 460–461.

34. Orwell, *CWGO 16*, p 89.

35. Orwell, *CWGO 14*, pp 234, 244–245, 361.

36. The attempt to rescue Jewish children from Vichy France that Orwell is referring to here was effectively sabotaged by Home Office stalling.

37. Bernard Wasserstein, *Britain and the Jews of Europe 1939–1943*, Leicester 1999, p 117. See also John Newsinger, 'The Labour Party, anti-Semitism and Zionism', *International Socialism* 153 (Winter 2017), pp 134–135. Gollancz's later pamphlet, *What Buchenwald Really Means*, published in early 1945 is in his collection.

38. Orwell, *CWGO 15*, p 110–11.

39. Orwell, *CWGO 15*, pp 303–304.

40. Orwell, *CWGO 17*, p 147. After the war, Reed was to emerge as a full-blown Holocaust denier and a champion of the Protocols of the Elders of Zion as the key to understanding the world. He emigrated from Britain to the more congenial South Africa in 1948 and later strongly supported the attempt by Ian Smith to sustain white rule in Southern Rhodesia. See Richard Thurlow, 'Anti-Nazi Antisemite: the Case of Douglas Reed', *Patterns of Prejudice* 18, 1 (1984).

41. Orwell, *CWGO 17*, p 61, 362.

42. Fyvel, *Personal Memoir*, p 180.

43. Benjamin Balint, *Running Commentary: The Contentious Magazine that Transformed the Jewish Left into the Neo-Conservative Right*, New York 2010, pp 33–36.

44. For an interesting discussion of Orwell's views on Palestine see Giora Goodman, 'Orwell and the Palestine Question', *The European Legacy* 20, 4, 2015.

45. Orwell, *CWGO 18*, p 482.

46. See Newsinger, 'The Labour Party...', and David Cesarani, *Justice Delayed: How Britain Became a Refuge for Nazi War Criminals*, London 1992.

Chapter 4

1. Roger Moorhouse, *The Devil's Alliance: Hitler's Pact with Stalin 1939–1941*, London 2014, p 14.

2. Orwell was to read the memoirs of one of these unfortunates, Margarete Buber-Neuman in the course of 1949. She had joined the German Communist Party in 1921, fleeing to Russia together with her husband when the Nazis came to power. They were both arrested in the course of

1938. She never saw her husband again. She was imprisoned in Siberia until 1940 when she was included in a group to be handed over to the Gestapo. She recalls the sheer disbelief that this could be happening expressed by her fellow prisoners, in particular, the Jewish Communist and the young worker from Dresden who had been smuggled out of Germany after a street clash in which a Nazi had been killed. Those arrested had all blamed him for the killing as they thought him safe. 'His fate was certain', she observed. She spent five years in the Ravensbrueck concentration camp, both shunned and threatened by her Communist fellow prisoners for her supposed Trotskyism and towards the end of the war was fearful that she would once again fall into Russian hands and face continued years of imprisonment at best and execution at worst. See Margarete Buber-Neuman, *Under Two Dictators*, London 1949, p 166. The book was published by Gollancz.

3. Noreen Branson, *History of the Communist Party of Great Britain 1927–1941*, London 1985, pp 262–263.

4. Ruth Dudley Edwards, *Victor Gollancz*, London 1987, p 301.

5. Francis Beckett, *Enemy Within: The Rise and Fall of the British Communist Party*, London 1995, p 90.

6. Kevin Morgan, *Against Fascism and War: Ruptures and Continuities in British Communist Politics 1935–1941*, Manchester 1989, pp 87–88.

7. Kevin Morgan, *Harry Pollitt*, Manchester 1993, p 112.

8. Among those who rallied in support of the Soviet invasion of Finland were the youthful Stalinists Eric Hobsbawm and Raymond Williams who published a 16 page pamphlet defending Russian aggression, *War on the USSR,* in February 1940.

9. Orwell, *CWGO 12*, p 271.

10. Orwell, *CWGO 12*, pp 7, 138.

11. Orwell, *CWGO 12*, pp 90–91, 99, 101, 106.

12. Orwell, *CWGO 14*, pp 218–219.

13. A Labour Candidate, 'R Palme Dutt v, Harry Pollitt' in Victor Gollancz ed, *The Betrayal of the Left*, London 1941, p 188.

14. John Strachey, 'Totalitarianism' in Gollancz, ed., *The Betrayal*, pp 191, 194–195, 200, 202, 205.

15. Victor Gollancz, 'An Immediate Programme', in Gollancz, *The Betrayal*, pp 246, 249, 250, 259, 261; Victor Gollancz, 'Epilogue: On Political Morality', in Gollancz, *The Betrayal*, p 301.

16. George Orwell, 'Fascism and Democracy', in Gollancz, *The Betrayal*, pp 207, 213, 215.

17. George Orwell, 'Patriots and Revolutionaries', in Gollancz, *The Betrayal*, pp 235, 239–240, 241, 245.

18. Victor Gollancz, *Russia and Ourselves*, London 1941, pp 39, 43.

19. For the 'Searchlight' Books see John Newsinger, *Orwell's Politics*, Basingstoke 1999, pp 70–86.

20. Robert Colls, *George Orwell: English Rebel*, Oxford 2013, pp 145, 153–154, 178.

21. George Orwell, *The Lion and the Unicorn*, London 1941.

22. The current Duke of Westminster, 26 year old Hugh Richard Louis Grosvenor is worth £9.52 billion and is the richest man under thirty in the world. His twenty first birthday celebrations cost some £5 million at a time of government imposed austerity'! His wartime ancestor, Hugh Richard Arthur Grosvenor, was well known for his 'anti-Semitic and pro-Nazi views' and had to be personally warned off by Churchill about opposing the war. See Richard Griffiths, *What Did You Do During the War?: The Last Throes of the British Pro-Nazi Right*, London 2017, pp 213–214.

23. Orwell, *The Lion*, London 1941 For Orwell's defence of constitutional monarchy in *Partisan Review* see CWGO 19, pp 68–70.

24. Orwell, *CWGO 14*, p 282.

25. According to Colls, the 1944 Education Act democratised British education. See Colls, *George Orwell*, p 153. This would, of course, come as something of a surprise to the likes of David Cameron, Boris Johnson and others. Indeed to just about everyone.

26. CWGO 16, pp 56–57.

27. CWGO 17, pp 302–303.

28. CWGO 12, p 199.

29. CWGO 13, pp 110–111. Woodcock described NOW as 'a fusion of avant-garde writing and militant pacifism. Later on when anarchism was inevitably added to the mixture, NOW became a literary organ for the wartime dissident literary left'. See George Woodcock, *Letter to the Past*, Don Mills 1982, p 210.

30. David Goodway, *Anarchist Seeds Beneath the Snow*, Liverpool 2006, p 140.

31. Orwell, *CWGO 13*, pp 392–400.

32. Orwell, *CWGO 14*, pp 213–214.

33. George Woodcock, *The Crystal Spirit*, London 1967.

34. Orwell, *CWGO 15*, p 216.

35. He apologised somewhat belatedly to Symons for his 'quite unjustified statement' in the pages of *Partisan Review* in the winter of 1944. See *CWGO 16*, pp 411–412.

36. Orwell, *CWGO 13*, pp 406–407. Orwell confided to Comfort that he had not mentioned Plowman by name because they were old friends and that Plowman did try to fight against his anti-Semitic prejudices, if not always successfully. He was to later review a volume of Plowman's letters, published as *Bridge into the Future*, where he argued that Plowman's 'deeds were better than his opinions', noting that before the war he had advocated 'unlimited Jewish immigration into Britain – a plan which was never put into operation, but which might have averted the death or suffering of millions of people'. See *CWGO 16*, p 494.

37. Griffiths, pp 81, 85, 117; Ethel Mannin, *Brief Voices*, London 1959, p 50. Before the outbreak of war, Mannin had warned against 'the real menace in rabid anti-Fascism' and had actually proclaimed that she would give 'Hitler and Mussolini and Franco the earth . . . if it would save the world from war'. See her *Privileged Spectator*, London 1938, p 294.

38. Mark Gilbert, 'Pacifist Attitudes to Nazi Germany 1936–45', *Journal of Contemporary History* 37, 3 (July 1992), pp 493, 503, 504, 509; Richard Rempel, 'The Dilemmas of British Pacifists During World War II', *Journal of Modern History* 50, 4, 1978, p 1224.

39. Orwell, *CWGO 19*, p 282.

40. Orwell, *CWGO 16*, pp 193–194.

41. Vera Brittain, *One Voice: Pacifist Writings from the Second World War*, London 2005, pp 98, 114, 133, 178. The *Seeds of Chaos* had very little impact in Britain although she did get abusive letters and on one occasion had dog faeces pushed through her letter box. Her work had a much greater impact in the United States, where she was widely denounced by – among others – Eleanor Roosevelt. See Paul Berry and Mark Bostridge, *Vera Brittain*, London 2001, p 441. For an interesting discussion of this episode and the issues involved see in particular A C Grayling, *Among the Dead Cities*, London 2007, pp 182–206.

42. Orwell, *CWGO 16*, pp 195–196.

43. Orwell, *CWGO 17*, p 122. It is worth noticing that the most authoritative account of wartime bombing gives the number of civilian fatalities in Britain at 60,595 and estimates the number of German civilian fatalities at 353,000. See Richard Overy, *The Bombing War: Europe 1939–1945*, London 2013, pp 194, 475.

44. Orwell, *CWGO 16*, p 411.

45. For the Quit India movement see John Newsinger, *'The Blood Never Dried': A People's History of the British Empire*, London 2010, pp 160–166 and John Newsinger, *Orwell's Politics*, Basingstoke 1999, pp 15–16

46 Orwell, *CWGO 16*, p 157.

47. Orwell, *CWGO 16*, pp 412, 414.

Chapter 5

1. Orwell, *CWGO 12*, pp 380, 418, 419, 420, 421. His strictures regarding the Labour Party did not stop him from receiving a request from the Hampstead Garden Suburb Ward of the Hendon Constituency Labour Party, dated 5 October 1941, asking him to allow them to nominate him as their Parliamentary candidate!

2. Orwell, *CWGO 13*, p 302.

3. See the Chapter 'Tribune and the Making of Animal Farm' in Bernard Crick, *George Orwell*, London 1992, pp 441–472.

4. See Paul Anderson, ed., *Orwell in Tribune*, London 2006.

5. Robert Colls, *George Orwell English Rebel*, Oxford 2013, pp 67, 172, 175, 178, 181, 193. For a review of Colls arguments and evidence see my 'Defusing George Orwell', *International Socialism* p 143, 2014.

6. Chris Harman, 'Tribune of the People 1', *International Socialism* 21 (Summer 1965), p 17.

7. According to one account, Cripps was a man of 'enormous wealth – he had inherited a fortune, married another and earned a third as one of the leading

barristers of his day'. See Clare Beckett and Francis Beckett, *Bevan*, London 2004, p 28.

8. Anderson, *Orwell in Tribune* p 14.

9. Tony Cliff and Donny Gluckstein, *The Labour Party: A Marxist History*, London 1996, pp 178–179, 189.

10. The *Daily Worker* casually dismissed him as 'an anti-soviet journalist' at the time. See John and Mary Postgate, *A Stomach for Dissent: The Life of Raymond Postgate*, Keele 1994, p 209. Postgate had, in fact, been a founding member of the Communist Party in 1920 and had been first deputy editor and then editor of its newspaper, *The Communist*, up until his resignation from the CP in May 1922.

11. Orwell, *CWGO 13*, pp 310–311.

12. Jennie Lee, *My Life With Nye*, London 1981, p 81.

13. Nicklaus Thomas-Symonds, *Nye: The Political Life of Aneurin Bevan*, London 2015, p 73. Michael Foot was another socialist who was welcomed into Beaverbrook's circle, indeed it was Bevan who recommended Foot for a job on Beaverbrook's *Evening Standard*. Even Orwell was invited to lunch with Beaverbrook in January 1946. He hoped to discuss Stalin who Beaverbrook had met if he got the chance: see *CWGO 18*, p 28.

14. Orwell, *CWGO 17*, p 311.

15. Beckett and Beckett, *Bevan*, p 44.

16. Anderson, *Orwell in Tribune*p 26.

17. Orwell, *CWGO 19*, pp 35–36, 38.

18. Anderson, *Orwell in Tribune*, p 27.

19. George Woodcock, *The Crystal Spirit*, Montreal 1984, p 13.

20. Richard Keeble, 'The Lasting is the Peripheral: Assessing George Orwell's As I Please column' in Richard Keeble and Sharon Wheeler, eds, *The Journalistic Imagination*, Abingdon 2007, pp 105, 110, 113.

21. Orwell, *CWGO 17*, p 398. Peter Davison provides the relevant extracts from the original report on pages 393–395.

22. Woodcock, *The Crystal Spirit,* pp 9–10, 11.

23. Anderson, *Orwell in Tribune*, p 28.

24. For a discussion of his experience and performance as war correspondent see Richard Keeble, 'Orwell as War Correspondent: a reassessment', *Journalism Studies* 2, 3 (2001).

25. Orwell, *CWGO 17*, p 264.

26. Orwell, *CWGO 19*, p 184.

27. Roy Hattersley, *Fifty Years On,* London 1997, p 2.

28. Orwell, *CWGO 17*, pp 245–249.

29. Orwell, *CWGO 17*, pp 339, 340.

30. T R Fyvel, 'The Years at Tribune', in Miriam Gross, ed., *The World of George Orwell*, London 1971, p 115.

31. Orwell, *CWGO 18*, p 28. In 1949, the American journalist, Virgingia Cowles published an account of Labour Britain that was intended to reassure American readers of the essential moderation of Labour's Revolution. As she pointed out, in Britain not only did you have Old Etonians in a Labour

Cabinet, but you also had trade union leaders in the House of Lords. And despite 'six years of total war and four years of a socialist government, English millionaires still manage to live on a more luxurious scale than the millionaires of almost any other country . . . The shadow of austerity has fallen lightly on the rich'. See Virginia Cowles, *No Cause for Alarm*, New York 1949, p 167.

32. Francis Beckett, *Clem Attlee*, London 1997, p 211. In 1950, Attlee actually typed up a list of the former public schoolboys, carefully noting the school attended, who had served in his government so far. This was purely for his own interest. Eton obviously came first with seven, Hailybury second with five, Winchester third with three, Marlborough, Wellington and St Paul's all with two each and Harrow, Cheltenham, Tonbridge, Dulwich, Rugby and Oundle, all with one each (p 277).

33. A public school educated Labour Prime Minister being installed in the House of Lords as Earl of a working-class area of London seems in many ways to capture the essence of British Labourism in its heyday. It is difficult to imagine any other European reformist party as being capable of perpetrating anything quite as grotesque.

34. Orwell, *CWGO 18*, pp 286–287.

35. Orwell, *CWGO 19*, pp 237, 250.

36. Julian Symons, 'Orwell, a Reminiscence', *London Magazine* (September 1963), pp 43–44.

37. Michael Foot, *Loyalists and Loners*, London 1987, p 201.

38. Simon Hoggart and David Leigh, *Michael Foot*, London 1981, p 74.

39. James Thomas, *Popular Newspapers, the Labour Party and British Politics*, Abingdon 2005, pp 15–16, 31–32.

40. Hoggart and Leigh, *Michael Foot*, p 70.

41. A J P Taylor, *Beaverbrook*, London 1972, p 598.

42. Michael Foot, *The Uncollected Michael Foot: Essays Old and New 1953–2003*, London 2003, p 319.

43. John Newsinger, 'The Labour Party, anti-Semitism and Zionism', *International Socialism* 153 (2017), pp 137–138, 139–140. For Crossman's Zionism see pages 140–142.

44. T R Fyvel, *George Orwell – A Personal Memoir*, London 1983, p 142.

45. Orwell, *CWGO 18*, pp 289–291.

46. Orwell, *CWGO 19*, pp 180–183. For Zilliacus's break with the CP over the Tito-Stalin split see Archie Potts, Zilliacus: A Life for Peace and Socialism, London 2002, pp 113–122.

47. For a discussion of the series and its importance see John Newsinger, *Orwell's Politics*, Basingstoke 1999, pp 150–151.

48. Orwell, *CWGO 19*, pp 163–167.

49. James Hinton, *Labour and Socialism: A History of the British Labour Movement 1867–1974*, Brighton 1983, p 176.

50. Cliff and Gluckstein, *The Labour Party*, p 235.

51. Thomas-Symonds, *Nye*, p 184.

52. Orwell, *CWGO 19*, pp 436–443.

Chapter 6

1. James Smith, *British Writers and MI5 Surveillance*, Cambridge 2013, p 111.
2. Scott Lucas, *Orwell*, London 2003, p 110. See also his *The Betrayal of Dissent: Beyond Orwell, Hitchens and the New American Century*, London 2004.
3. John Sutherland, *Orwell's Nose: A Pathological Biography*, London 2016, pp 105, 111. Even Sutherland himself describes the idea of an attempt being made to recruit Orwell to MI5 as 'the most far-fetched of speculations' and does not present any evidence for it whatsoever, but nevertheless puts it forward as a possibility, however remote. This, of course, indicates one of the problems of writing about this particular world of smoke and mirrors, where almost any speculation can gain traction.
4. Smith, *British Writers* pp 112–124. See also Richard Lance Keeble, 'Orwell, *Nineteen Eighty Four* and the Spooks' in Richard Lance Keeble, ed., *Orwell Today*, Bury St Edmunds 2012, pp 151–161.
5. J Calvitt Clarke, *Russia and Italy Against Hitler*, Westport 1991, pp 77, 146–148.
6. Angel Vinas, 'September 1936: Stalin's Decision to Support the Spanish Republic', in Jim Jump, ed., *Looking Back on the Spanish Civil War*, London 2010, p 147.
7. For a recent discussion see Daniel Kolwalsky, 'Operation X: Soviet Russia and the Spanish Civil War', *Bulletin of Spanish Studies* 91, 1–2, 2014.
8. Robert J Alexander, *The Right Opposition: The Lovestoneites and the International Communist Opposition of the 1930s*, Westport 1981, pp 223, 225. One of the problems for Antonov-Ovseenko was that not only was he officially welcomed to Barcelona by the POUM leader, Andres Nin, acting on behalf of the Catalan government, but that they knew each other from when Nin had lived in Moscow and they had both supported Trotsky against Stalin. He affected not to know Nin. Despite his best efforts at demonstrating his loyalty to Stalin, including endorsing the slaughter of many former comrades, Antonov-Ovseenko was himself recalled to Moscow a few months after the May 1937 uprising and was arrested in October 1937 and shot sometime the following year. When Orwell reviewed Frank Jellinek's *The Civil War in Spain*, for the *New Leader* on 8 July 1938, he could not resist sarcastically noticing Jellinek's quoting 'approvingly a denunciation of the POUM by . . . Antonov-Ovseenko'. As he put it, 'the speed with which the angels in the Communist mythology turn into devils has its comic side' so that Antonov-Ovseenko is 'now on trial as a Trotskyist!' See Orwell, *CWGO 11*, p 173. The Soviet Ambassador, Marcel Rosenberg was also recalled and subsequently shot. Indeed, many of those who faithfully implemented Stalin's Spanish mini-'Terror' were themselves to be shot. See Karl Schlogel, *Moscow 1937*, Cambridge 2013, pp 107–108. Even some of the low level foreign agents operating in Spain fell victim to Stalinism sooner or later with the Irishman, Brian Goold, dying in the Gulag in January 1942, and David Crook being imprisoned for five years during the Cultural Revolution in China. For Goold see Barry McLoughlin, *Left to the Wolves: Irish Victims of*

the Stalinist Terror, Dublin 2007, pp 168–195 and for Crook see his online autobiography: David Crook, Hampstead Heath to Tian An Men: The autobiography of David Crook (www.davidcrook.net).

9. Jonathan Haslam, *The Soviet Union and the Struggle for Collective Security in Europe 1933–39*, Basingstoke 1984, p 116.

10. For Orlov in Spain see Boris Volodarsky, *Stalin's Agent: The Life and Death of Alexander Orlov*, Oxford 2015, pp 238–291.

11. Gordon Bowker, *George Orwell*, London 2003, pp 216– 224. Bowker's is the best account of this episode that we have so far. Tapsell later made clear to a number of ILP members that he did not take seriously the 'Trotsky Fascist' slander directed against the ILP and that he considered the provocations of the Spanish Communists as responsible for the May uprising. He was later killed in combat, although one leading member of the International Brigades, Fred Copeman, was convinced he had, in fact, been murdered by the Communist secret police for what he might reveal of their activities, rather than killed in the fighting which was the official story. See James K Hopkins, *Into the Heart of the Fire: The British in the Spanish Civil War*, Stanford 1998, pp 287–288.

12. Orwell, *CWGO 11*, pp 34–35.

13. Michael Shelden, *Orwell*, London 1991, p 295.

14. Richard Rees, *A Theory of My Time*, London 1956, p 96; Richard Rees, *For Love or Money*, London 1960, p 153.

15. For Georges Kopp see Marc Wildemeersch, *George Orwell's Commander in Spain: The Enigma of Georges Kopp*, London 2013 and Don Bateman, 'Georges Kopp and the POUM Militia', *Revolutionary History* 14, 1.

16. See Rob Stradling, 'The Spies Who Loved Them: The Blairs in Barcelona 1937', *Intelligence and National Security*, 25, 5 2010, p 650.

17. John Newsinger, 'The Death of Bob Smillie', *Historical Journal*, 41, 2, 1998, pp 575– 578.

18. Orwell, *CWGO 11*, p 64.

19. Peter Davison, *The Lost Orwell*, London 2006, p 83.

20. See Tom Buchanan, 'The Death of Bob Smillie: A Reply', in *Historical Journal*, 43, 2, 2000. See also Gidon Cohen, *The Failure of a Dream: The Independent Labour Party from Disaffiliation to World War II*, London 2007, pp 186–188.

21. Bowker,*George Orwell*, p 224.

22. Orwell, *CWGO 11*, pp 35–36. For British intelligence's surveillance of and attempt to infiltrate the ILP contingent, see Cohen, *The Failure*, pp 179–180.

23. For Frankford see in particular Jeffrey Meyers, *Orwell: Life and Art*, Urbana 2010, pp 75–80.

24. Orwell, *CWGO 11*, pp 82–85.

25. Cohen, *The Failure*, p 139.

26. Orwell, *CWGO 11*, p 41.

27. Keeble, *Orwell*, pp 154–155.

28. W J West, ed., *Orwell: The War Commentaries*, London 1986, p 19.

29. For Burgess and Smollett at the BBC and their work on behalf of the Soviet Union see Stewart Purvis and Jeff Hulbert, *Guy Burgess: The Spy Who Knew Everyone*, London 2016, pp 145–159. While he was suspicious of Smollett, as they point out, Orwell seems not to have had 'any suspicions about Burgess' (p 159). See also W J West, *Truth Betrayed*, London 1987, pp 45–64. And for an assessment of Smollett's successes at the Ministry of Information and the suspicion this aroused back in Moscow where it was considered as pointing to him being a double–agent see Christopher Andrew and Vasili Mitrokhin, *The Mitrokhin Archive: The KGB in Europe and the West*, London 2000, p 158.

30. See Richard Keeble, 'Orwell as War correspondent: a reassessment', *Journalism Studies* 2, 3, 2001.

31. See Geoff Andrews, *The Shadow Man: At the Heart of the Cambridge Spy Circle*, London 2016.

32. Paul Lashmar and James Oliver, *Britain's Secret Propaganda War 1948–1977*, London 1998, p 95.

33. Ibid., p 26.

34. Paul Lashmar and James Oliver, *Britain's Secret Propaganda War 1948–1977*, London 1998, pp 26–27, 37.

35. Richard Aldrich, *The Hidden Hand: Britain, America and Cold War Secret Intelligence*, London 2001, p 131. There is a growing academic literature on the IRD but see in particular Hugh Wilford, *The CIA, the British Left and the Cold War*, London 2003; Andrew Defty, *Britain, America and Anti-Communist Propaganda 1945–53*, Abingdon 2004; John Jenks, *British Propaganda and News Media in the Cold War*, Edinburgh 2006; and Lowell Schwartz, *Political Warfare Against the Kremlin: Us and British Propaganda Policy at the Beginning of the Cold War*, Basingstoke 2009.

36. Richard Lance Keeble, *Covering Conflict,: The Making and Unmaking of the New Militarism*, Bury St Edmunds 2017, p 55.

37. For the Attlee government's imperial policy see John Newsinger, *The Blood Never Dried: A People's History of the British Empire*, London 2010, pp 168–172, 174–179, 209–219, 224–230.

38. Wilford, *TheCIA*, p 63.

39. For the full list see the 2006 Supplement to the *Complete Works*, Davison, *The Lost Orwell*, pp 140–151.

40. Ibid.

41. Orwell, *CWGO 20*, p103.

42. Davison, *The Lost Orwell*, pp 147–148; CWGO 20, p 103.

43. K E Holme , *Two Commonwealths*, London 1945, pp 28, 36–37.

44. Christopher Hill, 'Stalin and the Science of History', *The Modern Quarterly* 8 1953, pp 209, 212.

45. Andrew Rubin, 'Orwell and Empire: Anti-Communism and the Globalization of Literature', *Alif: Journal of Comparative Poetics* 28, 2008, pp 83, 86. As Rubin puts it, Orwell was 'certainly aware of the dubious political uses which *Animal Farm* could be put to'.

46. Orwell, *CWGO 18*, pp 154–155.

47. For the 'Lovestoneites see Alexander, *The Right Opposition* ,and Ted Morgan, *A Covert life: Jay Lovestone Communist, anti-Communist and Spymaster*, New York 1999.

48. Eric Thomas Chester, *Covert Network: Progressives, the International Rescue Committee and the CIA*, New York 1995, pp 1, 3, 6. Chester goes on to document IRC involvement in CIA operations against the Cuban Revolution, including the Bay of Pigs invasion, in the Vietnam War and in the US intervention against the Russian occupation of Afghanistan.

49. Lucas, *Orwell*, p 116.

50. Tony Shaw, '"Some Writers are More Equal than Others": George Orwell, the State and Cold War Privilege', in Rana Mitter and Patrick Major, eds, *Across the Blocs: Cold War Cultural and Social History*, London 2012, p 156.

51. Daniel J Leab, *Orwell Subverted: The CIA and the Filming of Animal Farm*, Philadelphia 2007, pp 79–80.

52. Orwell, *CWGO 17*, pp 416–418.

53. George Woodcock, *The Crystal Spirit*, New York 1984, pp 17–19.

54. Daniel W B Lomas, *Intelligence Security and the Attlee Governments 1945–1951*, Manchester 2017, pp 186–189, 192.

55. Richard Aldrich and Rory Cormac, *The Black Door: Spies, Secret Intelligence and British Prime Ministers*, London 2016, p 143. Attlee was absolutely in favour of covert operations abroad and, as Aldrich and Cormac point out, it was he who set in motion preparations for the coup in Iran that was to eventually overthrow the elected government and restore the Shah in 1953! (pp 156–157).

56. Jim Phillips, *The Great Alliance: Economic Recovery and the Problems of Power 1945–1951*, London 1996, pp 72–77, 107–112.

57. See Ken Young, 'Cold War Insecurities and the Curious Case of John Strachey', *Intelligence and National Security* 29, 6 2014 and Giora Goodman, 'The British Government and the Challenge of McCarthyism in the Early Cold war', *Journal of Cold War History* 12, 1, 2010.

58. Rhodri Jeffreys-Jones, *We Know all About You: The Story of Surveillance in Britain and America*, Oxford 2017, pp 111–112.

59. Lomas, pp 202–206.

60. Joan Mahoney, 'Civil liberties in Britain during the Cold War: The Role of Central Government', *American Journal of Legal History* 33, 1 1989, p 97.

61. See Mark Clapson, 'The rise and fall of Monica Felton, British town planner and peace activist, 1930s to 1950s', *Planning Perspectives* 30, 2, 2015. She published a pamphlet, *What I Saw in Korea* on her return and later a book, *That's Why I Went*, London 1953.

62. Aldrich and Cormac, *The Black Door*, p 145.

63. Orwell, *CWGO 20*, p 52.

64. Orwell, *CWGO 19*, p 301.

65. The imprisonment of people for having in their possession *Homage to Catalonia*, *Animal Farm* and *Nineteen Eighty-Four* is something that is seriously under-researched, but John Rodden has pointed us in the right direction in his *Scenes from an Afterlife: The Legacy of George Orwell*,

Wilmington 2003. Here he tells of Baldur Haase, an East German, who got 3 years for being in possession of *Nineteen Eighty-Four*, and Milan Simecka, a Czech, who got two years for translating it into Czech as late as the 1970s (pp 68–74, 142). There were undoubtedly many more.

Chapter 7

1. Orwell, *CWGO 20*, p 92.
2. Stephen Spender, *The Thirties and After: Poetry, Politics, People 1930s–1970s*, New York 1979, p 75.
3. John Sutherland, *Stephen Spender*, London 2004, p 351.
4. Orwell, *CWGO 19*, p 88.
5. T R Fyvel, *George Orwell: A Personal Memoir*, London 1983, p 165.
6. Orwell, *CWGO 20*, p 136.
7. Fyvel, *A Personal Memoir*, p 167.
8. David Caute, *Politics and the Novel During the Cold War*, London 2016, p 90.
9. John Rossi, 'America's View of George Orwell', *Review of Politics*, 43, 4, 1981, p 577.
10. A L Morton, *The English Utopia*, London 1952, pp 208, 212–213.
11. Alaric Jacob, 'Sharing Orwell's Joys – But Not His Fears' in Christopher Hollis, ed., *Inside the Myth: Orwell, Views from the Left*, London 1984, p 81.
12. Kevin McDermott and Matthew Stibbe, 'Stalinist Terror in Eastern Europe: problems, perspectives and interpretations' in Kevin McDermott and Matthew Stibbe, eds, *Stalinist Terror in Eastern Europe*, Manchester 2010, pp 1–14.
13. Adam Westoby, *Communism Since World War Two*, London 1981, p 73.
14. Borhi, 'Stalinist terror in Hungary 1946–1956', McDermott and Stibbe, *Stalinist Terror*, p 132.
15. Alison Macleod, *The Death of Uncle Joe*, London 1997, pp 99–100. She was a journalist on the *Daily Worker*.
16. Josefa Slanska, *Report on My Husband*, London 1969, pp 165–166.
17. McDermott and Stibbe, *Stalinist Terror*, p 7.
18. Jonathan Miles, *The Nine Lives of Otto Katz*, London 2010, pp 377–398. For Smollett see Christopher Andrew and Oleg Gordievsky, *KGB: The Inside Story*, London 1990, pp 345–346.
19. James Klugman, *From Trotsky to Tito*, London 1951, pp 36–37, 43, 85. In his recent biography of Klugman, Geoff Andrews reveals how he had worked for the NKVD as a 'talent spotter' from 1937, something agreed to by Harry Pollitt himself. And while at SOE, he had done everything he could to champion the cause of Tito and the Partisans, even suppressing intelligence reflecting favourably on the rival Chetniks. Klugman spent decades in fear of exposure, arrest and imprisonment. He was editor of *Marxism Today* until 1977. See Geoff Andrews, *The Shadow Man*, London 2015, pp 119–120, 135, 168, 221–223.
20. Morton, *The English Utopia*, pp 211–212.

21. E P Thompson, William Morris and the Moral issues Today', *Arena* 2, 8 1951 (online at www.marxists.org/archive/thompson-ep/1951/william-morris.htm).

22. Edith Bone, *Seven Years Solitary*, London 1957, pp 30, 55, 58, 61, 64, 71, 108, 121, 173.

23. Malcolm MacEwen, *The Greening of a Red*, London 1991, pp 186–187.

24. Isaac Deutscher, '1984 – The Mysticism of Cruelty' in Raymond Williams, ed., *George Orwell: A Collection of Critical Essays*, New Jersey 1974, pp 119–132.

25. Peter Davison, *The Lost Orwell*, London 2006, p 143.

26. Chris Harman, *Class Struggle in Eastern Europe 1945–83*, London 1983, pp 161–185.

27. Francis Beckett and Tony Russell, *1956: The Year That Changed Britain*, London 2015, pp 46–47.

28. Paul Hogarth, *Drawing on Life*, London 2002, p 33, 44–45.

29. For the New Left see Michael Kenny, *The First New Left: British Intellectuals After Stalin*, London 1984 and Lin Chun, *The British New Left*, Edinburgh 1993.

30. John McIlroy, 'John Saville and Stalinism: An Exploration' in Paul Flewers and John McIlroy, eds, *1956: John Saville, E P Thompson and The Reasoner*, London 2016, pp 375–382.

31. E P Thompson, 'Through the Smoke of Budapest', *The Reasoner* 3 reprinted in Paul Flewers and John McIlroy, ibid., pp 266–284.

32. Andy Croft, 'A sack of potatoes or freedom fries? Orwell in the twenty-first century', *Socialist History* 26, 2004, p 98. This article is one of two in a Forum feature in the journal, 'In search of Orwell'. The other article is the current author's 'The other Blair'.

33. E P Thompson, 'Outside the Whale' in E P Thompson and others, *Out of Apathy*, London 1960, pp 158–181. For an interesting discussion see also Scott Hamilton, *The Crisis of Theory: E P Thompson, the new left and postwar British politics*, Manchester 2011, pp 49–86.

34. Orwell, *CWGO 19*, p 86.

35. Orwell, *CWGO 12*, pp 101–106.

36. Daphne Patai, *The Orwell Mystique: A Study in Male Ideology*, 1984. For a somewhat disillusioned revisiting of Orwell twenty years later, see her 'Third Thoughts about Orwell' in Thomas Cushman and John Rodden, eds, *George Orwell into the Twenty-First Century*, Boulder 2004.

37. Gordon Bowker, *George Orwell*, London 2003, p 431.

38. Orwell, *CWGO 17*, p 238.

39. Orwell, *CWGO 16*, pp 304–305.

40. Orwell, *CWGO 16*, pp 173–174.

41. Orwell, *CWGO 18*, pp 471–472.

42. Dan Hitchens, 'Orwell and Contraception', *First Things: A Monthly journal of Religion and Public Life*, April 2016, p 19.

43. George Woodcock, *The Crystal Spirit*, Montreal 1984, p 261.

44. Orwell, *CWGO 16*, pp 222–224.

45. See John Newsinger, *Orwell's Politics*, Basingstoke 1999, pp 130–135.

46. "'You're Only a Rebel from the Waist Downwards": Orwell's View of Women' in Peter Stansky, ed., *On Nineteen Eighty-Four*, New York 1983, p 118.

47. George Orwell, *Nineteen Eighty-Four*, London 1989, pp 131–132.

48. Kingsley Amis, *Memoirs*, London 2004, pp 231–232. See also his novel *The Anti-Death League*, London 1966

49. This episode even gets a mention in Dominic Sandbrook's *White Heat: A History of Britain in the Swinging Sixties*, London 2009, p 581.

50. John Sutherland, *Orwell's Nose*, London 2016, pp 43–45.

51. Hilary Spurling, *The Girl From the Fiction Department: A Portrait of Sonia Orwell*, London 2002.

52. George Orwell, *Nineteen Eighty-Four*, pp 229–230.

Conclusion

1. Orwell, *CWGO 19*, p 166.

2. For a retracing of Orwell's steps in *The Road* today see Stephen Armstrong, *The Road to Wigan Pier Revisited*, London 2012.

3. Orwell, *CWGO 12*, p 263.

4. Ritchie Calder, *The Lesson of London*, London 1941, pp 13, 33.

Index